# THE

# LITERARY

# MIND

# THE

# LITERARY

# MIND

MARK TURNER

OXFORD UNIVERSITY PRESS
NEW YORK   OXFORD

Oxford University Press

Oxford    New York

Athens   Auckland   Bangkok   Bogotá   Buenos Aires   Calcutta
Cape Town   Chennai   Dar es Salaam   Delhi   Florence   Hong Kong   Istanbul
Karachi   Kuala Lumpur   Madrid   Melbourne   Mexico City   Mumbai
Nairobi   Paris   São Paulo   Singapore   Taipei   Tokyo   Toronto   Warsaw

*and associated companies in*

Berlin    Ibadan

Library of Congress Cataloging-in-Publication Data
Turner, Mark.
The literary mind / Mark Turner.
p.  cm.   Includes bibliographical references and index.
ISBN 0-19-512667-X (pbk.)
1. Literature—Philosophy.  2. Cognitive science.   I. Title.
PN49.T77   1996
801'.92—dc20    95-50366

1 3 5 7 9 10 8 6 4 2
Printed in the United States of America

# ✌ PREFACE ✎

IF YOU ARE BROWSING this paragraph in a bookstore, glance at the people around you. They are thinking, searching, planning, deciding, watching the clock, walking to the register, buying books, talking to friends, and wondering why you are looking at them. None of this seems literary.

But to do these things, they (and you) are using principles of mind we mistakenly classify as "literary"—*story, projection,* and *parable.* We notice these principles so rarely in operation, when a literary style puts them on display, that we think of them as special and separate from everyday life. On the contrary, they make everyday life possible. The literary mind is not a separate kind of mind. It is our mind. The literary mind is the fundamental mind. Although cognitive science is associated with mechanical technologies like robots and computer instruments that seem unliterary, the central issues for cognitive science are in fact the issues of the literary mind.

*Story* is a basic principle of mind. Most of our experience, our knowledge, and our thinking is organized as stories. The mental scope of story is magnified by *projection*—one story helps us make sense of another. The projection of one story onto another is *parable,* a basic cognitive principle that shows up everywhere, from simple actions like telling time to complex literary creations like Proust's *À la recherche du temps perdu.*

We interpret every level of our experience by means of parable. In this book, I investigate the mechanisms of parable. I explore technical details of the brain sciences and the mind sciences that cast light on our use of parable as we think, invent, plan, decide, reason, imagine, and persuade. I analyze the activity of parable, inquire into its origin, speculate about its biological and developmental bases, and demonstrate its range. In the final chapter, I explore the possibility that language is not the source of parable but instead its complex product.

Parable is the root of the human mind—of thinking, knowing, acting, creating, and plausibly even of speaking. But the common view, firmly in place for two and a half millennia, sees the everyday mind as unliterary and the literary mind as optional. This book is an attempt to show how wrong the common view is and to replace it with a view of the mind that is more scientific, more accurate, more inclusive, and more interesting, a view that no longer misrepresents everyday thought and action as divorced from the literary mind.

*College Park, Md.*                                                                    M. T.
*November* 1995

# ॐ ACKNOWLEDGMENTS ॐ

THE JOHN SIMON GUGGENHEIM MEMORIAL FOUNDATION and the University of Maryland supported the writing of this book during 1992–1993, while I was a visiting scholar of the Department of Cognitive Science, the Department of Linguistics, and the Center for Research in Language at the University of California, San Diego. Their support made it possible for me to prepare for publication research I had presented in public lectures during earlier years. The book was completed during my year as a fellow of the Center for Advanced Study in the Behavioral Sciences, in 1994–1995. I am grateful for financial support provided during that period by the Andrew W. Mellon Foundation.

Scholars at the University of California, San Diego, to whom I am indebted include Seana Coulson, Jeff Lansing, Gilles Fauconnier, Adele Goldberg, Robert Kluender, Ronald Langacker, Jean Mandler, and Nili Mandelblit. I am also indebted to Claudia Brugman, Jane Espenson, Charles Fillmore, Mark Johnson, Paul Kay, George Lakoff, Eve Sweetser, and Leonard Talmy.

Gilles Fauconnier and I discovered independently a range of problems in conceptual projection that convinced us of the need for a new approach. Our collaboration resulted in the theory of conceptual blending. We presented its elements at the October 1993 Cognitive Linguistics Workshop and later in a technical report and articles. I thank Gilles Fauconnier for permission to include in chapters 5 and 6 some of our results. Anyone who knows the extreme velocity of Fauconnier's intellect will understand why credit for insights achieved during our collaboration cannot be partitioned (especially since many other people have been involved in the discussions), but also why I owe a net intellectual debt. I take responsibility for the version of the theory I present here.

I am grateful to Antonio Damasio, Hanna Damasio, and Gerald Edelman for conversations on the relationship of the study of language to the study of the brain. I also thank Hallgjerd Aksnes, David Collier, Raymond W. Gibbs, Jr.,

Edward Haertel, Mardi Horowitz, Suzanne Kemmer, Robert Keohane, Tanya Luhrmann, and Francis-Noël Thomas for comments. Kathleen Much, staff editor at the Center for Advanced Study in the Behavioral Sciences, made helpful suggestions on some of the chapters. It has been my good fortune to have Cynthia Read as my editor at Oxford University Press.

# Ꙩ CONTENTS ꙮ

# THE

LITERARY

MIND

# BEDTIME WITH SHAHRAZAD

THERE WAS ONCE a wealthy farmer who owned many herds of cattle. He knew the languages of beasts and birds. In one of his stalls he kept an ox and a donkey. At the end of each day, the ox came to the place where the donkey was tied and found it well swept and watered; the manger filled with sifted straw and well-winnowed barley; and the donkey lying at his ease, for the master seldom rode him.

It chanced that one day the farmer heard the ox say to the donkey: "How fortunate you are! I am worn out with toil, while you rest here in comfort. You eat well-sifted barley and lack nothing. It is only occasionally that your master rides you. As for me, my life is perpetual drudgery at the plough and the millstone."

The donkey answered: "When you go out into the field and the yoke is placed upon your neck, pretend to be ill and drop down on your belly. Do not rise even if they beat you; or if you do rise, lie down again. When they take you back and place the fodder before you, do not eat it. Abstain for a day or two; and thus shall you find a rest from toil."

Remember that the farmer was there and heard what passed between them.

And so when the ploughman came to the ox with his fodder, he ate scarcely any of it. And when the ploughman came the following morning to take him out into the field, the ox appeared to be far from well. Then the farmer said to the ploughman: "Take the donkey and use him at the plough all day!"

With this story, the vizier, counselor to the great Sassanid king, Shahriyar, begins to advise his daughter. The vizier's daughter is Shahrazad, known to us as the gifted and erotic storyteller of the thousand and one nights, whose genius and beauty will make her famous. But at the moment, she has told no tales. She has not offered herself to Shahriyar as a wife or given him any of the multiple pleasures of her bed. She is merely the vizier's daughter, and her father would like to keep it that way. For the last three years, it has been his grim daily task to execute Shahriyar's queen of the day before and procure for him another virgin.

The trouble began when Shahriyar discovered that his first wife was unfaithful. In sorrow, he abandoned his throne to roam the world. He unwillingly became involved in a distasteful episode that convinced him that no woman can be trusted. He returned to his kingdom, ordered his wife to be slain, and redefined "married life."

The situation in the kingdom is very bad; rebellion is simmering, and the vizier is running out of virgins. Shahrazad offers herself as the next bride, but not as the next victim. She is far too well bred ever to place her father in the awkward position of having to execute his own child. Instead, she will marry King Shahriyar and by telling him marvelous stories free him of the need to behead each morning the woman he had taken as his virgin bride the preceding afternoon. Her hope is to begin once again the daily royal wedding tale, but this time to replace its local, twisted finish with the more common and traditional ending.

Her image of her wedding night is unusual, in keeping with her circumstances: After sex with the king, she will begin a story, supposedly for her younger sister Dinarzad, but really meant for the king's ears. She will time its climax to be interrupted by the breaking of dawn so that the king, to hear the rest of the story, will have to postpone her execution by a day. She hopes to repeat this trick for as many days as it takes. Some of her stories will be veiled parables. Some will carry King Shahriyar beyond his bleak interior landscape. Some will be symbols of what could be. All will have an amazing and wonderful surface.

The vizier fears that his daughter will merely suffer. True to his character and to his role, he does not say so directly, but instead tells her a story of a donkey who, proud of his intelligence, schemes to trick the master of the farm into excusing the sweet, simple ox from labor. The scheme works, but not as the donkey expected. The wealthy farmer orders the donkey driven into the field to work in the ox's place.

In using a story to warn Shahrazad, the vizier engages in narrative imagining, a form of thinking before acting. In trying to change her mind through story, he unwittingly endorses the very strategy he asks her to reject—to try to change the king's mind through stories.

Narrative imagining—story—is the fundamental instrument of thought. Rational capacities depend upon it. It is our chief means of looking into the future, of predicting, of planning, and of explaining. It is a literary capacity indispensable to human cognition generally. This is the first way in which the mind is essentially literary.

The vizier asks Shahrazad to think before acting by imagining a story and then evaluating it. He traces the consequence of her action forward to disaster, implying that Shahrazad should abandon her plan. In doing so, he puts to domestic use a fundamental cognitive activity: story.

But there is something odd here. The vizier does not say, "Look, daughter, this is your current situation: You are comfortable, so comfortable that you have the leisure to get interested in other people's problems. But if you keep this up, you will end in pain." Instead, he says, "Once upon a time there was a comfortable donkey who got interested in the problems of the ox. The donkey, who thought he was the sharpest thing ever, gave some clever advice to the dullard ox. It worked amazingly well, at least for the ox, but it had unfortunate consequences for the donkey. Before you know it, the ox was lolling about in the hay of contentment while the donkey was sweating and groaning at the ox's labor."

The vizier presents one story that projects to another story whose principal character is Shahrazad. We, and Shahrazad, are to understand the possible future story of Shahrazad by projecting onto it the story of the ox and the donkey. The punch line is that Shahrazad is the donkey. This projection of one story onto another may seem exotic and literary, and it is—but it is also, like story, a fundamental instrument of the mind. Rational capacities depend upon it. It is a literary capacity indispensable to human cognition generally. This is the second way in which the human mind is essentially literary.

One special kind of literature, parable, conveniently combines story and projection. Parable serves as a laboratory where great things are condensed in a small space. To understand parable is to understand root capacities of the everyday mind, and conversely.

Parable begins with narrative imagining—the understanding of a complex of objects, events, and actors as organized by our knowledge of *story*. It then combines story with projection: one story is projected onto another. The essence of parable is its intricate combining of two of our basic forms of knowledge—story and projection. This classic combination produces one of our keenest mental processes for constructing meaning. The evolution of the genre of parable is thus neither accidental nor exclusively literary: it follows inevitably from the nature of our conceptual systems. The motivations for parable are as strong as the motivations for color vision or sentence structure or the ability to hit a distant object with a stone.

Literary parables are only one artifact of the mental process of parable. Proverbs frequently present a condensed, implicit story to be interpreted through projection: "When the cat's away, the mice will play," "Once burned, twice shy," "A poor workman blames his tools," "Don't get between a dog and his bone." In cases like these, the target story—the story we are to understand—is not even mentioned overtly, but through our agile capacity to use both story and projection, we project the overt source story onto a covert target story. "When the cat's away, the mice will play," said at the office, can be projected onto a story of boss and workers. Said in the classroom, it can be projected onto a story of teacher and students. Said of sexual relationships, it can be projected onto a story of infidelity. With equal ease, we can project it onto stories of a congressional oversight committee and the industries regulated by that committee, a police force and the local thieves, or a computer security device and the computer viruses it was intended to control. If we find "When the cat's away, the mice will play" out of context, in a book of proverbs or in a fortune cookie, we can project it onto an abstract story that might cover a great range of specific target stories and muse over the possible targets to which it might apply. "Look before you leap" similarly suggests an abstract story that applies to indefinitely many target stories.

The ease with which we interpret statements and construct meanings in this fashion is absolutely misleading: we feel as if we are doing no work at all. It is like listening to a speaker of English utter scores of syllables a minute: We use complicated unconscious knowledge to understand the speech but feel as if we are passive, as if we merely listen while the understanding happens by magic. With parables and proverbs, just as with language itself, we must see past our apparent ease of understanding if we are to locate the intricate unconscious work involved in arriving at these interpretations.

To study mind, we must become comfortable with the fact that mind generally does not work the way it appears to. This sounds paradoxical. We expect our introspective sense of mind to serve as a reasonable guide to the actual nature of mind. We expect it to give us a loose picture that, once enhanced by science, will represent the workings of mind. But it is instead badly deceptive. Our loose picture of mind is a loose fantasy. Consciousness is a wonderful instrument for helping us to focus, to make certain kinds of decisions and discriminations, and to create certain kinds of memories, but it is a liar about mind. It shamelessly represents itself as comprehensive and all-governing, when in fact the real work is often done elsewhere, in ways too fast and too smart and too effective for slow, stupid, unreliable consciousness to do more than glimpse, dream of, and envy.

Fables like Aesop's, cautionary tales like the vizier's to his daughter Shahrazad, veiled indictments like the one the prophet Nathan delivers to King David in 2 Samuel 12:1-7 ("You are the man"), epithets like "wing-footed Hermes," conceits in metaphysical poetry, and extended allegories like *Everyman* or *Pilgrim's Progress* or the *Divine Comedy* all consist of the combination of story and projection. Even stories exceptionally specific in their setting, character, and dialogue submit to projection. Often a short story will contain no overt mark that it stands for anything but what it purports to represent, and yet we will interpret it as projecting to a much larger abstract narrative, one that applies to our own specific lives, however far our lives are removed from the detail of the story. Such an emblematic story, however unyieldingly specific in its references, can seem pregnant with general meaning.

The projection of story operates throughout everyday life and throughout the most elite and sacred literature. Literary critics, observing it at work in exceptional literary inventions such as the *Faerie Queene* or *The Rime of the Ancient Mariner* or *Through the Looking Glass* or *The Wasteland*, have from time to time proposed that these spectacular inventions are not essentially exotic, but rather represent the carefully worked products of a fundamental mode of thought that is universal and indispensable. Parable—defined by the *Oxford English Dictionary* as the expression of one story through another—has seemed to literary critics to belong not merely to expression and not exclusively to literature, but rather, as C. S. Lewis observed in 1936, *to mind in general*. If we want to study the everyday mind, we can begin by turning to the literary mind exactly because the everyday mind is essentially literary.

Parable is today understood as a certain kind of exotic and inventive literary story, a subcategory within the special worlds of fiction. The original Greek word—παραβολή (*parabole*), from the verb παραβάλλειν (*paraballein*)—had a much wider, schematic meaning: the tossing or projecting of one thing alongside another. The Greek word could be used of placing one thing against another, staking one thing to another, even tossing fodder beside a horse, tossing dice alongside each other, or turning one's eyes to the side. In these meanings, παραβάλλειν is the equivalent of Latin *projicere*, from which we get the English "to project" and "projection."

I will use the word *parable* more narrowly than its Greek root but much more widely than the common English term: *Parable is the projection of story*. Parable, defined this way, refers to a general and indispensable instrument of everyday thought that shows up everywhere, from telling time to reading Proust. I use the word *parable* in this unconventional way to draw attention to a misconception I hope to correct, that the everyday mind has little to do with literature. Although literary texts may be special, the instruments of thought used to invent and interpret them are basic to everyday thought. Written works called narratives or stories may be shelved in a special section of the bookstore, but the mental instrument I call narrative or story is basic to human thinking. Literary works known as parables may reside within fiction, but the mental instrument I call parable has the widest utility in the everyday mind.

We can learn a surprising amount about story, projection, and parable in everyday life by considering for a moment the fictional lives of the fictional vizier and Shahrazad. The vizier is in a terrible position, on the edge of dealing with his daughter's life or death, the complex mind of his king, and the fate of his country. He is called on to foresee, a basic human mental activity, and he is supposedly the national master at foresight. He is the vizier. He has had unparalleled experience in crucial foresight when there is no second chance. He is fully exposed in his roles as both father and adviser. A failure at this moment will destroy absolutely everything. He turns, naturally, to the most powerful and basic instruments he possesses: story and projection. His motivation is absolute, since he knows that to succeed at her scheme, Shahrazad will have to outperform him at his own professional practice her first time out, under conditions more unfamiliar and dramatic than anything that has accompanied his own feats of forethought and persuasion. Yet the contest is unequal: She is a rank novice while he is the reigning grand master.

Shahrazad sees everything at stake, too, but from a different viewpoint: It is her country, her king, her father, her sisters (literally and figuratively), and sooner or later, no doubt, her own virginity and life, whether she volunteers them or not. It is also, potentially, in narrative imagination, her marriage, her children, her future, her genius, her life story. A failure will destroy absolutely everything. She too turns naturally to the most powerful and basic instruments she possesses: story and projection. These are the powers of mind she will live by, not only in the drama of her execution or reprieve, but also in the minute details of her storytelling nights.

It is a recurrent tale: The cautious parent sees all the danger while the adventurous child sees all the opportunity. They stand in conflict at just that moment in their lives when the parent's power is ebbing and the child's capacity is rising. The child, of course, will have her way. Her father must step back into the condition of hope. Shahrazad has always been in his hands. Now he will be in hers. In this story, repeated in every generation, the child is confident and ambivalently thrilled at the prospect of having her capacity put to the test in action, to see whether she can succeed where her parent has failed, while the parent is nearly overcome with fear yet sustained by the secret thought that if anyone can do it, it's his kid.

I imagine Shahrazad at this moment as prescient, knowing just how good she is and just what powers and opportunities she possesses that are beyond her father's capacity to imagine. Her presentiment comes from her own use of foresight through narrative imagining. But not even she, for all her looking into the future, can know that her performance during the next thousand and one nights will bring her a reputation as the greatest literary mind ever. Along with that other fictional author, the Homer of the *Odyssey*, she will become a paragon of human imaginative superiority.

If Shahrazad and the vizier could know of her fame down to our age, it would probably mean less to them than would its implication that her daring idea succeeds, which further implies that tomorrow morning her head will not fall beneath her father's sword. She will live, not happily ever after—this is an adult story—but for the appropriate temporal space of risk and terror, intimacy and pleasure, until she and Shahriyar are visited by the Destroyer of all earthly pleasures, the Leveler of kings and peasants, the Annihilator of women and men.

&

The story of Shahrazad presents to us in miniature the mental patterns of parable:

*Prediction.* The vizier imagines the consequences of an event, namely the story that follows the donkey's intrusion into the affairs of the ox and the farmer. By projection, he is at the same time imagining the story that would follow Shahrazad's proposed intrusion into the affairs of the virgins and Shahriyar. Narrative imagining is prediction.

*Evaluation.* If the event whose consequences we imagine is an intentional act, we can evaluate the wisdom of that act by evaluating those consequences. The vizier not only predicts the consequences of Shahrazad's proposed intrusion, he thereby evaluates its wisdom. Narrative imagining is evaluation.

*Planning.* Shahrazad imagines a goal: to stop Shahriyar. She intends to "succeed in saving the people or perish and die like the rest." It so happens that she has a second goal: to establish a sound marriage with King Shahriyar. It is convenient that achieving the second goal automatically achieves the first. She constructs in imagination a narrative path of action that leads from the present situation to the sound marriage. This story is her plan. Narrative imagining is planning.

*Explanation.* We often need to explain how something "came about." We appear to do this by constructing a narrative path from a prior understood state to the state we need to explain. Shahrazad's plan to change Shahriyar depends upon a prior explanation, of how Shahriyar the happily married king became Shahriyar the destroyer of women. This explanation consists of the narrative that starts with Shahriyar the happily married king and ends with Shahriyar the destroyer of women. Narrative imagining is explanation.

*Objects and events.* We recognize small stories as involving objects and events. This raises a problem: The world does not come to us with category labels—"This is an object," "This is an event." How do we form conceptual categories of objects and events?

*Actors.* We recognize certain objects in stories as actors. This raises another problem: The world does not come labeled with little category signs that say "This is an actor." How do we form conceptual categories of actors?

*Stories.* We recognize stories as complex dynamic integrations of objects, actors, and events. But again, we do not recognize each story as wholly unique. Instead, we know abstract stories that apply to ranges of specific situations. How do we form conceptual categories of stories?

*Projection.* The tale of the ox and the donkey, in which the donkey helps the ox but then suffers in the ox's place, is offered as a source tale to be projected onto the story of what will happen should Shahrazad be foolish enough to try to help the suffering virgins. The power of this projection is obvious, but how it works is a mystery. How do we project one story onto another? What is the cognitive mechanism of parable?

*Metonymy.* In the tale of the ox and the donkey, the sifted straw is metonymic for luxury—that is, it stands for luxury—and the plough and the millstone are metonymic for labor and suffering. We know this without conscious evaluation. We know, for example, not to take the sifted straw as metonymic for yellow things, or the plough and millstone as metonymic for man-made artifacts. This seems obvious and even automatic, but how we make metonymic associations is mysterious.

*Emblem.* The vizier and his daughter stand as emblems or instances of parent and child; their conflict stands as an emblem or instance of generational conflict. What is an emblematic narrative?

*Image schemas.* When we think of one thing, for example, the donkey's pride and nosiness, as "leading to" another, such as his suffering, we are thinking image-schematically. This particular image schema—"leading to"—is basic to story. It consists of movement along a directed path. The points on the path correspond to stages of the story: We say, "What point have we reached in the story?" The "path" of the story "leads from" its "beginning" "to" its "end." What are image schemas and what are their roles in the literary mind?

*Counterparts in imaginative domains.* The vizier, in warning his daughter, has a mental model of the present. He imaginatively blends it with a hypothetical scenario in which Shahrazad goes to Shahriyar. Mentally, he develops that blend into a robust picture of a hypothetical future. These two narrative mental spaces, of the vizier's present reality and the hypothetical future, are separated in time and in potential. But there are conceptual connections between them as well as differences. In the mental space of the present, the role of vizier's elder daughter and the role of Shahriyar's wife do not have the same inhabitant. But in the mental space of the hypothetical future, they do, which is to say, the vizier is imagining a future in which the person who happens to inhabit the role of vizier's elder daughter also happens to inhabit the role of Shahriyar's (temporary) wife. The vizier, expressing these connections, could say, "If you marry Shahriyar, I will have to kill you," and we would know that the cause of the killing would not be his anger at his daughter for having disobeyed him but instead his obligation as vizier to execute whoever inhabits the role of Shahriyar's wife. We understand these mental space connections as well as the vizier, instantly, despite their complexity. If Shahrazad were to say, "If I marry Shahriyar, you will be surprised; you will be grandfather to the next king," we as well as the vizier would know immediately the connections between Shahrazad's mental space of the present and her mental space of the future. Constructing these mental space connections is amazingly literary and complicated. Shahrazad's mental space of the future, for example, includes a father who remembers his previous mental space of the future and who knows that it does not accord with his mental space of the present reality in the way it was supposed to. How do we construct narrative mental spaces and establish such connections between them?

*Conceptual Blending.* The ox and the donkey talk. Talking animals are so common in stories as to seem natural. Why do they arise in imagination and why should they seem natural? This apparently idle question turns out to be both essential to the investigation of mind and profoundly difficult to answer. Conceptual blending—in this case, the blending of talking people with mute animals to produce talking animals—is a basic process of thought. How does it work? What is its range?

*Language.* The parable of the ox and the donkey is expressed in language. Where does the structure of our language "come from" and what is its relation to parable?

We imagine realities and construct meanings. The everyday mind performs these feats by means of mental processes that are literary and that have always been judged to be literary. Cultural meanings peculiar to a society often fail to migrate intact across anthropological or historical boundaries, but the basic mental processes that make these meanings possible are universal. Parable is one of them.

## 2

# HUMAN MEANING

> Hamlet: Do you see yonder cloud that's almost in shape of
> a camel?
> Polonius: By th'mass, and 'tis like a camel indeed.
> Hamlet: Methinks it is like a weasel.
> Polonius: It is backed like a weasel.
> Hamlet: Or like a whale.
> Polonius: Very like a whale.
>
> *William Shakespeare, Hamlet*

IN THE TALE of the ox and the donkey, it is easy to see that we are dealing with *story, projection*, and *parable*. It is harder to see these capacities at work in everyday life, but we always use them. The rest of this book explores how the human mind is always at work constructing small stories and projecting them.

Story, projection, and parable do work for us; they make everyday life possible; they are the root of human thought; they are not primarily—or even importantly—entertainment. To be sure, the kinds of stories we are apt to notice draw attention to their status as the product of storytelling, and they often have an entertaining side. We might therefore think that storytelling is a special performance rather than a constant mental activity. But story as a mental activity is essential to human thought. The kinds of stories that are most essential to human thought produce experience that is completely absorbing, but we rarely notice those stories themselves or the way they work because they are always present.

This conjunction of what is absorbing but unnoticed is not as weird as it sounds. Human vision, for example, produces content that is always psychologically absorbing to everyone—we are absorbed in our visual field, no matter what it contains—but only a neurobiologist is likely to notice the constant mechanisms of vision that create our visual field. What everyone notices are some exceptional products of vision: A fireworks display seems more interesting than an empty parking lot, even though vision uses the same mechanisms to see both of them. We almost never notice the activity of vision or think of vision as an activity, but if we do, we must recognize that the activity of vision is constant and more important than anything we may happen to see.

Story as a mental activity is similarly constant yet unnoticed, and more important than any particular story. In the next three chapters, we will analyze some very basic abstract stories and some very basic patterns of their projection. We will find that the same basic mechanisms of parable underlie a great range of examples, from the everyday to the literary.

The basic stories we know best are small stories of events in space: The wind blows clouds through the sky, a child throws a rock, a mother pours milk into a glass, a whale swims through the water. These stories constitute our world and they are completely absorbing—we cannot resist watching the volley of the tennis ball. Our adult experience actually revolves around pouring the drink into the cup, carrying it, watching the bird soar, watching the plane descend, tracking the small stick as the stream carries it away.

As subjects of our prolonged conscious investigation, however, these small spatial stories may seem hopelessly boring. We are highly interested in our coherent personal experiences, which are the product of thinking with small spatial stories, but we are not interested in the small spatial stories themselves. When someone says, "Tell me a story," he means something unusual and interesting. *King Lear* is a "story"; *Peter Rabbit* is a "story." Someone pouring coffee into a cup is not a "story." Why waste time thinking about a human being pouring liquid into a container? This small spatial story takes place billions of times a day, all over the world, with numbing repetition. No one who pours the liquid thinks it is an interesting story; what is the point?

We must adopt a scientific perspective to see why something we already know how to do without effort or conscious attention can pose an extremely difficult and important scientific puzzle. The capacity for recognizing and executing small spatial stories is—like the capacity to speak, to see color, or to distinguish sounds— an obvious and deceptively easy capacity. In fact, it presents the chief puzzle of cognitive science. How can five billion different human beings all recognize and execute small spatial stories?

Even the most boring person can do it, so we have a hard time imagining that the capacity can be interesting. We devalue it as we devalue any plentiful resource. Since it is universal instead of scarce, the calculus of supply and demand must fix its price at zero. But it is actually worth whatever it is worth to be a human being because if you do not have this capacity, you do not have a human mind.

These small stories are what a human being has instead of chaotic experience. We know how they go. They are the knowledge that goes unnoticed but makes life possible. We do not need to worry about our movements or our interaction with the world because we have absolute confidence in these stories. They are so essential to life that our mastery of them must be almost entirely unconscious; from a biological point of view, we cannot be trusted to run them consciously. In important moments, we had better not notice them, just as we had better not notice mechanisms of vision while we are fleeing a predator. We have in fact no practical need to analyze them. Biologically, they must be *unproblematic,* making them seem intellectually boring. But they become intellectually interesting the moment we lack them.

These stories are inventions. They are essential, but they are invented. This conjunction of adjectives may seem paradoxical if we think of essential things (like a heartbeat) as compulsory or necessary and invented things (like a light bulb) as optional. In that way of thinking, what is essential and what is invented must be contraries. But although these small spatial stories are inventive constructions of the human mind, they are not optional. The necessary biology and the necessary experience of any normal human infant inevitably produce a capacity for story in the infant. It is not possible for a human infant to fail to achieve the concept of a container, for example, or liquid, or pouring, or flowing, or a path, or movement along a path, or the product of these concepts: the small spatial story in which liquid is poured and flows along a path into a container. Our core indispensable stories not only can be invented, they must be invented if we are to survive and have human lives.

We can see their status as inventions by contrasting them with alternative representations of the world. When we watch someone sitting down into a chair, we see what physics cannot recognize: an animate agent performing an intentional act involving basic human-scale categories of events like *sitting* and objects like *chair.* But physics offers a representation of the world that leaves out agency, motive, intentionality, and a range of structure that is part of the conceptual equipment of everyone, including physicists. The basic elements of physics are not tied to the human scale; *sitting* and *chair* are elements of story but not elements of physics. The fundamental units of physics exist at levels that are foreign to us—subatomic quarks, metrics of space-time, integrations from zero to infinity. Where physics offers an impenetrable but accurate physical description in the form of a wave equation, story offers Einstein sitting in a chair.

In our small stories, we distinguish objects from events, objects from other objects, and events from other events. We categorize some objects as belonging to the category *person* and other objects as belonging to the category *chair*. We recognize what a person does with a chair as belonging to the category *sitting*.

We understand our experience in this way because we are built evolutionarily to learn to distinguish objects and events and combine them in small spatial stories at human scale in a way that is useful for us, given that we have human bodies. This is what the human brain does best, although a divine intelligence with a God's-eye view might have no use for the human concepts *object* and *event*, no use for human perceptual categories of kinds of objects and events, and no use for small spatial stories.

There is a general story to human existence: It is the story of how we use story, projection, and parable to think, beginning at the level of small spatial stories. Yet this level, although fully inventive, is so unproblematic in our experience and so necessary to our existence that it is left out of account as precultural, even though it is the core of culture. When it is left out of account, the human condition can appear to have no general story. As Clifford Geertz has observed,

> It is necessary then to be satisfied with swirls, confluxions, and inconstant connections; clouds collecting, clouds dispersing. There is no general story to be told, no synoptic picture to be had. Or if there is, no one, certainly no one wandering into the middle of them like Fabrice at Waterloo, is in a position to construct them, neither at the time nor later. What we can construct, if we keep notes and survive, are hindsight accounts of the connectedness of things that seem to have happened: pieced-together patternings, after the fact.

But Geertz's claim that there is no general story is itself a general story not of what we know but of how we know, and his story is possible only because there is already in place, behind it, a general story about human thought. The general story is that human beings construct small spatial stories and project them parabolically. Geertz's story depends upon this general story: Like Hamlet and Polonius, he gives us small spatial stories in which we recognize clouds that collect or disperse, shapes that we assign to categories of objects, pieces that we put together, liquids or gases that swirl and flow together, vistas that we see, and so on; and he encourages us to use the mental process of parable to project these small spatial stories we know and must know since we are human onto the story of human culture and knowledge. His description of the absence of a general story begins with small spatial stories and projects them parabolically onto stories of human thought. Its compelling use of story, projection, and parable demonstrates the general story of the human condition—a story whose existence it denies.

## IMAGE SCHEMAS

How do we recognize objects, events, and stories? Part of the answer has to do with "image schemas." Mark Johnson and Leonard Talmy—followed more recently by Claudia Brugman, Eve Sweetser, George Lakoff, Ronald Langacker, me, and many others—have analyzed linguistic evidence for the existence of image schemas. Image schemas are skeletal patterns that recur in our sensory and motor experience. *Motion along a path*, *bounded interior*, *balance*, and *symmetry* are typical image schemas.

Consider the image schema *container*. Like all image schemas, it is minimal. It has three parts: an interior, an exterior, and a boundary that separates them. We experience many things as containers: a bottle, a bag, a cup, a car, a mountain valley, rooms, houses, cupboards, boxes, chests, and drawers. Two of our most important containers are our heads and our bodies.

We use the image schema *motion along a path* to recognize locomotion by people, hands reaching out to us, our own hand reaching out, a ball rolling, milk pouring into a cup.

Simple image schemas can combine to form complex image schemas. For example, the *goal* of the *path* can be the *interior* of a *container*. This combination produces the complex image schema *into*. Alternatively, the *source* of the *path* can be the *interior* of a *container*, producing the complex image schema *out of*. The *path* can intersect a *container*, producing the complex image schema *through*.

There are many other image schemas we use to structure our experience, and thereby to recognize objects and events and place them in categories. Leonard Talmy originally analyzed image schemas of force dynamics such as *pushing*, *pulling*, *resisting*, *yielding*, and *releasing*. Other dynamic image schemas include *dipping*, *rising*, *climbing*, *pouring*, and *falling*.

Image schemas arise from perception but also from interaction. We *perceive* milk flowing into a glass; we *interact* with it flowing into our bodies. We recognize a category connection between one door and another, one chair and another, one ball and another, one rock and another, one event of *pouring* and another not only because they share image schemas of shape or part-whole structure, but also because our image schemas for interacting with them are the same. Our image schemas for *interacting* with an object or an event must be consistent with our image schemas for *perceiving* it if perception is to provide a basis for action.

To recognize several events as structured by the same image schema is to recognize a category. We have a neurobiological pattern for throwing a small object. This pattern underlies the individual event of throwing a rock and helps us create the category *throwing*. We have a neurobiological pattern for reaching out and picking something up. This pattern underlies an individual event of reaching out and picking something up and helps us create the category *reaching out and picking up*.

Every time such a pattern becomes active it is slightly different. If we think of how often we reach out to pick up a glass and under what different conditions the event takes place, we see how varied the actual event is in its exact details each time it occurs. Our bodies are at slightly different orientations to the glass; the glass is slightly nearer or farther away; the glass sits on a slightly different surface; there may be obstructions to be avoided; the glass has a slightly different shape or weight or texture. We recognize all of the individual events of picking up a glass as belonging to one category in part because they all share a skeletal complex image schema of dynamic interaction.

Partitioning the world into objects involves partitioning the world into small spatial stories because our recognition of objects depends on the characteristic stories in which they appear: We catch a ball, throw a rock, sit in a chair, pet a dog, take a drink from a glass of water.

## PROJECTING IMAGE SCHEMAS

Parable often projects image schemas. When the projection carries structure from a "source" we understand to a "target" we want to understand, the projection conforms to a constraint: The result for the target shall not be a conflict of image schemas.

For example, when we map one rich image onto another, the (relevant) image schemas of source and target end up aligned in certain ways. It may seem obvious when we say someone's head is hanging like a wilted flower, or when Auden describes a solitary man weeping on a bench and "Hanging his head down, with his mouth distorted, / Helpless and ugly as an embryo chicken," that the verticality schemas in the source images (flower and chicken) and target image (human head) should align. It may seem equally obvious that part-whole relationships in source and target images should align, that a bounded interior should project to a bounded interior, that directionality of gaze should correspond in source and target, that relationships of adjacency should correspond, and so on. But in fact it is not at all obvious, however natural it seems. The specific details of the rich images need not correspond, but the relevant image schemas are lined up.

When we project one concept onto another, image schemas again seem to do much of the work. For example, when we project spatiality onto temporality, we project image schemas; we think of time itself, which has no spatial shape, as having a spatial shape—linear, for example, or circular. We like to think of events in time, which also have no spatial shape, as having features of spatial shapes—continuity, extension, discreteness, completion, open-endedness, circularity, part-whole relations, and so on. This way of conceiving of time and of events in time arises by projecting skeletal image schemas from space onto time.

We think of causal relations as structured by spatial image schemas such as *links* and *paths*. These image schemas need not be static. For example, we have a dynamic image schema in which one thing comes out of another, and we project that image schema to give structure to one of our concepts of causation, as when we say that Italian *emerged from* its mother, Latin. Abstract reasoning appears to be possible in large part because we project image-schematic structure from spatial concepts onto abstract concepts. We say, for example, "Shame *forced* him to confess," even though no physical forces are involved. Forms of social and psychological causation are understood by projection from bodily causation that involves physical forces. This is parable.

## SEQUENCES

A woman sees a rock, moves toward it, bends down, picks it up, and stands back up. Her legs, body, and arms begin an amazingly intricate sequence of movements. Her hand releases the rock, which follows a trajectory through the air to hit the window, which shatters.

The brain is extremely good at constructing refined and intricate sequences of movement and then executing them, as when we run to catch a baseball. William H. Calvin's *Cerebral Symphony* is a meditation upon whether this capacity might be considered the one central capacity of human intelligence. As Calvin shows, running and walking are marvels of the brain's ability to compose and execute motor sequences. We share the capacity for such sequencing of bodily action with other species. But peculiarly human mental activities also depend upon sequencing. Composing or recognizing a musical phrase, speaking or listening to a sentence, and telling or understanding a story are all examples of our ability to recognize or execute a sequence that counts as a whole. The sequential nature of speech has historically been recognized as one of the defining features of language. Many cognitive scientists have observed that the human brain is uncommonly sophisticated in its capacity for constructing sequences.

To recognize small spatial stories requires us to recognize not only objects involved in events, but also sequences of these situations. The ball is pushed; it rolls; it encounters an obstacle; it knocks the obstacle over, or the obstacle stops the ball. In another small spatial story, our father's hand grasps an object and moves the object to a position in front of us; the hand releases; the hand withdraws; we reach out; we touch the object; we grasp the object; we put it into our mouth; we release it; we remove our hand; we chew it; we swallow it.

In recognizing small spatial stories, we are recognizing not just a sequence of particular objects involved in particular events, but also a sequence of objects *that belong to categories* involved in events *that belong to categories*. Every time our father places food in front of us, both his actions and the food will be somewhat different, and our actions in response will be somewhat different. But we recognize the objects and events as essentially the same, as belonging to the same category. We recognize a general story. Our experiences differ in detail, but we make sense of them as consisting of a repertoire of small spatial stories, repeated again and again.

These small spatial stories are routinely held together by one or more dynamic image schemas. Consider a fish jumping out of the water through an arc and back into the water, a baseball hit from a bat to fly through an arc into the stands, a rock thrown to hit a distant object, a bird flying from one tree to another. All of these sequences are structured by the image schema of a point moving along a directed path from a source to a goal. This dynamic image schema inherently carries with it a sequence of spatial situations. Consider the image schema of something moving to the edge of a supporting plateau and falling off. This is a temporal sequence combining image schemas. There is no end to the number of particular small spatial stories it structures: a ball rolling off a deck, a keg rolling off a dock, a puddle of tea pouring off the side of a table, a human being walking off a roof.

## EXECUTION, RECOGNITION, IMAGINATION

Most of our action consists of executing small spatial stories: getting a glass of juice from the refrigerator, dressing, bicycling to the market. Executing these stories, recognizing them, and imagining them are all related because they are all structured by the same image schemas.

If we see someone pick up a stone and throw it at us, we do not need to wait for the stone to hit us before we can recognize the small spatial story and respond to it. We recognize small spatial stories on the basis of partial information. When we duck, it is because pattern completion tells us the possible end of the small spatial story in which we are hit by the stone. Suppose we see nothing but a stone smashing into a window. We immediately look in the direction from which the stone came to see who or what threw it. Suppose we see only someone's arm go back, and a few seconds later, a stone hitting a window. We can imagine the intermediate sequence in the story. Finally, suppose we see none of the story, but only imagine it with our eyes closed. In this last case, the recognition of the small spatial story has been activated without perception of any of its parts.

## PREDICTION, EVALUATION, PLANNING, EXPLANATION

We duck when we see someone cock an arm to throw a stone at us because we are predicting: we recognize the beginning sequence of a small spatial story, imagine the rest, and respond. Narrative imagining is our fundamental form of predicting

When we decide that it is perfectly reasonable to place our plum on the dictionary but not the dictionary on our plum, we are both predicting and evaluating. Evaluating the future of an act is evaluating the wisdom of the act. In this way, narrative imagining is also our fundamental form of evaluating.

When we hear something and want to see it, and walk to a new location in order to see it, we have made and executed a plan. We have constructed a story taking us from the original situation to the desired situation and executed the story. The story is the plan. In this way, narrative imagining is our fundamental cognitive instrument for planning.

When a drop of water falls mysteriously from the ceiling and lands at our feet, we try to imagine a story that begins from the normal situation and ends with the mysterious situation. The story is the explanation. Narrative imagining is our fundamental cognitive instrument for explanation.

## ANIMACY AND AGENCY

Small spatial stories involve events and objects. We recognize some of these objects as animate actors. From time to time it has been considered philosophically embarrassing that we think of animate actors as causes in themselves. Objects and events seem to have a claim on objective existence, but animacy and agency seem almost supernatural and suspicious as elements of a scientific theory. Many attempts have been made to reduce animacy and agency to simple matters of objects and events. We have eliminated river gods and wind deities and tree spirits from our descriptions of the natural world. But small spatial stories are often populated with animate actors that show no sign of disappearing. What are they?

Prototypical actors—human beings and many animals—are recognized as self-moving and as capable of sensation. Self-movement, like all movement, is recognized by means of dynamic image schemas: we recognize an event of self-movement when we recognize it as conforming to an image schema of self-movement. It is more difficult to say how we recognize sensation by actors other than ourselves, since we can have only our own sensations, not theirs. We can perceive their movements but we cannot perceive their sensations. We must infer their sensations by analogy with ourselves: they appear to move in reaction to sensations just as we would. We recoil when startled; we track a visual stimulus; we turn from an unpleasant smell. They appear to do the same things. We see the cat jump backward in surprise or move when it recognizes a bird, and we infer the cat's sensations from its movements. Recognizing objects (other than ourselves) as having sensations depends in this way upon recognizing them as self-moving: we can infer their sensations from their self-movements. This is already parable: We see a small spatial story in which an actor other than ourselves behaves in certain ways, and we project features of animacy and agency onto it from stories in which we are the actor.

Prototypical objects can be moved. Objects that are prototypical actors are perceived as able to move themselves and able to move other objects. If actors move objects, what moves the actors? What is the source of their movement? One answer that has come up historically is *the soul*. The soul is what moves the body. The body is the object the soul moves as a consequence of its own self-movement. In *On the Soul*, Aristotle surveys theories on the nature of the soul, showing that in nearly all of them, soul is regarded as having movement and sensation. His survey testifies to the antiquity and durability of recognizing actors as movers and sensors. This abstract concept of the soul is created by a parabolic projection. We know the small spatial story in which an actor moves a physical object; we project this story onto the story of the movement of the body. The object projects to the body and the actor projects to the soul. In this way, parable creates the concept of the soul.

When Aristotle writes of self-movement, he appears to be thinking of movement complexes, because something that is self-moving uses its capacity for self-movement often, making the trajectory of its movement irregular. A horse, for example, does not move the way a cannon ball moves or the way an apple falls from a tree or the way a ball rolls down a smooth incline: the horse moves here and there, to one side and the other, moving its head this way and that. The movement of a person or an animal looks like a complex of many movements, resulting in a complex trajectory. In short, the image schema for recognizing the self-movement of an actor is more detailed than the image schema for recognizing the "self-movement" of the ripe apple's fall to the ground.

We detect *self-movement* by an object when we recognize an image schema of movement not caused by external forces. We detect *animacy* when this image schema is a complex of a number of movements. We detect *caused motion* when we recognize a complex dynamic image schema in which the motion of one object causes the motion of another object. We detect *animate agency* when we recognize an image schema of *animacy* combined with an image schema of *caused motion*, as when a baby reaches out (animacy) and picks up the rattle (caused motion). The causal object in an image schema of *animate agency* is usually recognized as an *actor*.

These recognitions do not stand up scientifically. We know that the wind may move variously and blow the leaves in subtle and varied patterns, or that the acid may eat the metal violently and erratically, thus fitting image schemas characteristic of actors, yet we do not want to place the wind and the acid in the same category with human beings and animals. But our reluctance to do so shows only that when we acquire a sophisticated scientific knowledge, we discount the validity of some of our recognitions. For virtually the entire history of human cognition, it has seemed plausible to regard the wind as an honorary actor because although it lacks sensation, it has the image schemas of animate agency. To the intelligent newborn child, the jouncy voice-activated mobile above the crib that moves when the child vocalizes may seem to be an excellent candidate for *actor*.

## RESEARCH ON IMAGE SCHEMAS

The term *image schema* was proposed by Mark Johnson, but the notion has a long lineage and many current cousins. Here, I review some of the most salient research. In "Further Reading on Image Schemas" I list some general introductions to image schemas as well as the specific works I cite in this section.

IMAGE SCHEMAS IN THE BRAIN. It is relatively easy to see image schemas at work in behavior and language. To walk in the rain, we must go *outside* our *house-container* so we will not be *under* a roof that *stops* the rain from *falling down onto* us, and we must *move* along a *path out of* doors.

It is harder to locate image schemas at work in the brain, but there are early indications. The cerebellum, for example, has traditionally been recognized as a specialized part of the brain suited for neuronal group patterns whose activation results in sequences of precisely timed and coordinated movement, like throwing a curve ball or touch-typing a common word or playing a theme on the piano. What we would like to know is how such brain patterns for spatial movement are connected across modalities: When we see someone throw a rock at a window, the visual image schemas according to which we recognize and understand the event are presumably connected to the kinesthetic image schemas according to which we perform the event, the auditory image schemas that belong to the event, and the tactile image schemas of touching the rock. Theories of connections between such image schemas have only recently been developed and remain speculative. Antonio Damasio has proposed a neurobiological model of "convergence zones" that might have something to say about such cross-modal integration. His model "rejects a single anatomical site for the integration of memory and motor processes and a single store for the meaning of entities or events. Meaning is reached by time-locked multiregional retro-activation of widespread fragment records. Only the latter records can become contents of consciousness." Because a higher-order convergence zone is cross-modal, it offers a site for activating different neuronal patterns corresponding to the identical image schema across different modalities.

The most specific evidence of image schemas in the brain comes from reports of what are known as "orientation tuning" columns. The primary visual cortex responds to moving bars of light in an interesting way: A given neuron will have a preferred "orientation tuning"—it will respond best to a bar at a given angle. Other neurons in the column appear to have the same preferred stimulus, so that the column constitutes a neuronal group of cells that fire together in time in an organized manner to recognize a line at a preferred angle. Different orientation columns prefer different angles. In this way, orientation tuning columns work like neurobiological image schemas for structuring certain kinds of visual experience and for understanding it. These orientation tuning columns in the primary visual cortex are connected to neuronal groups in another, separate visual map, known as V2, and these two connected visual maps respond coherently to the same preferred stimulus, which suggests that image schemas in primary visual cortex are coordinated with analogous image schemas in V2.

Gerald Edelman's theory of neuronal group selection offers a suggestion for a general neuroscientific explanation of image schemas. In simplistic outline, it has the following logic. A sensory sheet (like the retina) projects to various regions of the nervous system (called "maps"). For any particular map, repeated encounter with a stimulus results in changes in synaptic strengths between neurons in the map, thus forming up ("selecting") certain neuronal group patterns in that map that become active whenever the stimulus is encountered. For any particular stimulus object, there will be many neuronal group patterns in many maps. (For example, there are different maps for different modalities, like vision, and for different submodalities, like form, motion, and color.) These various neuronal group patterns in the various maps are linked through another hypothetical neurobiological process Edelman calls "reentrant mapping": a given stimulus will result in activity in many maps, and these activities are linked reinforcingly through "reentry."

For example, an image schema for *container* would be a coordinated dynamic interaction across neuronal group patterns in various maps that arose through experiential selection and reentry during encounters with a great variety of things that gradually came to be categorized as containers exactly *because* we take them to share this dynamic interactional image schema. The image schema itself needs no translation: it is meaningful, when activated, as corresponding to this category.

It would be a mistake to overwork or overinterpret these beginning results. It is not clear how to connect the evidence for image schemas in the study of the mind to the evidence for image schemas in the study of the brain. Perhaps the neurobiological analogue of an image schema is not one neuronal group pattern but rather the complex interaction of several neuronal group patterns in different sites, all coordinated. The best evidence to date of the specific nature of image schemas still comes from the study of language.

IMAGE SCHEMAS IN BASIC-LEVEL CATEGORIES. Outside the neurosciences, psychological studies are beginning to provide evidence for the role of image schemas in categorization and cognition. Psychologists Eleanor Rosch and Carolyn Mervis and a range of associates have made insightful discoveries in the last fifteen years concerning the conceptual categories of concrete objects. Rosch and her colleagues showed that there is one level of abstraction around which most information is organized. They call it the "basic" level—the level of concepts like *dog, table, car, tree, house, bicycle, spoon,* and *giraffe.* The basic level, essentially, is the level at which we partition our environments into objects with which we interact in small spatial stories: *chair, door, knife, ball, rock.* Rosch presents evidence that the basic level is the highest level at which category members share overall perceived shapes and the highest level at which members call for similar interactional motor patterns. Since these overall shapes and these interactional patterns are image schemas, Rosch's work provides evidence for the role of image schemas in structuring perceptual and conceptual categories. Although the tradition of research on "basic-level" categories is controversial, none of the controversy detracts from this essential point.

IMAGE SCHEMAS IN DEVELOPMENTAL PSYCHOLOGY. In a 1992 article in *Psychological Review* called "How to Build a Baby: II. Conceptual Primitives," Jean Mandler presents evidence for image schemas from clinical experiments in developmental psychology. She claims that infants develop concepts of animacy and agency on the basis of image schemas. The image schemas she proposes are closely equivalent to those we have considered above.

Mandler attempts to explain how the developing infant might go from forming discriminable perceptual categories to using them for thought. She proposes that certain kinds of perceptual information are recoded into forms that represent meanings. This recoding produces a set of image schemas that serve as conceptual primitives (in the sense of being foundational, not in the sense of being atomic, unitary, or without structure). She proposes that infants form an image schema of self-motion ("an object is not moving, and then, without any forces acting on it, it starts to move"), of animate-motion (motion with an irregular trajectory), of self-moving animate (a complex combination of the previous two), of caused motion (a trajector impinges on an object and it then moves), and of agency (a combination of the image schemas of animacy and caused motion, in which an animate object moves itself and also causes another object to move.)

Mandler, in essence, proposes a general psychological process whereby perceptual experience is redescribed "into an image-schematic form of representation" used in building concepts.

## NARRATIVE AND THE BODY

At conception, an individual human being carries an individual genetic endowment (genotype) that arose under evolutionary pressures of selection and that guides her individual brain as it develops in its changing environments. That genotype cannot determine the fine specifics of point-to-point wiring and activity in the individual brain, but it can (and must) contribute to setting up a nervous system that will reach certain target values under experience. That genotype must do this because of Darwinian pressures: Genes that lead to less competent brains will be selected against. The genes implicitly provide target values for the developing brain. Those values derive implicitly from the history of selection on our ancestors. The particular target values that have arisen in our species are, at a minimum, stable regulation of homeostasis and metabolism, dispositions toward survival and reproduction, bodily movement in space, perceptual categorization, and the recognition and execution of small spatial stories. The combined operation of genetic influence and necessary experience of the sort inevitable for any normal human infant with a human body in a human environment leads to the ability to recognize and execute small spatial stories.

Seen in this way, narrative imagining, often thought of as literary and optional, appears instead to be inseparable from our evolutionary past and our necessary personal experience. It also appears to be a fundamental target value for the developing human mind.

## ᴈ 3 ᴇ

# BODY ACTION

But Apollo took from them the day of their return

αὐτὰρ ὁ τοῖσιν ἀφείλετο νόστιμον ἦμαρ

*Homer, the Odyssey*

Iɴ ᴛʜɪs ᴄʜᴀᴘᴛᴇʀ and the next, we will begin to map the basic parabolic terrain of the everyday mind. We will look at fundamental and extremely common patterns of parable that are essential to everyday thought, reasoning, and action, and that show up in literary examples for the reason that literature takes its instruments from the everyday mind. We will see some extremely basic abstract stories and some extremely common projections of those stories. Any single detail of these many related projections may look as if it could interest only the specialist, but taken together, these details provide an overall picture of the importance of parable in the everyday mind.

We begin by looking at stories that involve actors engaged in bodily action. Often a spatial story has no actor. The small spatial story of a wall's collapsing from age, for example, has no actor. Often a spatial story has many partial or potential actors and many intricate events that are brought about by no single distinct actor. The story of a bridge's giving way after years of use is such a story. Unfamiliar or complicated event-stories like these are easy to grasp by projection from simple action-stories we already know. Parable, by projecting simple action-stories onto unfamiliar or complicated event-stories, extends the range of action-stories.

Parable extends story through projection. One type of extremely fundamental projection projects action-stories onto event-stories. George Lakoff and I named this general pattern EVENTS ARE ACTIONS. An action is an event with an actor.

26

EVENTS ARE ACTIONS guides us in projecting familiar action-stories onto event-stories with or without actors. EVENTS ARE ACTIONS is a special case of parable: The source story is an action-story; the target story is any kind of event-story, including action-stories.

We can observe an example of this kind of parable in the first few lines of the *Odyssey*, where Homer refers to the thoughts of Odysseus and to the sad fates of his shipmates as they sailed homeward toward the island of Ithaka:

> Many were the men whose cities Odysseus learned and whose
>     minds he came to know,
> Many were the cares he suffered inwardly upon the sea,
> Hoping for his own life and the return of his crew.
> He could not save them, although he wanted to.
> Their own blind folly destroyed them.
> Idiots, they ate the cattle of Apollo.
> But Apollo took from them the day of their return.

> πολλῶν δ᾽ ἀνθρώπων ἴδεν ἄστεα καὶ νόον ἔγνω,
> πολλὰ δ᾽ ὅ γ᾽ ἐν πόντῳ πάθεν ἄλγεα ὃν κατὰ θυμόν,
> ἀρνύμενος ἥν τε ψυχὴν καὶ νόστον ἑταίρων.
> ἀλλ᾽ οὐδ᾽ ὣς ἑτάρους ἐρρύσατο, ἱέμενός περ·
> αὐτῶν γὰρ σφετέρῃσιν ἀτασθαλίῃσιν ὄλοντο,
> νήπιοι, οἳ κατὰ βοῦς Ὑπερίονος Ἠελίοιο
> ἤσθιον· αὐτὰρ ὁ τοῖσιν ἀφείλετο νόστιμον ἦμαρ.

The shipmates, returning from the Trojan War, sailed toward Ithaka with Odysseus, but in their wanderings they died at various times and in various ways. None of them made it home to Ithaka. This is a complicated spatial story of a journey, structured by the image schema of a directed path from a source (Troy) to a goal (Ithaka). For each of the shipmates, the progress along the path halts before the goal is reached. Many events of death occur in the elaborate story of this journey, with no single clear agency responsible for all of them. Homer chooses to present this complicated spatial event-story of a journey through parable: He projects onto it a simple spatial action-story in which there is one actor, Apollo, who is responsible for all these deaths. The source story is an action-story not of a journey but rather of an actor's physical manipulation of an object: Apollo, god of the sun, "takes" "something" "away from" the shipmates. What he takes away is conceived as an object: "the day of their return." This looks highly literary, and of course it is, since this parable intricately projects a story of physical manipulation onto a story of a journey. But parabolic projections occur in literature because they are already indispensable in the everyday mind.

In everyday conception, we often project a spatial action-story onto a spatial event-story. We might say, for example, that a duplicating machine *chewed up* a document. The target story is a physical and spatial event without an actor: A document is damaged in a copying machine. The source story is a physical and spatial action with an actor: The actor chews food. We understand the target event-story of *damage* by projection from the source action-story of *eating*. *Chewing* in the source story is projected onto the *mechanical process of copying* in the target story; *food* is projected onto the *document; chewer* is projected onto *the copying machine.* An action-story of *eating* is thus projected parabolically onto an event-story of *damage.*

We can say of a sailor exposed to the elements at sea that the sun *tortured* him and that he was *beaten mercilessly* by *savage* winds. The story of an actor who tortures someone by burning him is projected onto the story of the sailor's becoming sunburned. The story of a savage actor's mercilessly *beating* a victim is projected parabolically onto the story of forcible gusts of wind *impinging* on the sailor.

Many everyday event-stories lack causal actors. EVENTS ARE ACTIONS can turn them into action-stories: We complete the event-story to include a causal actor by projecting the actor in the action-story onto a nonactor in the event-story. The nonactor becomes thereby a metaphorical actor, usually a person. The duplicating machine becomes a *chewer.* The sun becomes a *torturer.* The wind becomes a *savage and merciless beater.*

Not just any element of the event-story can receive projection from the actor in the action-story. Not just any action-story can be projected in just any way to cover just any event-story. There are constraints on parable. Not surprisingly, these constraints depend on the image schemas we use to structure the event-story and the action-story.

## THE IMAGE-SCHEMATIC STRUCTURE OF EVENTS

We appear to understand an event as having its own "internal" structure: It can be punctual or drawn out; single or repeating; closed or open; preserving, creating, or destroying entities; cyclic or not cyclic, and so on. This internal structure is image-schematic: it is rooted in our understanding of small spatial stories. Technically, this internal structure of an event is called its "aspect." I will refer to it loosely as its "event shape." We think of a season as coming around again, time as progressing along a line, a search as going on, a sale as closed, a blink as punctual (like a spatial point). None of these events has the literal spatial or bodily form we associate with it, but we use these image schemas to structure and recognize these events.

In addition to "event shape," events also have causal structure, which is also image-schematic. Causation by physical force, for example, is typically understood through image schemas of force dynamics. When the force of the sledgehammer causes the door to fall, or a punch causes a boxer to fall, or a gust of wind topples the tree, we understand all of these events as instances of a particular image schema of physical force dynamics, which is why we can say of all of them that the first entity (sledgehammer, boxer, wind) "knocked" the other entity (door, opponent, tree) "down." Phrases like "The tidal wave swept the resort away," "The telephone pole crushed the car," "The roof gave in when the tree fell on it," "The river cut a new path," and similar expressions all portray causal events through image schemas of physical force dynamics.

Leonard Talmy has shown that image schemas of force dynamics are also used to structure nonphysical causation, as when we say, "The sight of blood *forced* him to run," "His ambition *propelled* him to excess," or "The committee finally gave *in* and *collapsed*." Causes are often understood by projecting onto them image schemas of force dynamics.

Some causes are understood by projecting onto them the image schema of *movement along a path*. First consider physical causation. A physical event of movement often involves a change of location. We are in one location, and then we are in another. The change is caused by our movement along a path. We say, "The road led us from the mountaintop to the valley floor," and understand it to mean that first we were in one situation, the mountaintop, and then we were in a different situation, the valley floor, and that going from one location to the other constituted a change of situation, and that the cause of this change in situation was movement along the path. Now consider nonphysical causation. The image schema of movement along a path can be projected onto nonphysical causation, as when we say, "The economy sank to its lowest point." The initial situation (strong economy) is understood by projection from the beginning of the path, and the final situation (bad economy) is understood by projection from the endpoint of the path. Both situations are understood by projection from spatial locations. The causal relation connecting the first situation to the second situation is understood image-schematically as a path between the first location and the second. Of course, "path" causation and "force-dynamic" causation usually go together. In "Fear *drove* him *to* a situation he otherwise would have *avoided*," we have both.

We also recognize the elements and parts of an event as standing in certain relations to each other, such as ability (actors are able to perform actions), obligation or necessity (a command may require the action), possibility (some condition may allow the actor to perform the action), and so on. Relations of these sorts are referred to technically as "modal" structure. These relations too are understood through projection from physical image schemas. When we think of someone as able to deal with a difficulty, we say, "He can *break* through that *psychological barrier* if he wants to." In that case, will is understood as a physical force and difficulty as a physical barrier, where the physical force (will) is strong enough to break through the barrier (difficulty). Alternatively, we might say, "He can *overcome* that if he tries." In that case, will is understood as a physical force and difficulty as a physical barrier, where the physical force (will) is strong enough and oriented suitably to flow over the physical barrier (difficulty). In either case, we know from the force-dynamic image schema that the force continues past the point of the barrier. It is therefore an inference that someone who "breaks through" or "overcomes" a "barrier" will continue along his "path" toward his "destination."

The projection of an action-story onto an event-story depends on the projection of the image schemas of the first story onto the second story.

## IMAGE SCHEMAS AND INVARIANCE

Just as we categorize events according to shared image schemas and actions according to shared image schemas, so we project action-stories onto event-stories in accord with their image schemas. We project image-schematic structure from the action-story to give structure to the event-story, but under a constraint: The result shall not be a clash of image-schematic structures in the target. Let us consider an example, Robert Browning's poem "Porphyria's Lover," which begins:

> The rain set early in to-night,
>   The sullen wind was soon awake,
> It tore the elm-tops down for spite,
>   And did its worst to vex the lake.

In the source action-story, there is a causal link between the actor who tears something down and the event of tearing down. This structure is image-schematic. In the target event-story, there is a causal link between the wind and the falling of the trees. This structure is image-schematic. Projecting one onto the other creates no clash in the target, since they match. But we could not say, for example, "The transparency of the wind tore the treetops down for spite," without provoking objection or offering an explanation, because the expression asks us to project an image-schematic causal link in the action-story onto two things in the event-story that we cannot think of as causally linked. Anyone who found the expression unobjectionable would have to be interpreting the target inventively

so as to find such a causal link between the transparency of the wind and the fall
ing of the trees.

The event in which standing objects are torn down by a person has an event
shape structured by image schemas; the event in which elms are toppled in the
wind has an event shape structured by the identical image schemas. Projecting
the first onto the second creates no image-schematic clash. But we could not
say, for example, "It wore the treetops down for spite," to express the same event-
story, because the action of *wearing down* has an image-schematic event shape
incompatible with the image-schematic event shape of *wind forcing trees over*.

In general, conceptual projection from a source to a target is not arbitrary: it
is guided by the principle of avoiding an image-schematic clash in the target.
This principle is called "the invariance principle." We will encounter it often in
our investigation of parable. It does not require that the image schema projected
from the source already exist in the target before the projection, but instead that
the result of the projection not include a contradiction of image schemas.

In Browning's poem, a spatial event-story of trees falling before the wind is
understood by parabolic projection from a spatial action-story of someone tearing something down intentionally. The instrument of this projection is EVENTS
ARE ACTIONS, which invites us to personify something in the event that is causally related to the event. Browning takes advantage of that possibility to personify
the wind.

## EURIPIDES'S *ALCESTIS*

In Browning's poem, we saw a spatial action-story projected onto a spatial event-
story. A spatial action story can also be projected onto a *nonspatial* event story.
In Euripides's *Alcestis*, Apollo has arranged for Admetus to live beyond his
appointed moment of death, provided he can produce a volunteer to die in his
place. His wife, Alcestis, has volunteered. The play opens on the day of her
death.

An event of death is not essentially a spatial story. Certainly, a corpse may
be buried, so that the body moves from one spatial location to another, but the
event of death is conceptually independent of any such movement. Yet we routinely conceive of the event-story of death parabolically by projection from the
action-story of someone's departing, willingly or not, as when we say "He's gone"
or "He's left us" to indicate that someone has died: the spatial action-story of
departure is projected onto the nonspatial event-story of death.

There is an image-schematic event shape associated with the standard conception of death: Something that has existed goes out of existence forever. There
is also an image-schematic event shape associated with the standard conception

of departure without chance of return: Someone who has been present goes away forever. The image-schematic structure of the event shape of death accords with the image-schematic structure of the event shape of departure; therefore, projecting the action-story onto the event-story does not create a clash in the target.

In any particular event-story of death, there will be a particular cause: illness, disease, injury, old age. We count all of them as instances of a general cause, Death-in-general. The notion that Death causes dying follows from our general conception of causal tautology: Death causes dying, Hunger causes hungering, Lust causes lusting, Desire causes desiring, Sleep causes sleeping. In all of these, an event of a certain kind is caused by an abstract causal element. In an event-story of dying, Death-in-general causes the particular death. In an action-story of departure, there can be an actor who *causes* someone to depart. If we project the person who departs onto the person who dies and the actor who causes the departure onto Death-in-general, we personify Death-in-general while preserving causal relationships. In "He left us," we project the person who departs onto the person who dies. In "Death took him," we additionally project the actor who enforces the departure onto Death-in-general.

The general personification of Death-in-general as an actor can be made more specific, depending on which action-story we project. In *Alcestis*, Death is personified in a number of ways. At one point, Death is personified as Thanatos, a wrestler who intends to take Alcestis away by dragging her body down to the halls of the dead. Heracles, a houseguest of Admetus's at the time, waits in hiding for Thanatos to appear at the grave, pounces on him, and wrestles him into yielding. In this personification, Death is an actor who tries to enforce the departure but fails.

Much earlier in the play, we have witnessed Alcestis "die." After her death, she lies in state, to be visited by her father-in-law and mother-in-law. Admetus and his father have a nasty quarrel over which of them bears responsibility for her death: The father, quite old, has refused to die in the place of his son. During this spat, Alcestis lies between them, dead. How can Alcestis be saved from death later by Heracles if indeed we have already seen her die? The answer is that in *Alcestis* death is conceived of as a complicated event with stages. Consequently, the action-story that is projected onto the event-story of death is equally complicated and has stages—it contains various actions and various actors. The complicated event-story of death involves not only the body's going underground but also the body's going limp because it no longer has a soul.

The event-story of the body's going underground is understood by projection from the action-story of Thanatos's dragging the body away. But the different event-story of the body's going limp is understood by projection from a different action-story of departure: The soul leaves the body and goes down to Hades. This departure of the soul involves a team of two actors, neither of them Alcestis. Alcestis sees these two actors as she is "dying" on stage. The first actor is an assistant to her departure: Charon, the ferryman, who is waiting to carry her soul over the river Styx. He leans on his pole, calling to her, hurrying her along. "Why are you so slow?" he asks.

The other actor, teamed with Charon, attempts to *force* Alcestis to depart on her parabolic journey from this life. Alcestis says:

> I feel a hand grasping my hand,
> Leading me—don't you see him?—leading me
> To the home of the dead. He has wings;
> His eyes glow dark under his frowning brow.
> What are you doing? Let me go.
> I am treading a fearful path; I am terrified.

> ἄγει μ' ἄγει μέ τις—οὐχ ὁρᾷς;—
> νεκύων ἐς αὐλὰν
> ὑπ' ὀφρύσι κυαναυγέσι
> βλέπων πτερωτὸς Ἅιδας.
> τί ῥέξεις; μέθες. οἵαν
> ὁδὸν ἁ δειλαιοτάτα προβαίνω.

In *Alcestis*, Death-in-general is personified not as a single agent but rather as a series of enforcers and assistants involved in the action-story of departure. The complicated event-story of Alcestis's death is not essentially spatial; the action-story of departure projected onto it is entirely spatial.

## APOLLO AND THE SHIPMATES

The story of Apollo and the shipmates in the *Odyssey* is another case in which a spatial action-story is projected onto a complicated event-story. The source action-story is Apollo's taking something from the shipmates. The body action in this case is not primarily *movement of a body through space*, as in *Alcestis*, but rather *manipulation of physical objects*.

Grasping a physical object so as to control it is a common body action performed by an actor. If we grasp a physical object, we can do what we want with it: We can put it into our mouth, throw it, throw it away, give it away, put it into a pocket, enjoy it as we wish. When a physical object is within our reach, only a small movement separates us from grasping it and controlling it. Reaching for a

physical object, or moving near to it so as to reach for it, is a body action accessory to grasping it and therefore to controlling it. These are some of the earliest
spatial stories learned by a child. In them, the child is the actor. Grasping a physical object so as to control it often seems to be the central story of the infant
imagination

It is common to project action-stories of grasping and controlling physical
objects onto other event-stories. Conditions we control and enjoy correspond
parabolically to physical objects we grasp, possess, and control. We can say of
someone that he *has* a wonderful office when in fact it is owned legally by his
employer; that an opportunity was *handed to him on a platter;* that he is *having* a
good time; that he *grabbed* the chance; that he *holds* a good job.

Within the logic of objects and grasping, something reliably within our grasp
is subject to our control. When we project an action-story of grasping, we project
this logic. Thus we can say of an elected official that he *has* his voting district *in
his hip pocket,* implying that he controls it. An object that we almost grasp is
almost under our control. We project this inference, and so can say of a job
candidate that he *has one hand on* the job but has not yet *got* it.

If something is near enough to us to be grasped and we have not yet grasped
it but see no obstruction to doing so, then we are close to controlling it but do
not yet control it. Projecting this logic, we can say of a thinker that the solution
to the problem he is working on is *easily within his reach.* We know that a lost or
discarded physical object was once in our grasp or reliably within our grasp but
is no longer; we controlled it but now do not. Thus we can say that someone *lost*
his job or *threw away* an opportunity. Something we give away is no longer under
our control, so we can say that someone *gave up* the chairmanship. Something
that is taken away is no longer under our control, so we can say that someone's
job was *taken away.*

If we grip an object or otherwise make it impossible for someone else to grasp
and manipulate the object, then we prevent anyone else from controlling it. Thus
we can say that someone has a *firm grip on* first place or that her *grip on* the seat
in the Senate cannot be *broken* or that she has the championship *all locked up* or
that he has a *lock* on her affections.

In all of these cases, the spatial body action of grasping is projected onto
situations that are not principally bodily or spatial. Projecting the actor from
the source story personifies something in the target story. Suppose we map the
body action of *taking away* onto the event-story of *becoming unemployed.* Then
the state of being employed corresponds to a physical object. Enjoying that state
corresponds to having the physical object in our grasp. Ceasing to enjoy that
state corresponds to having the physical object removed from our grasp. Something causally related to this change of state can be personified as the actor of

that change. We can say that *a machine took* our job *away* or *recession took* our job *away*, thus projecting the actor of *take away* onto the machine or the recession.

A physical object that we expect will remain reliably within our grasp is also under our control, to the extent that our expectation is correct. If the object is in our hip pocket or all locked up, we can think of ourselves as having it at our disposal. Alternatively, if we are able to reach the object and see no obstruction, we imagine ourselves, narratively, as able to grasp it and control it. When someone, to our surprise, removes the object, as when a pickpocket steals our watch or a thief breaks the lock or someone pops out of nowhere to grab the object and run away, we feel that an actor has spatially removed a physical object from within our reliable grasp and control. Thus we can say that the happy little boy bending to pick up the penny *had* it until the last second when his older sister *took it away from him*, even though the boy never touched the coin. Parabolically, we can say of someone nearing retirement that his secure old age was *stolen from him* by a crooked labor union whose president embezzled from the pension fund, even though the employee had not yet reached old age or retired. We can say that the weather *took our sailing trip away* from us, even though we had not yet launched the boat. In this case, the weather is personified: the weather is the actor of the taking.

In the story of Odysseus's shipmates, homecoming is a state to which they look forward. They expect to be able to enjoy that state. Parabolically, it is a physical object within their grasp. The cancelation of the possibility corresponds parabolically to the *taking away* of an object. An epic story of events, deaths, and dashed expectations is understood by parabolic projection from a simple story of body action in space, in which Apollo takes something away from the shipmates. Apollo acts justly, says Homer. The shipmates had been warned to conduct themselves respectfully as they journeyed home, but, ignoring the advice of Odysseus, they turned savage and raided a herd of cattle. The cattle belonged to Apollo. They took what was his; in response, he takes what was theirs.

## MOVERS AND MANIPULATORS

We have seen EVENTS ARE ACTIONS guide us in projecting the action-story of a journey. In this projection, states correspond to locations, so that the state of being alive corresponds to being present *here* and the state of being dead corresponds to having departed for a different location. Changes of state correspond to changes of location that are caused by spatial movement.

We have also seen EVENTS ARE ACTIONS guide us in projecting the action-story of reaching, grasping, holding, and taking physical objects. In this projection, states correspond to physical objects. We can grasp or fail to grasp a physical object; we can lose it or keep it. Parabolically, we can *obtain* or fail to *obtain* a state; we can *get* or fail to *get* a job; or we can *lose* a job or *keep it.*

These are two alternative ways to conceive of a state, as a *location* or as an *object,* but they combine and reinforce each other. In our spatial experience, we routinely *journey* to a *point* near a physical *object* in order to *grasp* it. We must walk to the coffee cup in order to pick it up. The state of having a physical object thus often involves two parts: *moving* toward it and *grasping* it. They go together in our experience, and they go together in the parabolic projection of stories of body action. Thus we can say of a job candidate that he had *almost arrived at the point* of *having the job in hand,* and feel no conceptual collision, even though we are projecting both movement and manipulation. We journey to an object and grasp it; parabolically, we journey to a state and have it.

In both cases, we project a routine spatial story of body action onto a story that may not necessarily be spatial.

## UNDERSTANDING NONSPATIAL EVENTS

EVENTS ARE ACTIONS guides us in understanding a wide range of event-stories by parabolic projection from spatial stories of body action. Sometimes the target event-story is itself a spatial action, with an actor or actors. When a ball is thrown in the direction of a receiver but another receiver intercepts it, this is certainly a spatial action-story, with actors. But through EVENTS ARE ACTIONS, we can project a *different* spatial action-story onto it, one in which the interceptor "takes" the ball "away" from the intended receiver. Of course, the intended receiver never had the ball, so the interceptor does not literally "take" it from him; and of course, the ball may have never been near the intended receiver, and the interceptor may in fact have carried the ball *closer* to the intended receiver in catching it, so the "away" is also metaphorical. The naturalness of the projection is so deep that it requires some scrutiny before we see that one spatial story of action is being projected onto a different spatial story of action. In the tale of the ox and the donkey, it is easy to see that one story is projected onto another; here, it is much harder to see, except under analysis. But the mental instruments are the same.

Sometimes the target event is not an action-story. The small story of what the sun and waves do to the sailor, and the small story of what the rain does to the elms and the lake, are spatial events where the causes are not actors but can correspond parabolically to actors in a spatial action-story.

Sometimes the target event-story is not clearly spatial or even physical. Consider mental events. They are of course physical in the sense that they consist of neurobiological events, but we rarely if ever conceive of an idea as physical. Usually, we conceive of an idea as neither physical nor spatial. Nor do we routinely conceive of it as a literal actor. But an idea can correspond parabolically to an actor in a spatial action-story. The idea can become, parabolically, an actor performing a spatial action, as when we say, "An idea came to me unbidden," "An idea seized me," or "An idea grabbed hold of me." We can turn our thoughts parabolically into actors of movement who "elude" us or "outrun our ability to express them."

So far, we have considered cases where the source story is a spatial story of body action. We have seen that such a source story can be projected onto stories of spatial action with actors, onto stories of spatial events without actors, and onto stories of nonspatial events. We will see in what follows that the scope of projection of spatial stories is much wider still.

# 4

# FIGURED TALES

Memory would come like a rope let down from heaven to draw me up out of the abyss of not-being, from which I could never have escaped by myself.

*Marcel Proust, Remembrance of Things Past*

Mind like a floating white cloud

*Ezra Pound, Cantos*

Time hath, my lord, a wallet at his back
Wherein he puts alms for Oblivion.

*William Shakespeare, Troilus and Cressida*

How all occasions do inform against me.

*William Shakespeare, Hamlet*

The fundamental things apply
As time goes by.

*Herman Hupfeld*

## ACTORS ARE BODY ACTORS

Events are actions guides us in projecting a story of action onto any kind of event-story, whether it has actors or not. The projected action is usually body action. The target event may be spatial or not. We have seen a story of *chewing* projected onto a story of *damage in the copy machine*, a story of *beating* projected onto the story of the sailor's exposure to the elements, a story of *tearing down* projected onto the story of elmtops falling in high winds and rain, a story of a *departure* involving many actors projected onto a story of death, and a story of *one person taking a physical object away from another* projected onto the epic story of the deaths of Odysseus's shipmates.

## ACTORS ARE MOVERS

One of the most common uses of EVENTS ARE ACTIONS is to project stories of body motion onto other action-stories. EVENTS ARE ACTIONS thus has a special subset: ACTORS ARE MOVERS. It is a general projection. Specific projections develop from it. Many of them are common and have become conventional. Several were noted as separate items by George Lakoff and Mark Johnson.

ACTORS ARE MOVERS is a dynamic, flexible, self-reinforcing pattern for projecting stories of body motion onto stories of action. Below is a list of common projections that arise from it. The list is not exclusive—the general projection invites creativity. The list is not obligatory—most of it can be ignored as we recruit what we need and modify or elaborate it. Elements on the list overlap considerably and sometimes imply each other. Crucially, the examples on this list are not mere figures of speech. They are not specific to language. They are expressions in language of the mental processes I call parable. They all concern the projection of a basic abstract story of movement by an actor under his own power onto a different story of action, whether or not it involves movement. These projections show up constantly in both everyday language and literary language because they are general cognitive processes indispensable to human thought and action.

Actors Are Actors Moving under Their Own Power

> She is a *mover* in the entertainment industry.
> Action is absolutely necessary but the president appears to be *paralyzed*.

Action Is Motion by an Actor under His Own Power

> She *walked right into* a dismal job.
> She *went ahead* and gave her opinion.

States (of Actors) Are Spatial Locations (That Actors Can Be In)

> He sees financial security as being *far off in the distance*.
> We cannot *return to* former conditions.

Being in a State Is Being in a Spatial Location

> He is *in* retirement.

He *left* physics to *go into* medicine at the age of thirty and *stayed there* for the rest of his career.

### Change of State (by an Actor) Is Change of Location (by an Actor)

He *came out of* retirement.

He made a *lateral* career *move*.

### Impediments to Action Are Impediments to Motion

He's *carrying* too many responsibilities to *get far*.

She started to speak, but his glare *stopped* her.

### Goals Are Spatial Locations We Try to Reach

I finally *reached* a solution.

They *stopped short* of their goal.

### Forgoing a Goal Is Forgoing a Journey to a Spatial Location

I was *headed toward* a degree in mathematics but then decided that my interests lay in a *different direction*.

She imagined that she wanted to be a lawyer, but when she was *nearly there*, she took a good, hard look at the reality of it and *fled*.

### Means to Goals Are Paths to Destinations

No *avenues* have been found to alleviate the suffering.

No one knows how to do this; we need a *trail-blazer*.

### Progress toward the Goal Is Movement toward the Destination

We are *getting there*.

I have been *held up* by all I have to do, but I will be *further along* soon.

### Quicker Means Are Paths That Can Be Traveled More Quickly

The *quickest way* to get this is to buy it at the store.

Yet I do fear thy nature. / It is too full o' th' milk of human kindness / To catch the nearest *way*. (Lady Macbeth on Macbeth)

### Causes of Actions Are Causes of Self-Powered Movement

Ambition *spurred* him to pick up the pace.

The company has ways of making you feel *very uncomfortable* if you *stay in* the same position for long.

The pattern is clear. A little looking will uncover many further projections: Effects of Actions Are Effects of Self-Powered Movement ("The prior accord ended up *trampled*"), Manner of Acting Is Manner of Movement ("He came to the realization *haltingly*"), and so on and on.

## ACTORS ARE MANIPULATORS

Self-powered *movement* is one fundamental subcategory of body action. A second fundamental subcategory is literal *manipulation* of physical objects. Manipulation—in this literal sense—can involve grasping, pushing, pulling, shaking, and so on. As infants, we observe that we can reach for an object, grasp it, manipulate it, push it, and shake it. We recognize other objects as intentional actors at least in part on the basis of recognizing them as capable of performing these actions.

One of the most common uses of EVENTS ARE ACTIONS is to project stories of bodily grasping and manipulation onto other action stories. EVENTS ARE ACTIONS thus has a second special subset: ACTORS ARE MANIPULATORS. It is a general projection. Specific projections develop from it. Many of them are common and have become conventional. Several of them were noted as separate items by Lakoff and Johnson. Again, the following list of common projections is meant only to suggest possibilities that arise under this general projection; its elements overlap and imply each other. Again, the examples on this list are not mere figures of speech. They are not specific to language but reveal mental processes of parable that show up in both everyday language and literary language because they are general cognitive patterns of projection. In this case, the projections carry a basic abstract story of manipulation onto a different story of action.

Actors Are Manipulators

He's got his *fingers into* everything.
*Hands off* my business!

Action Is Grasping

I *took* the opportunity.
I finally *got my hands on that house*.

States Are Physical Objects

He *has* the nomination *in the bag*.
Love is hard to *hold on to*.

Enjoying or Controlling a State Is Grasping the Object

He has a *firm grip* on the situation.
The new contract *took my vacation away* from me.

Change of State Is Change of Grasping

I *had* the game *completely in my grasp* but then I let it *get away from me*.
He *throws* his chances *away*.

### Impediments to Action Are Impediments to Grasping

I can't *have* that job.

Bob's already got it *locked up*.

### Goals Are Physical Objects One Tries to Grasp

He's headed for the job of news editor and he is going to *get it*, and when he does, no one is going to be able to *take it away from* him. He tried to *take* the lead.

### Forgoing a Goal Is Forgoing Grasping the Object One Wishes to Grasp

Why don't you *put the cruise aside* for a while until you can enjoy it? She let that chance *go by*.

### Means to Goals Are Aids to Grasping

Ask the supervisor to *hold that job* for you until you are free to *take it*. Persuade the office to *set that trip aside for you* so that no one else will *take it* before you can.

### Progress toward the Goal Is Improved Positioning for Grasping

He is *positioning himself* to *snatch* that job *without anybody's noticing*.

### Quicker Means Are Quicker Ways of Grasping

He keeps *creeping up* on the topic. I think he should ask his boss directly to *give it to him*.

### Causes of Action Are Causes of Manipulating an Object

He was *juggling* too many projects and finally had to *release* some of them *to* other managers.

Again, the pattern is clear. A little looking will uncover many further projections: Effects of Actions Are Effects of Manipulating an Object ("The vice-presidency is *up for grabs* because Juanita *let go* of it"), Manner of Acting Is Manner of Grasping ("He *seized* the opportunity"), and so on and on.

## BODY TALK

The most thorough analysis of a special case of ACTORS ARE MANIPULATORS is Michael Reddy's foundational study of how we project the story of manipulating objects onto the story of communicating. In his detailed 1979 inquiry, which established both the original perspective and much of the methodology of later cognitive scientific work on conceptual projection, Reddy demonstrated that a story of communication is routinely understood by projection from a story of body action, specifically manipulation. One person, the speaker, puts a physical object, the meaning, into a container, language, and sends it along a conduit to another person, the hearer, who then opens the container, language, to extract the object, the meaning, so as to have it—that is, to know it. We say "My head is full of ideas that I am trying to put into words," "He couldn't get his ideas across," "I got a lot out of the book," "I can't extract your meaning," and so on. In all of these cases, action-stories of manipulation are projected onto action-stories of communication.

## ACTORS ARE MOVERS AND MANIPULATORS

Self-powered movement overlaps with manipulation of physical objects. To manipulate an object, we often must go to it, move our arm and hand toward it, grasp the object, and manipulate it. Someone who is "going for the football" is usually moving his entire body in the direction of the ball, moving his hands toward the ball, and intending to grab the ball and manipulate it. Movement and manipulation combine naturally in our experience and in our conceptual categorizing of ourselves and other actors.

These two special cases of EVENTS ARE ACTIONS—ACTORS ARE MOVERS and ACTORS ARE MANIPULATORS—are therefore compatible. If we say of a chess match, "Observers thought that white would *take* the draw, but his next move made it clear he was *heading for* a win," we have an example of the overlap of the two special cases. We project physical objects in spatial locations onto *draw* and *win*. We project effort to move in their direction onto trying to obtain them. We project *both* a self-powered mover and a manipulator of physical objects onto the chess player.

This pattern of overlap might be called ACTORS ARE MOVERS AND MANIPULATORS. Since shaking is a particularly energetic kind of manipulating, it is not surprising that highly active and effective actors are colloquially referred to as "movers and shakers."

## A THINKER IS A MOVER AND A MANIPULATOR

Eve Sweetser has examined the case in which we project the action-story of movement and manipulation onto the story of thinking. She calls this pattern THE MIND IS A BODY MOVING THROUGH SPACE. Most of it derives from the more general projection ACTORS ARE MOVERS AND MANIPULATORS.

For example, when we wish to tell the action-story of a mathematical or scientific discovery, we can say that the thinker *began from* a certain assumption, was *headed for* a certain conclusion, *stumbled over* difficulties, *moved faster* or *slower* at various times, had to *backtrack* to correct mistakes, *obtained part of* the solution but was still *missing* the most important *part*, had a notion of *where to look for it*, began at last to *see* it, *followed it* as *it eluded* her, finally *got one finger on it, felt it slip nearly away*, but at last *got it*. Of course, after she has made the discovery, it becomes *hers*. This is a case in which an actor in a nonspatial story of thinking is understood by projection from a spatial action-story of moving and manipulating.

There is a second highly productive scenario of A THINKER IS A MOVER AND A MANIPULATOR in which the body is not moving through space but rather manipulating objects as instruments, tools, or aids to fabrication. When we talk of cognitive "instruments" or conceptual "tools" or of "piecing together a story," we are understanding the action of thought by projection from the body action of manipulation, specifically manipulation for the purpose of manufacture. We may "apply" a principle in the way we "apply" a template. We may "carve" out a theory in the way we "carve" a statue out of wood or stone.

## HOMER, DANTE, BUNYAN, SACKS, SAINT JOHN OF THE CROSS, PROUST, POUND

Writers often use A THINKER IS A MOVER AND A MANIPULATOR to create parabolic stories of mental events. Any work presenting a "journey of the soul," such as Bunyan's *Pilgrim's Progress* or Dante's *Divina Commedia*, uses this projection. Some writers blend the parabolic journey of the mind with a detailed travelogue: As Odysseus descends to the underworld, as Marlow journeys deeper down the river into the heart of darkness, or as the various voices of travel in Pound's *Cantos* roam over lands and times, we interpret the travel story as literally spatial for the body of the traveler and parabolic for the mind of the traveler.

In *A Leg to Stand On*, Oliver Sacks tells a story of a mental journey. It takes place aboard a train. When his real train is stuck in a siding, he considers how neurology is stuck: "I withdrew now from musing and gazing as the train pulled into a siding, and returned to Head's *Studies in Neurology*." When Sacks makes a conceptual breakthrough that allows the old neurology to move into a new era, the train takes off: "And now, I realized, after a long hour of stasis, we had emerged from the siding, and we were moving again." Those last four words refer to a blend of three journeys: the literal train journey, the parabolic journey of the discipline of neurology, and Sacks's personal parabolic journey of intellectual discovery.

Some writers are explicit about the parable. Saint John of the Cross, in a poem of eight stanzas titled "En una noche oscura"—commonly translated "The Dark Night of the Soul"—presents the story of his soul's union with God as a story of a journey along the path of spiritual negation. His mind, or soul, is a traveler; the mental process is vertical ascent by the secret ladder; the night is a guide; and spiritual union is a bodily embrace against the breast. Saint John of the Cross wrote hundreds of pages, gathered into two books—*The Ascent of Mount Carmel* and *The Dark Night*—in the form of commentaries explaining explicitly that the eight stanzas of this poem are a projection of a spatial action-story of movement and manipulation onto a nonspatial story of religious transformation. The commentary in these two books never advances beyond the first line of the third stanza of the poem.

Other writers are less explicit about their use of A THINKER IS A MOVER AND MANIPULATOR. Perhaps the most famous representation of mental events in twentieth-century literature is the opening of Marcel Proust's *À la recherche du temps perdu*, the *ouverture*, in which he describes his experiences of memory and dreaming. In it, Proust repeatedly asks us to project the story of a mover in space onto the story of a thinker. Mental states are physical locations, and a change from one mental state to another is a change of spatial location: "I would bury the whole of my head in the pillow before returning to the world of dreams"; "my mind, striving for hours on end to break away from its moorings, to stretch upwards . . ." To consider memories is to linger in space above or before them and to view them: "And even before my thought, lingering at the doorstep of occasions and shapes, had identified the dwelling together with the events . . ."

At times, he presents the effect of memory on his mind as a story in which an object comes to him, which he then uses as an aid to help *his mind move* from one state to another:

I was more destitute than the cave-dweller; but then the memory—not yet of the place in which I was, but of various other places where I had lived and might now very possibly be—would come like a rope let down from heaven to draw me up out of the abyss of not-being, from which I could never have escaped by myself; in a flash I would traverse centuries of civilisation. . . .

J'étais plus dénué que l'homme des cavernes; mais alors le souvenir—non encore du lieu où j'étais, mais de quelques-uns de ceux que j'avais habités et où j'aurais pu être—venait à moi comme un secours d'en haut pour me tirer du néant d'où je n'aurais pu sortir tout seul; je passais en une seconde par-dessus des siècles de civilisation. . . .

## EVENTS ARE BODY ACTORS

The target story in EVENTS ARE ACTIONS need not be an event performed by an actor. It can be an event without actors, or an event with many indistinct actors, or an event that happens to a human being. Consider, "The recession is coming at me and will hammer me when it gets here; it will beat me to a pulp." Here, the actor in the source story is projected onto the event, the recession. The physical object that the actor hammers is projected onto the human being. With a slight shift, we can use a source story with several actors and project those actors onto both the recession and the human beings it will affect: "If we can just dodge it long enough, it may weaken, and we may get away unharmed."

## EVENTS ARE MOVERS

When the actor in a story of movement is projected onto an event that is not an actor, we have EVENTS ARE MOVERS, a common variety of EVENTS ARE ACTIONS. It includes projections like the following:

> Events Are Actors (Moving under Their Own Power) and Occurrence Is Motion (by an Actor under His Own Power)
> This recession is an *opponent* whose *progress* we cannot stop.
> Time *marches* on.
> The recession *crept up* on California and delivered an unexpected wallop.

Once the mover is projected onto the event, the rest of the projections follow: The event can have goals that are spatial locations it tries to reach; means to those goals will be paths to destinations; and so on.

## EVENTS ARE MANIPULATORS

When the actor in a story of manipulation is projected onto an event that is not an actor, we have EVENTS ARE MANIPULATORS, a common variety of EVENTS ARE ACTIONS. It includes projections like the following:

> Events Are Manipulators and Occurrence Is Manipulation
> The recession is *spinning us around*.
> The economy is *yanking us left and right*.
> The drought is *strangling* us.
> The bad weather this season has *picked our pockets*.

Once the mover is projected onto the event, the rest of the projections follow.

## EVENTS ARE MOVERS AND MANIPULATORS

We saw that parable can project a mover and manipulator onto any kind of actor. Similarly, parable can project a mover and manipulator onto any kind of event: "The recession *crept up* on us and then *put a chokehold on* the business."

Stories of our interaction with other actors can be projected onto event-stories that include us. Events can help us, hinder us, hurt us. Events can assist someone, give her a boost, throw her into a situation she isn't prepared for. Unemployment can knock somebody flat. Jealousy becomes a green-eyed monster to be confronted, addiction an opponent to be wrestled. The farmer can steal land from the desert, and every summer the desert can try to take it back. The sailor can fight a murderous sea that tries to steal his life and his livelihood.

The most ubiquitous special case of EVENTS ARE MOVERS AND MANIPULATORS is DEATH IS A MOVER AND MANIPULATOR: it comes upon you, and you become a physical object it manipulates. It takes you away, unless, of course, your friend Heracles owes you a favor, which he repays by physically preventing death from reaching you and seizing you and taking you away.

Time, too, can be understood as a mover and manipulator. Time catches up with you, wears you down, races against you, stops you, takes your youth away, your beauty away, your friends away, and your family away. Time may also, of course, be on your side and bring you comfort and success.

## PROJECTING SPATIAL STORIES

Action is not the only kind of story. Everywhere we look, we see spatial stories that do not contain animate actors. We see a wall collapse from age, water run downhill, leaves blowing in the wind. These are spatial stories.

They also can be projected. I call the general pattern of their projections EVENTS ARE SPATIAL STORIES. It naturally overlaps with EVENTS ARE ACTIONS to such an extent that they may appear to be identical. But EVENTS ARE ACTIONS can project nonspatial action-stories (like a story of thinking or dreaming or suffering), and EVENTS ARE SPATIAL STORIES can project stories without actors, so neither is entirely contained in the other.

Leonard Talmy showed in a series of papers in the 1970s and 1980s that we frequently project spatial stories—especially force-dynamic stories—onto stories of nonspatial events. Eve Sweetser, in an analysis compatible with Talmy's, considered the special case in which we project spatial stories onto stories of mental events. Some of Talmy's and Sweetser's results are incorporated into the work George Lakoff and I did on EVENTS ARE ACTIONS and into the further analysis of what I call EVENTS ARE SPATIAL STORIES. Some individual facets of EVENTS ARE SPATIAL STORIES were first noticed by George Lakoff and Mark Johnson in 1980. The results summarized below come from many scholars, including, among others, Leonard Talmy, Eve Sweetser, George Lakoff, Mark Johnson, Jane Espenson, and me.

EVENTS ARE SPATIAL STORIES includes all the projections of spatial action-stories we saw in EVENTS ARE ACTIONS, but it also includes projections of spatial stories without actors. These are exactly the sort of projections Talmy originally analyzed:

Changes Are Spatial Movements

The building has *fallen* into disrepair.
The market *crashed.*

Causes Are Forces

The global slowdown was like mud *forcing* the American economy to stop.

Occurrence Is Motion and Cessation Is Stopping

The drought has been *going on* for a long time, but we hope it will *stop* soon.

Contrary Causality Is Opposing Force

State decree cannot *force* the drought to end, and Federal money won't *stop* the drought, either. Only rain in the Sierra will *put an end* to the drought.

In "The building has fallen into disrepair," a spatial story of *falling* is projected onto the rather different spatial story of roof tiles breaking, paint chipping, and windows cracking. In "The global slowdown pushed the American economy into recession," a spatial story of physical forces on physical objects and the consequent change of their spatial location is projected onto a nonspatial story of economics.

## AS TIME GOES BY

Stories take place in time. Stories of change over time can be understood by projection from stories of body action—time becomes a causal mover and manipulator: "Time hath, my lord, a wallet at his back, / wherein he puts alms for Oblivion."

A story of change over time may alternatively be understood by projection from a spatial story without actors. Time is then an object rather than an actor. For example, time might be a river, which moves "current" events along.

We can oscillate back and forth between viewing time as a moving actor and viewing time or specific times as moving objects. Time can be a moving actor with a wallet at his back or a collection of "approaching" hours and "upcoming" minutes. Time can be viewed as moving toward the past ("The days raced by us") or as moving toward the future, either as an actor ("But at my back I always hear / Time's winged chariot hurrying near," "Time is a runner we cannot outrun") or as an object ("Time keeps on slipping into the future").

In summary, we have considered the following cases where the projected story is spatial:

| Source Story | Target Story | Examples |
|---|---|---|
| Spatial Action | Spatial Action | Someone who intercepts a ball is said to "*take* the ball *away* from the intended receiver." |
| Spatial Event | Spatial Action | A warrior is said to "rain down" blows upon his enemy. |
| Spatial Action | Spatial Event | "The sullen wind . . . tore the elm-tops down for spite." Death in *Alcestis.* "Time hath a wallet at his back." |
| Spatial Event | Spatial Event | The roof tiles have cracked, the paint has chipped, the windows have cracked; we say the house has "*fallen* into disrepair." |
| Spatial Action | Nonspatial Action | "In solving the equation, he *leapt over* every *obstacle* known to have *stopped* previous mathematicians." |
| Spatial Event | Nonspatial Action | "His concentration *blotted out* (or *dissipated*) his fears." |
| | | Ezra Pound in the *Cantos* refers to "Mind like a floating white cloud." |
| Spatial Action | Non-Spatial Event | "The recession *caught up* with the university budget and *flattened it with a single blow.*" |
| Spatial Event | Nonspatial Event | "The economy *sank.*" |

## PROJECTING NONSPATIAL STORIES

In everyday thought, we routinely project spatial stories onto nonspatial stories of social, political, and mental events. When people agree to act as allies, for example, we say they are *aligned*, they *pull together*, they vote *as a bloc*, they *support* each other, they *stand* together. When they conspire to defeat someone, we say they are *arrayed against* him. In these cases, we project spatial stories of force onto nonspatial stories of social, political, and mental alliance. Similarly, when we conceive of people conspiring by *banding together* to vote *against* someone, thus *forcing him* into defeat, we are projecting a spatial story of force onto a nonspatial story of conspiracy.

But projection can happen multiply, repeatedly, and recursively. A nonspatial story that was the target of projection from a spatial story can in turn serve as the nonspatial source story for a further projection. In that second projection, the source is nonspatial (although the original spatial source story stands behind it). For example, conspiring to defeat someone is a nonspatial story; it can serve as a source to be projected onto other stories. We can say, for example, that the national economies are *conspiring against* a global recovery. A source spatial story of forces was originally projected onto a target nonspatial story of conspiracy; the nonspatial story of conspiracy is then the source projected onto a target nonspatial story of global economics.

Forces combining reinforcingly → Conspiring against

Conspiring against → Economics

In sum, the force-dynamic image schemas originally projected to the story of *conspiring against* are in turn projected to the story of *economics*.

Although multiple projections may seem on analysis to be complicated and to require a kind of algebra of the mind, it is only their analysis that gives us difficulty, not their occurrence in thought. When Hamlet says, "How all occasions do inform against me," modern readers sometimes interpret him as portraying "occasions" as "informers." They project a social action story of informing onto occasions, making them informers. But it is also the case that a spatial action-story is projected onto informing so that it can be "against."

Body Action → Social Action

(Exerting Force Against) (Informing)

Social Action → Events

(Informing) (All Occasions)

Multiple projections of this sort are nearly trivial for us, since they arise from common procedures of everyday thought. Hamlet's phrase is not a puzzle to these modern readers, but rather a particularly lucid and compelling expression.

Multiple projection often arises when body action is projected onto mental action (A THINKER IS A MOVER AND A MANIPULATOR) and the mental action is then projected to an event-story. If someone observes, "The sky has been thinking about raining all day, and now it looks as if it's finally getting around to it," we have a projection of the spatial story of movement (*getting around to it*) onto the nonspatial story of mental action (*deciding*) and we have additionally a projection of the nonspatial story of mental action (*deciding*) onto the spatial story of an event without actors (*raining*). Through concatenated projection, the sky becomes a thinking actor, and its thinking is understood as a spatial *getting around to* deciding to rain, even though it is possible that we have not seen a single thing move in the sky all day.

## EVIDENCE AND LIMITS

It might seem plausible to abstract from these analyses a general claim: Nonspatial stories and their further projections are always grounded in spatial and bodily stories. The extreme form of this claim is that abstract thought and reasoning are always grounded, through a kind of archeology of the mind, in spatial and bodily stories. Although not clearly false, this claim is too extreme for the available evidence.

We may say comfortably that our understanding of spatial and bodily stories is so rich, and our powers of parable so developed, that imagination can project spatial and bodily stories at will to any point of the conceptual compass. We may also say comfortably that for many abstract concepts, the spatial and bodily instances are the archetypes. Everyday thought contains conventional projections of spatial and bodily stories onto stories of society and mind and onto abstract reasoning. Their traces are routinely carried in language. Preliminary models are beginning to take shape of how the brain might develop both perceptual and conceptual categories of spatial and bodily stories. No equally specific preliminary models are at hand of how the brain might develop categories of stories of society and mind that are independent of the categories of spatial and bodily stories. These facts make it plausible that our understanding of social, mental, and abstract domains is formed on our understanding of spatial and bodily stories. But plausibility is the most we can assert on this evidence.

It is impressive and remarkable that we can always project from spatial and bodily stories onto social, mental, and abstract stories. It is equally impressive and remarkable that conversation about social, mental, and abstract stories will almost always elicit spatial and bodily projections ("He is *cracking up*," "I *let go* of that option a long time ago"). In contrast, conversation about spatial and bodily stories ("The house paint is flaking") may extend indefinitely without ever eliciting projections from social, mental, or abstract stories.

And yet no one ever has any difficulty projecting social, mental, or abstract stories onto spatial and bodily stories. We can say easily that the flaking paint is "losing its nerve" in the face of the storm; that our lunch is "disagreeing" with our stomach; that the floorboards are "conspiring" to break free of the underflooring. Nonetheless, these expressions seem less idiomatic than those based in spatial and bodily stories.

Given our robust capacity to project from stories of society or the mind, how would we know whether spatial and bodily stories are always basic to understanding? This appears to be one of the profoundly tantalizing and difficult open questions in the study of the mind.

## THE STORY OF BIRTH

The story of birth is complex, universal, and familiar. It is found at the core of both secular and holy literature. It is a spatial story in which one physical body comes out of another. It is equally a spatial story of action in which the mother is an intentional actor. It is also a biological if not spatial story in which mother and father are biological causes. Birth, or more accurately, progeneration, is a story with several acts, from conception through gestation to birth. Extra acts are often added: courtship, nurturing, bonding, early development.

Various parts of the story of birth are structured by spatial image schemas. The first image schema in the story of birth is *one thing coming out of another*. The mother is conceived of as a *container* that has a body inside it. The interior body exits, creating two distinct bodies where only one existed before. The second image schema is *an object emerging from its source material*. The mother's body is conceived of as a biological source material; the child emerges from it. A third image schema is *motion along a path from a source to a goal*. The child, at birth, departs its point of origin along a bodily way to a point outside the mother's body. A fourth is *link*: The spatial path from mother to child is statically realized in the form of an umbilical cord, which is understood as an asymmetric spatial link between mother and child. A fifth is *spatial growth:* The body that is interior to the mother-container begins from next to nothing, and grows, forcing its mother-container to become convex.

The extraordinary richness of the story of birth has made it perhaps the premier example of a familiar and powerful story that is projected onto other stories. Stories of progeneration are often projected onto causal stories, in accord with the invariance principle. We may speak of a "brainchild" or say, "Necessity is the mother of invention." We may say, with Wallace Stevens, "The moon is the mother of pathos and pity," or simply, "Ignorance is the mother of suspicion." We may say, "Italian is the eldest daughter of Latin." This range of causal projections is to be expected: the story of birth happens to include a set of image schemas that are, quite independently of the story of birth itself, routinely projected to causation. It is easy to think of nonbirth sources for "The tax cut *came out of* desperation," "His ambitions *emerge* directly *from* his greed," "One thing *led* to another," "Health is *linked* to diet," and "The problem is *growing*." These image schemas associated with causation are all contained in the story of birth and combined there in a coherent manner. This convenient combination makes the story of birth highly useful in thinking about causation. The story of birth moreover has an additional feature useful in thinking about causation—*inheritance*. We say that a figurine "inherits" its shape from the mold or that a computer program "inherits" its slowness from the language in which it is written.

In *Death Is the Mother of Beauty*, I listed the ways in which we routinely project stories of birth onto other stories, in everyday language and elite literary texts. Milton presents the story of the origin of Satan, Sin, and Death as a primordial history in which Sin—Satan's daughter—springs from his brow. Satan later fathers a son, Death, incestuously upon his daughter Sin. Gower adds to this odd family extra offspring—the vices. The Bible and therefore Gower and Milton all present the curse on humanity as a story of progeneration and inheritance: We all inherit the curse from Adam and Eve. Blake explains human psychology and emotions through an elaborate and exquisite story of a family tree. Spenser explains human psychological dispositions through stories of births. Hesiod's history of the cosmos, like nearly all early cosmogonies, is a story of progenerations. The list of such texts is long.

In *Death Is the Mother of Beauty*, I discussed constraints—later generalized into the invariance principle—on the projection of progeneration. A parent and a child have a spatial distinction and an aspectual duration over time, and this structure can be projected onto only those stories that can have compatible image-schematic structure. For example, given default conceptions of basketball or baseball, it would be infelicitous to say that a woman basketball player was the mother of the basket she just sank or that a baseball player was the father of the home run he just hit. These events are not thought of as having a suitable aspectual duration. Betsy Ross, however, could be called the mother of the American flag.

A mother and a child are also thought of as acquiring high spatial distinction at birth. If we watch a cloud as it shifts nearly imperceptibly into a slightly different shape and are asked to project the story of birth onto the story of the cloud, it would take considerable invention to do so in a way that projected this distinction between parent and child.

The spatial distinction between mother and child is also thought of as arising in a manner that is relatively singular and punctual. The moment of birth is distinguished from what comes before and what comes after. If the shifting of the cloud appears continuous, with no points of singularity, it would be even more difficult to project the story of birth onto it.

In these and a variety of related ways, parable is constrained: Not just anything can be projected in just any way. We have choice in our conception of the source, in our conception of the target, and in what is to be projected from one to the other. We are constrained to line these choices up so as to avoid an image-schematic clash in the target.

We are free to project image-schematic structure onto the target where the target is indeterminate. If we wish to convey a causal link between A and B where the relation between A and B is indeterminate, we may say, "B is the child of A." We may say, "Violence is the child of fear," or we may claim with Blake that ignorance is the child of sloth. In these cases, we do not violate image-schematic structure in the target, but we do create new image-schematic structure there.

An expression like "Italian is the daughter of Latin" raises no objection because projecting onto Latin and Italian the causal progenerative link between mother and daughter is compatible with our conception of the historical relationship of these languages. But if someone says, "Italian is the mother of Latin," and we project *causal link* from the source story of birth, it will take extraordinary invention to find a way in which something we can refer to as "Italian" can be viewed as causally prior to something we can refer to as "Latin." Stretching our imaginations, we might come to consider that the study of Italian can lead to the study of Latin, so that *learning Italian* can be the mother of *learning Latin*. Had we failed to locate this causal connection from "Italian" to "Latin," we would have been obliged to backtrack to reconsider how some other, noncausal structure could be projected from the story of birth onto the story of Latin and Italian so as to arrive at a meaning that could plausibly have been suggested by "Italian is the mother of Latin." The boundaries of our invention in conceiving the source, conceiving the target, and projecting from one to the other are governed by the invariance principle: we are constrained to avoid creating an image-schematic clash in the target.

The story of birth involves inheritance of physical attributes and character traits. We project these stories of inheritance parabolically onto stories of how features came to exist. We say, "Italian inherits many things from Latin, including vocabulary and gender."

We can conceive of members of a family as sharing attributes and traits: not every member of a family shares a given attribute or trait, but attributes and traits run through families according to the intricate logic of inheritance. We commonly project this logic onto other stories. We call someone a "child of the Age of Reason" to imply that he shares features with his personified parent. When we describe someone as "a child of Nature," "a child of the modern age," or "a daughter of the hills," we are projecting *inheritance* from the story of progeneration onto stories having nothing to do with progeneration.

These projections take literary form only because the everyday mind is fundamentally literary. We can see the continuity between everyday thought and literary thought by looking at expressions of popular culture, like the following. In January 1993, a major computer corporation launched an intensive advertisement campaign for a new laptop computer. Ads for the laptop appeared in many markets and in many media. An airline passenger might have opened Delta's glossy in-flight magazine to a slick two-page ad for the machine. In flight magazines are designed, of course, to appeal to thousands of potential customers from all social stations, many of whom have never read a poem except at the point of a pedagogical gun, and even then hated it. In-flight magazines hawk cologne, cruises, air cleaners, anti-wrinkle suitbags, nightlife in Vegas, medicines to restore hair or prevent it from falling out, gift notions, personalized mailing labels, lingerie, ingenious labor-saving devices for every imaginable pointless activity in the home or the office, alcohol, retirement communities, and an eerie assortment of richly vulgar and sometimes hysterically colored consumer items. The advertisement in this in-flight magazine carries a picture of the laptop in the center, and underneath, in large type,

Its mother was a mainframe.
Its father was a Maserati.

Everyone, of course, understands immediately that the laptop is being described as having the power and range we associate with a mainframe computer, and the sleek design, speed, and excitement we associate with a Maserati racing car. The laptop *inherits* these attributes. The logic of inheritance as part of the story of birth is so routinely projected onto other stories that it has its own conventional joke construction: "What do you get when you cross a such-and-such with a so-and-so?" In most instances of this construction, such-and-such and so-and-so are not reproductive organisms, and when they are, they usually do not mate naturally. Milton uses the projection of inheritance onto theology when he conceives of Sin as inheriting what he imagines to be the "feminine" aspects of Satan (beauty, seduction, persuasion, blandishment) and of Death as inheriting what he imagines to be the "masculine" aspects of Satan (direct power, absolute courage, arrogance, violence, strength). Later, when Satan intends to exit the gates of Hell, which are guarded by Sin and Death, Sin with honeyed speech endeavors to dissuade him, while Death laconically threatens to destroy him.

The ad copy for the laptop widens the story of progeneration to include genetics and evolution. Its opening sentence reads, "As they say, it's all in the genes." The laptop's button for moving a pointer on the screen is described as doing "what a mouse would do with a few million more years of evolution." We are asked to project a detailed story of progeneration onto an extraordinarily complex story of technological development.

The ad for the laptop evokes inherited attributes quite unlike those Milton found useful. The slick, sleek Maserati, powerful and mobile, unbelievably quick, welcome everywhere but never tied down, driven by its driver and responsive to its driver's every wish, is, in this parable, a father who passes these attributes by inheritance to the laptop. The ad wants you to understand that the laptop gets around and takes you with it: it "begs you to take it anywhere. And once you own one, that's exactly what you'll do." It "blows the doors off its competition." It "sports a screaming 486 processor," but "it's built for comfort too." Its button for moving the pointer is described as the "world's smallest stick shift."

The awesome mainframe, conceived of as a machine of great potential and scope, can be understood as a *mother* who passes these attributes on to her laptop-offspring. These may be more common associations of *mother* than one might think. They help to explain the aptness of expressions such as "mother lode" and "motherboard." Saddam Hussein of Iraq made a statement before the Gulf War that was translated as a threat to the allied forces: if they attacked Iraq, they would suffer "the mother of all battles." Although there was considerable confusion over how to interpret this threat, many Americans understood *mother* in this phrase as connoting tremendous power and potential, something not to be trifled with. That a mainframe might be thought of as a mother seems appropriate for any number of reasons. This particular electronic mother passes her power and potential to her offspring, the laptop, by inheritance.

The corporation that made the new laptop risked its image, the success of its new product, and an immense amount of money on the expectation that everyday readers of this ad would understand a detailed and complicated projection, carrying a robust story of birth parabolically onto a sophisticated story of computer research and development. For the ad to be effective, its readers would have to understand this projection instantly and recognize it as singularly apt. The corporation gambled that parable is a fundamental human cognitive capacity, universal, powerful, and familiar. Of course, as we have seen by now, this is no gamble at all.

*In these chapters are seeds for research projects.*

*Is parable a fundamental human cognitive capacity, universal, powerful, familiar?*

# 5

# CREATIVE BLENDS

> . . . nor did Alice think it so *very* much out of the way to
> hear the Rabbit say to itself, "Oh dear! Oh dear! I shall be
> too late!" (when she thought it over afterwards, it occurred
> to her that she ought to have wondered at this, but at the
> time it all seemed quite natural).
>
> *Lewis Carroll, Alice's Adventures in Wonderland*

WE TYPICALLY CONCEIVE of concepts as packets of meaning. We give them
labels: *marriage, birth, death, force, electricity, time, tomorrow.* Meanings
seem localized and stable.

But parable gives us a different view of meaning as arising from connections across more than one mental space. Meaning is not a deposit in a concept-
container. It is alive and active, dynamic and distributed, constructed for local
purposes of knowing and acting. Meanings are not mental objects bounded in
conceptual places but rather complex operations of projection, binding, linking,
blending, and integration over multiple spaces. Meaning is parabolic and literary.

We have seen that parable carries narrative meaning across at least two mental
spaces. In fact, other spaces are involved, and their involvement is not a modest
addition to parable, but instead its most important aspect. We can detect a hint
of this new aspect of parable by looking at a curious event in the tale of the ox
and the donkey: The ox and the donkey, like Alice's hurried rabbit, *talk*.

Talking animals are a conceptual blend. The talking ox and the talking donkey do not reside in the space that treats everyday farm labor and mute beasts of
burden, nor do they reside in the hypothetical space that treats the vizier's appre-
hension of Shahrazad's future disaster. Where, conceptually, do they reside? It
may seem perverse to ask this question. Talking animals are as natural as the

nursery. They are obvious in every national literature. But in the study of the mind, whatever looks natural is most suspect. Talking animals, seemingly so trivial, are created through a general and central parabolic activity of the everyday mind—blending. Blending has been studied in detail by Gilles Fauconnier and me jointly and separately, and by Seana Coulson, Nili Mandelblit, Todd Oakley, and Douglas Sun.

The blending involved in the tale of the ox and the donkey is extensive. Let us approach it by looking at the central inference of the tale. The central inference is that the donkey has outsmarted himself; he should have foreseen that, on a farm, the inevitable background of ploughing and milling requires work animals, so that if one work animal is excused, another becomes liable for the job. The donkey's failure to foresee the obvious likelihood that he will suffer justifies our judgment that he is too smart for his own good. His conceit makes him blind to the obvious. We blame him for being blind.

Can this central inference be constructed in the target space independently of projection? Can it be constructed in the source space and projected from source to target? The answers to these questions are no and no. This central inference does not arise in the target space independently of projection from somewhere, which is why the vizier exerts himself so ingeniously to project it. This central inference requires an agent who outsmarts himself *by failing to take account of inevitable and unavoidable background*. This inevitable and unavoidable background does exist in the source space: Farm labor is performed by work animals. But it does not exist in the target space. There, the counterpart of labor by work animals is suffering by wives, but Shahrazad explicitly disagrees that the suffering by the wives is inevitable in the way ploughing is inevitable on a farm. In this target space, she views King Shahriyar's practice as contrary to courtly decorum, to his own disposition, and to traditions of order. So does he. His subjects believe that only exceptional and remarkable events have led Shahriyar to this bizarre practice. They believe they are right to rebel against it. Secretly, he may think so, too. The enormity of his exceptional practice is unquestioned, which accounts in part for the plausibility of his discontinuing it under appropriately contrived conditions.

Shahrazad's plan to change Shahriyar's mind depends on bringing him to invoke traditional deeply held normative expectations—his own—against his recent abnormal behavior. In the source space, labor by work animals is inevitable background: standard, expected, and unavoidable. But in the target space, suffering by wives has the opposite status: abnormal, surprising, and possibly avoidable. According to the logic of this target space, therefore, Shahrazad cannot be judged as blind for overlooking the inevitability of the background practice, because the inevitability does not exist; it is explicitly denied. Her denial is reinforced by the narrator of *The Thousand and One Nights*, who, before the vizier tells the tale of the ox and the donkey, classifies Shahriyar's behavior as quirky and unstable.

Because the inevitable background necessary for the central inference does not exist in the target, the central inference cannot arise in the target. We can not infer in the target that the inevitable background requires someone to suffer; that if Shahrazad manages to get the virgins off the hook, she must suffer in their place; or that Shahrazad is foolish for working against inevitable background. The central inferences of the tale of the ox and the donkey cannot arise in the target independently of projection. The vizier must construct them according to the logic of a different frame—farm labor—and then project the inference to the target without projecting the details of the frame that made it possible for him to establish it.

There are additional reasons that this central inference cannot arise in the target. The agent who outsmarts himself does so because he is blinded by pride. But this condition does not apply to Shahrazad in the target. Quite unlike her counterpart, the donkey, she does indeed see the risk and explicitly insists upon taking it. The donkey is foolish for blinding himself to the risk but Shahrazad looks at it without blinking. Again, the central inference of the tale of the ox and the donkey is simply unavailable exclusively from the target.

But the central inference is not available from the source, either. In the source space of farm animals, it is predictable that if one beast of burden is excused from ploughing and milling, another will be used. A human being on the farm who did not see this likelihood would be thought to have *failed* in not seeing it. But a donkey cannot see it. Much less can a donkey scheme or foresee. In the source, the inferences that a donkey is responsible for the ox's reprieve, that he should have foreseen how the ox's reprieve would result in his own grievous employment, and that he is to blame for having outwitted himself are simply unavailable. Farm animals do not have these capacities.

Where are the central inferences constructed? They are constructed in the blended space of animals with human characteristics. The blend includes abstract information that is taken as applying to both source and target, such as schematic event shape and force-dynamic structure. Additionally, specific information from both source and target is projected into the blended space. The scenario of ploughing and milling as inevitable background, the relation of work animals to this background, and the classification of the ox and the donkey as work animals come from the source space. From this information, we can deduce that when the ox is excused, the donkey is the likely replacement. We can deduce this only because the donkey is a donkey and a donkey can pull a plough, which is information from the source space. But to obtain the central inferences also requires that the donkey be intelligent, cunning, and able to articulate his complicated plan to the ox so that it can be acted upon. This information comes from the target space. The blended space incorporates intentionality, scheming, talking, foreseeing, and surprise from the target space. The result is an impossible blend with animals that are simultaneously beasts of burden and intentional agents with sophisticated mental capacities.

The central structure of this blended space does not come from the source space alone. The blended space has, for example, causal structure that cannot come from the source of the farm: The donkey's thought leads to a plan, which leads to the execution of the plan, which leads to the reprieve of the ox, which leads to the donkey's suffering; but this causal structure cannot come from the space that contains farm animals who do not plan. Only the causal relation between the ox's languor and the donkey's use as a plough animal can come from a space that contains regular farm animals. The blended space also has "modal" structure (of possibility, enablement, and so on) that cannot come from the source space of the farm: The donkey's cunning enables him to devise a plan, and his talking enables him to communicate; but farm animals are not cunning in this way and do not communicate in this way.

The vizier intends to project the causal and modal structure developed in the blend to the hypothetical story of Shahrazad and Shahriyar. He also wants to project the blend's framing of agents because it yields the judgment he prefers. The central inference in the blend is that the schemer blindly causes his own suffering through his pride and his schemes. It is this inference that the vizier wishes to see projected to the target, in the hope of dissuading his daughter from her plan. It cannot be projected directly from the source to the target because it does not exist in the source. It is instead constructed in a blended space, and then projected to the target.

In the previous four chapters, we used a model of projection from one space to another where the projection was direct, one-way, and positive. This model needs refinement. The refinement is blended spaces.

A blended space has *input spaces*. There is partial projection from the input spaces to the blend. In the tale of the ox and the donkey, the input spaces include the story of real farm animals and the story of Shahrazad. Sometimes, those input spaces will be related as source and target, in just the way we have seen so often. Crucially, blended spaces can develop emergent structure of their own and can project structure *back* to their input spaces. Input spaces can be not only *providers* of projections to the blend, but also *receivers* of projections back from the developed blend.

## BLENDED SPACES

In the tale of the ox and the donkey, the specific agent in the blended space who develops the cunning plan has four legs and enormous ears, eats barley, sleeps on well-sifted straw, and talks. We are not to project the specific attributes *four legs*, *enormous ears*, *eats well-winnowed barley*, and *sleeps on sifted straw* onto Shahrazad in the target space. *Talks* is projected onto Shahrazad in the target space, or rather, *talks* is returned to the target whence it came.

One of the great cognitive advantages of a blended space is its freedom to deal in all the vivid specifics—ploughing, straw, barns, planning, talking, deceiving—of both its input spaces. Although the blended space will conform to its own logic, it is free of various constraints of possibility that restrict the input spaces. By means of these specifics from both input spaces, the blended space can powerfully activate both spaces and keep them easily active while we do cognitive work over them to construct meaning. Upon that circus of lively information, the mind can dwell and work to develop a projection.

Let us consider a literary example, Dante's celebrated portrayal of Bertran de Born in the *Inferno*. While living, Bertran had instigated strife between the king of England and the king's son and heir, tearing father and son apart. When seen in hell, Bertran consists, spectacularly, of two parts: a headless body and its separate head. The body carries the head in its hand, lifting the head manually to talk to Dante on his journey through hell. Bertran cites his punishment as the appropriate analogue of his sin:

> Because I parted people so joined,
>   I carry my brain, alas, separated
>   from its root, which is in this trunk.
> Thus is to be seen in me the retribution.

> Perch'io parti' così giunte persone,
>   partito porto il meo cerebro, lasso!
>   dal suo principio ch'è in questo toncone.
> Così s'osserva in me lo contrapasso.

This is an impossible blending, in which a talking human being has an unnaturally divided body. The blend has many parts. First, there is a conventional metaphoric understanding: Dividing people socially is understood metaphorically as dividing a joined physical object. This metaphoric projection is not at all novel. We can say conventionally that a home wrecker has "come between" a married couple by creating "distance" between them. "Till death do us *part*" is not a vow to hold hands; "what God has *joined together*, let no man *put asunder*" does not mean that husband and wife are surgically sutured. We can speak of breaking a bond of business, a bond of belief, a bond of loyalty, a bond of trust. None of this inherently involves the specific information of dividing a head from a body.

In this conventional metaphor, spatial proximity, junction, and separation are projected to create an abstract generic space that applies to many different targets, including stories of social and psychological actions. We have already seen such a generic projection in the interpretation of "Look before you leap" as it appears on a slip in a fortune cookie: It suggests an abstract story that applies to many target stories—a business deal, a romantic involvement, even standing up to leave the restaurant. In general, we understand proverbs out of context by projecting a generic interpretation. These generic spaces are a new kind of mental space in addition to source and target input spaces. Impossible blending does not occur in them. The information they contain applies to both source and target input spaces. In the case of "separating" father and son, the generic space contains only a unit that is separated and an agent who causes the separation.

In Dante's portrayal of Bertran de Born, this generic space provides the beginnings for a much fuller space, a "blended" space. The blended space contains the abstract information of the generic space; it additionally contains specific information projected from its input spaces. Dante's blended space takes, from the target, the specific sin and sinner, and, from the source, the source *counterpart* of the sin: the separation of a joined physical object. *In the blended space, the source counterpart of the sin is visited upon the target sinner as punishment.* We can see the justice of this punishment: The sinner has his own sin visited upon him not literally but figurally; the projection to the sin is traced backward to its source, and this source analogue of the sin is visited upon the sinner. The specific information from the source input space—physical separation of a joined physical object—is applied impossibly to the target human being in a blended space. The blended space contains something impossible for both source and target: a talking and reasoning human being who carries his detached but articulate head in his hand like a lantern.

In the case of the portrayal of Bertran de Born, just as in the tale of the ox and the donkey, the power and even the existence of central inferences of the projection come not from the source input space and not from the target input space but only from the blended space. The portrayal of Bertran de Born is often quoted out of context as an example of the kind of horrible punishment found in the *Inferno*. It is not merely bad, but bad in a special way: unnatural, ghastly, violent, destructive of integrity. The bodily division is taken as a sign of this special kind of badness. To be sure, a sophisticated reader of this passage in its context may have already concluded that Bertran has sinned, given that he is in hell, and that his sin is of a particular sort, given his location in hell. But even such a reader may derive the central inferences from the portrayal itself rather than from an abstract definition of the sin.

Where does the inference arise that this scene signals this kind of badness? Let us consider the background metaphoric projection. In the source space, there may be nothing at all wrong with separating a joined physical object, like shelling a pistachio nut. In the target space, there may be nothing wrong with setting two people against each other, or, more specifically, in setting son against father (perhaps the father is an evil infidel warrior, for example). The background metaphoric projection does not necessarily carry the implication that division is wrong—social "parting" can be good. Many readers, informed of the relevant history, would not even agree that Bertran de Born's actions were sinful, much less treacherous. But we all know there is something ghastly and horribly wrong about a decapitated human body that operates as if it were alive. We see the amazing spectacle of Bertran carrying his detached head and interpret this division as symbolizing something unnatural, ghastly, violent, and inappropriately destructive. The inference is established in the blended space *before* Bertran de Born begins to tell his story to Dante in hell—which is to say, *before* we are told the history of the target space.

As we will see often, blending is not restricted to combining counterparts. In the set of metaphoric correspondences, the divided object in the source is the counterpart of the "divided" father and son in the target, not of Bertran de Born in the target. But in the blend, the divided object and Bertran de Born are combined.

Blends arise often in Dante. "Mahomet," regarded as the great schismatic who "divided" Christianity, has *split* himself in hell. The adulterers Paolo and Francesca, who yielded to the "forces" of passion, are *blown hither and yon* in hell by a *forceful* wind over which they have no control. The "uncommitted," whose sin was that they never took a "stand" or a "position," must *scurry* ceaselessly over a place that is—in Dante's scheme of cosmic geography—*nowhere*, lacking all status.

In all these cases, a source story (division, being swept away by wind, moving without stopping) has been projected onto a target story of a particular sin as a way of conceiving that sin. The punishment of that sin resides in a blended space that is fed by source and target input spaces. The punishment comes from the specifics of the source. The damned human being comes from the target. The specific information from the source is applied to the human being from the target in a blended space of retribution.

Dante's *Inferno* is an encyclopedic display of local blended spaces, but additionally, at a higher level, it is a single monumental synoptic blended space. Its target is the story of Dante's instruction in theology and philosophy. Its source is the story of a journey. The blended space combines all the aspects of the story of the journey with all the aspects of the story of instruction in theology and philosophy.

Dante's blended spaces are explicitly marked as exotic and literary. Blends of this sort are—like talking animals—vivid. Paradoxically, because they present striking spectacles, they may mislead us into thinking that blends are incongruous visual cartoons, unimportant to everyday thought. To be sure, cartoons that use blends are ubiquitous and familiar. Consider the cartoon of the angry character: His skin grows red from his toes to his head in the manner of a boiled thermometer; he flips his lid while steam shoots from his ears. This is certainly a blend, based on the conventional metaphoric projection that connects heated objects to angry human beings. But it is only one kind of blend, and not the most interesting kind. Most blending is covert and undetectable except on analysis. Most blends are unrelated to visualization, to exotic incompatibilities, to structural clash, or to emotion. The essential cognitive work done by blended spaces is often invisible.

Let us consider a slightly less exotic example of a blended space, from Shakespeare's *King John*. It occurs in a scene that involves no cartoonish impossibilities and no visualization of clashes. On the contrary, a member of the audience, watching the scene, would see only a messenger, looking fearful, who comes before the king. King John, recognizing the disturbance in the messenger's face, says:

> So foul a sky clears not without a storm.
> Pour down thy weather.

We could read this passage simply as asking us to project directly from source to target: The appearance of the sky projects to the appearance of the face; the bad weather projects to the bad message; the event of precipitation projects to the act of delivering the message; and so on. This projection is familiar to us as an instance of the conduit metaphor: a message is an object in a container; communication is transferring an object spatially from the speaker to the hearer.

So far, so good. But there is a more sophisticated customary reading. King John speaks these lines at a moment in the play when everything is falling apart, when there is a confrontation of the first magnitude over who or what is in command, and it is a question whether King John can survive the forces gathering against him. He has apparently just succeeded in having the rightful heir to the throne, Arthur, killed, which causes powerful nobles to defect, no doubt taking with them a worrisome following of lesser nobles. In certain subtle ways, King

John is becoming something other than king, increasingly represented as having never been king. He is a king who is not a king. The activities and economies King John normally commands are rapidly escaping him. He tries to command what he no longer commands. He may appear to be in command, events may happen that seem to conform to his command, but his command is losing status. He is not naïve—he realizes that his command is a conundrum. This is a subtle reading. To arrive at this reading requires a blended space, in which the messenger, the prime example of something absolutely under the king's command, is also nature, the prime example of something that is absolutely above the king's command. This is a combination of contraries impossible outside the blend. King John is commanding what he can command, but what he can command turns out to be simultaneously what he cannot command. The tension and instability in King John's command is presented symbolically. It is a powerful and significant paradox.

The blend necessary for this reading combines, from the source, the inevitable release of weather that is subject to no one's control, and, from the target, King John's intentional control over the intentional messenger. The manifest tension between the lack of control and the exercise of control provides the central inference of the subtle reading. But the tension is not in the source: in the source space that includes nature, human command plays no role at all, and King John is not mad like Lear and would not dream of trying to command the weather. The tension is not present in the target, either: King John can indeed command messengers absolutely to deliver their bad news. The tension cannot be imported to the target directly from the source because the target would defeat it: the messenger is absolutely and rigidly under the command of King John. Indeed, the messenger's complete subordination to the king in the target is reinforced by this very scene in which John commands and the messenger performs accordingly. We do not construe this passage as saying of the target that just as King John cannot command nature, so he cannot command the messenger. That is clearly false: He can and does command the messenger.

It is only in the blended space that King John is revealed in a situation of conflict: He both commands and lacks command at the same moment and in the identical respect. In the blended space, he is giving commands that are simultaneously appropriate and inappropriate, simultaneously routine and absurd. This is a fundamentally unstable position. It is the basis of the sophisticated reading that King John's command is profoundly troubled and conflicted.

The tension of the blended space is reinforced by a corollary blending of impossibilities. King John is above the messenger metaphorically, in the sense of having power over him. He is probably above him spatially: The messenger may be kneeling. By contrast, any human being on earth is below a raining sky both metaphorically and spatially: The human being is subject to the power of the sky and is also literally below it. In the blended space, King John is literally and figuratively above the messenger but literally and figuratively below the sky. He is simultaneously above and below the messenger-sky. This paradox is compacted into a single expression: "Pour down!" This would be a very odd thing to say to a messenger who is kneeling. In the source space of people and skies, John is simply below; in the target space of kings and their dominions, he is simply above. Only in the blended space is he both, a clash of the most significant violence.

This presentation of John as inhabiting an impossibly unstable position has been read as constituting the power and memorability of this passage, and as distinguishing it from insipid expressions such as "he has a stormy countenance." But the central inferences of this subtle reading are unavailable except from the blended space. The reading of these two lines as conveying on their own that something is seriously wrong in the structure of John's kingship comes neither from the source of weather and people nor the target of kings and messengers. It comes only from the blended space. The projection is not direct from source to target.

The work of this blended space involves disanalogy between the source and the target. We do not simply suppress lack of correspondence between source and target. On the contrary, information from the source that does not correspond to the target and cannot be projected onto the target is brought into the blended space exactly so we can understand the difference between the source and the target, and thereby recognize the clash. The projection is therefore significantly negative. We have seen that the projection is not direct; now we see that it is not essentially positive. The model of projection as direct and positive from source to target will not capture the central inference of these two lines.

The scene is profoundly ironic, exactly because in the blended space there is an ironic tension between the image schemas. Without the blend, there would be no tension, and without the tension, there would be no irony. To explain the cognitive result of irony in this case requires a model of conceptual projection that acknowledges the role of blended spaces.

We often encounter linguistic marks of blended spaces. The passage from *King John* contains a lovely example: "thy weather." Possessive pronouns like "thy" or "your" can be used with a noun to indicate possession and control, as in "thy riches" or "your coat," since riches and coats can be under human control. They can be used with a noun like "weather" to indicate association, as in "Your weather is better than mine." But in the blended space, they can exceptionally be used to indicate possession and control of "weather": The messenger-nature possesses and controls the message-weather. "Thy" with this meaning of control comes from the target; "weather" with its meaning comes from the source; "thy weather" combines vocabulary from the source and the target. But "Pour down thy weather" combines more than vocabulary: Semantically, the verb "pour" is connected to the weather of the source space, but its use in the imperative mode—to indicate command—comes from the target space, where one intentional agent can command a second agent to perform the action encoded in the verb. The single word "pour" in this sentence blends linguistic structure associated with both the source and the target.

Because I have introduced blended spaces with examples from the high literary canon—*The Thousand and One Nights*, Dante, and Shakespeare—it would be easy to make the mistake of thinking that blending is a special device of literature. The everyday mind is essentially literary. Everyday logic and language depend upon blending. Fauconnier and I originally demonstrated this point with the following example, taken from the world's premier sailing rag, *Latitude 38*:

> As we went to press, Rich Wilson and Bill Biewenga were barely maintaining a 4.5 day lead over the ghost of the clipper *Northern Light*, whose record run from San Francisco to Boston they're trying to beat. In 1853, the clipper made the passage in 76 days, 8 hours.

In the space of 1853, *Northern Light* makes a passage. In the space of 1993, *Great America II* makes the same passage, although, given the inevitable differences in weather and sea conditions in the two spaces, and the considerable differences in performance between a high-tech racing catamaran and a huge wooden clipper ship laden with cargo, they surely did not follow the identical course in detail. In neither space is there a race. But in the blended space, there is a race between *Great America II* and the ghost of *Northern Light*. Readers easily distinguish and manipulate these three spaces, and they know what each space is good for. No one imagines that the writer believes in ghost ships. No one imagines that, should *Great America II* capsize (as did its predecessor, *Great America*), *Northern Light* will come along from behind to rescue the rival crew.

Here we come to a fundamental widening of our investigation of parable. So far in this book, for the sake of pedagogical sequence, we have considered only those cases of parable where one of the stories is a source and the other is its target—the target is conceived, at least in part, by projection from the source. After looking at the principles of source-target parables, we detected the role of blended spaces: We saw that the source and the target are *inputs* to the blend and that the blend can project back to the *source* and *target input spaces*. Often, the essential projections go from the blended space to the *target input space*. This is the case for the tale of the ox and the donkey, for Dante, and for King John.

But now we see something quite new. *Input spaces* to the blend do not have to be related as *source* and *target*. Consider the boat race. Clearly this is conceptual projection from input stories, which I will call 1853 and 1993. In each story, there is only one boat, no race, and no chance of a "lead." Projecting structure from 1853 and 1993 to a blend helps us create a blended story of a boat race, where there are two boats, one with a "lead" over the other. That blended story helps us understand the relationship between the inputs. It gives us a way to integrate the entire situation into one blended story, without erasing what we know of its independent inputs. But 1853 is not a *source* for 1993; 1993 is not a *source* for 1853. Neither is a target for the other; neither is conceived by projection from the other. For example, we do not understand the catamaran by projection from the clipper ship the way we understand *Death-in-general* by projection from an *agent who enforces departure* or the way we understand a *cause* by metaphoric projection from a *mother*. Hereafter, I will speak of *input spaces* and *blended spaces*. When the input spaces are related as source and target, I will call them the *source input space* and the *target input space,* or, where there is no possibility of confusion, just *source* and *target*.

In parabolic blending, the input spaces are often rhetorically unequal. For example, in the boat race, it is 1993 that the reporter cares about and talks about. It is 1993 that he wants to understand and report fully. I will say that 1993 is the *topic space* of the parabolic projection. A topic space is not necessarily a target space. Nineteen ninety-three is a topic space but not a target space with 1853 as its source. It is possible, as we will see later, for there to be more than one topic space. It is also possible for the topic space to shift: If we are descendants of the captain of *Northern Light*, it may be 1853 that we care about understanding. It is even possible, as Seana Coulson has shown, for the source input space to be the topic space.

The blended space includes an imaginary race; inferences can be made in that blended space and projected to the topic space of 1993: *Great America II* is doing well, is moving fast enough, is accomplishing its goal. The blended space does not merely compare positions of two ships; it calls up the conceptual frame of a *race*. The blend therefore contains structure not contained in either of the two input spaces. This frame provides emotions and intentions of the crew and of fans, which can be transferred to the space of 1993. A victory party, with all the standard rituals and conventional photographs, was held for the crew of *Great America II* and reported in the customary fashion in *Latitude 38*. The blended space made a profound mark on the feelings and actions of everyone involved. The blended space left its trace on reality.

In the cases of Bertran de Born and the messenger in *King John*, impossible conjunctions were exploited inferentially—for example, we were able to draw an inference of irony from the discordant image schemas in the King John blend. But in the sailboat race, the impossibility of the two ships' racing is merely pragmatic—there is nothing in the structure of the race that is impossible, merely the extraneous difference in the years during which the two boats existed—and this merely pragmatic impossibility is irrelevant to the central inferences. Blends are in general not constructed merely to present some spectacular clash or exotic impossibility. Suppose someone says, "Four and a half days may seem like an insurmountable lead, but maybe it isn't: *Great America II* looks as if she will be becalmed when she enters the Caribbean, but *Northern Light* will have a gale behind her and could pick up enough time to sail right through *Great America II*." In this case, the blend incorporates fabulous elements impossible outside the blend, such as one ship's sailing through another unharmed, but that impossibility is merely pragmatic and we draw no inferences of irony from that impossibility.

The blended space of the boat race is not constructed exclusively by fusing counterparts from the input spaces. There are many counterpart connections between the space of 1853 and 1993: The catamaran and the clipper are counterparts, as are their courses, their starting points, and their destinations. Many of these counterparts are fused in the blend: The two courses are fused into one course, for example, the way the messenger in *King John* is fused with nature. But the catamaran and the clipper are not fused into each other in the blend. The catamaran and the clipper are distinct in the blend.

The passage in *Latitude 38* sets up an independent conceptual domain—of ghost ships and imaginary races. It is specific to the blend; it does not belong to either input space. This extra and fantastic conceptual domain helps us to notice the existence of the blend. But blended spaces do not have to set up their own independent conceptual domains and do not have to make us realize consciously that we are doing any blending. For example, the passage in *Latitude 38* could easily have read, "At last report, *Great America II* was 4.5 days ahead of *Northern Light*." Here, with the same blend but without the mention of phantom ships, we might not realize consciously that we have constructed the blend. Another way to set up the "impossible" blended space so as to provide the right inferences would be to exploit the standard counterfactual construction: "If the two ships were racing, *Great America II* would be 4.5 days ahead of *Northern Light* at this point."

Projecting inferences from the blend to an input space is not a simple matter of copying all of the inferences in the blend to the input space. We know how the blend connects to its input spaces, and we know how inferences in the blend correspond to inferences possible in the input spaces. Projecting inferences from the blend to an input space often involves selecting or translating them to fit the input space. For example, the inference in the blend that *Great America II* is a long way ahead of *Northern Light* is not appropriate for the space of 1993; but the corollary inference that *Great America II* is doing well is appropriate for the space of 1993, and can be projected from the blend to the space of 1993.

There are several different ways to make the appropriate inferences in the blend and project them appropriately to the space of 1993. For example, how do we construct a scenario in the blend in which *Great America II* is "4.5 days ahead" of *Northern Light*? There are several possibilities. In one reading, *Great America II* reached a particular geographical position after sailing a certain length of time, and *Northern Light* did not reach that position until it had sailed a length of time longer by 4.5 days. In another reading, *Northern Light* and *Great America II* sailed the same length of time, at the end of which *Northern Light* had reached a geographical position that *Great America II* had reached after sailing a length of time shorter by 4.5 days. It is tempting to imagine that these are equivalent statements of the same situation, but they are in general not, and, given the realities of sailing, they are in practice almost certainly not. In the first reading, the difference of 4.5 days comes from the space of 1853, and it is *Northern Light* that does the 4.5 days of sailing. In the second reading, the difference of 4.5 days comes from the space of 1993, and it is *Great America II* that does the 4.5 days of sailing.

In yet another reading, experts predict that *Great America II*, given its performance so far, should complete its voyage to Boston in a time that is 4.5 days less than the time of the voyage for *Northern Light*. In yet another reading, the distance between the positions of *Great America II* and *Northern Light* after each has sailed a certain length of time is what would be covered in 4.5 days at *Northern Light*'s average speed made good—its overall speed actually accomplished relative to the ground along the course line. In yet another, experts compute that *Northern Light*, under the weather and sea conditions in the relevant area faced by *Great America II* during the *past* several days, would have covered the relevant distance in 4.5 days. In another, experts compute that *Northern Light*, under the weather and sea conditions *coming up* for the next several days, would cover the relevant distance in 4.5 days. And so on. Any of these constructions can be established in the blended space, all of them leading to the inference, projectable to the space of 1993, that *Great America II* is succeeding in its ambition.

There are evident linguistic traces of this conceptual blending. In the blended space of the boat race, there are two boats simultaneously racing, and we can refer to them accordingly, but there are vestiges of *Northern Light*'s having come from a space that provides the landmark frame, so that in the blend, *Northern Light* provides the landmark and *Great America II* is conceived as a trajector relative to that landmark: We prefer to say, "*Great America II* is ahead of *Northern Light*," rather than "*Northern Light* is behind *Great America II*." For a real race, we might say either because in general either boat can be the landmark. The phrase "barely maintaining" also shows a trace of blending, since it presupposes intentionality: The crew of *Great America II* is trying to maintain a lead. By contrast, if *Northern Light* were ahead by a day in the blend, it would be strange to say, "The captain of *Northern Light* is barely maintaining his one-day lead," since the presupposed intentionality could not be projected back to the space of 1853 without some work to make it possible there, like the following: "Historically, the captain of *Northern Light* took the view that he had the fastest ship imaginable and that his record would stand forever. But now, he is barely maintaining a tiny lead over *Great America II* and may be proved wrong." It is important to see that the construction of the blend is not meant to erase or dispense with the input spaces. Blending provides a way to integrate efficiently and effectively over many spaces while maintaining the network of connections across all those spaces.

The same constraints of landmark and intentionality can be shown to operate in a case that involves metaphor. To understand, "President Franklin Delano Roosevelt accomplished a great deal in his first one hundred days, but President Clinton has accomplished by comparison little," we must build two mental spaces and an intricate comparison between them. Both of these mental spaces can themselves be understood through a conceptual metaphor according to which *accomplishment* is *travel along a path*. We might then say, "FDR covered a lot of ground during his first one hundred days. President Clinton by comparison has only just started to move." In one blended space, FDR is moving along a path whose locations are goals; reaching the location is accomplishing the goal. In the other blended space, President Clinton is beginning to move along a similar path. These two blends are conventional and share the identical generic space. These two blends can themselves be the input spaces to a new blended space, as when we say, two months after President Clinton has taken office, "Clinton was supposed to hit the ground running. He implied that he was going to accomplish as much in his first one hundred days as FDR accomplished in his. So far, Clinton has failed completely *to keep pace with* FDR."

"To keep pace with" requires the construction of a conventional blend that has both agents competing simultaneously along the same track. For most readers, this conventional blend will have been constructed and used entirely unconsciously. The construction of that conventional blend includes the connection of structures in the blend to corresponding structures in all of the spaces that led to it, so that we know the implications for Clinton in the space of 1992 of the fact that Clinton in the FDR-versus-Clinton blend does not "keep pace with" FDR in that blend.

We can force the blend into consciousness by drawing attention to it: "Clinton is in a race with the ghost of FDR"; alternatively, "At this rate, Clinton's term will be over before he gets anywhere near the finish line." We know implicitly that "the finish line" in the blend corresponds to FDR's degree of accomplishment on his hundredth day in office in the relevant input space of "FDR's first year in office" (beginning March 4, 1993). But protest will arise if we say, "So far, FDR has succeeded completely at keeping well ahead of Clinton." We could say this of a real race, but not of this blended race, because in the blend, some aspects of intentionality from the input spaces are indispensable for the reasoning in the blend, but only certain aspects of that intentionality are allowed to enter the blend. Yet this restriction is not simple. If we knew of a passage in President Roosevelt's diary in which he represents himself as competing with all presidents, past and future, and then claims that he has set a record for accomplishment in his first one hundred days that no other president will ever be able to equal, then we might be able to say without provoking protest, "So far, FDR has succeeded in staying well ahead of Clinton."

Structure that is developed in a blended space can change our view of the input spaces, as in the following riddle, which Arthur Koestler attributed to psychologist Carl Dunker:

> A Buddhist monk begins at dawn to walk up a mountain. He stops and starts and varies his pace as he pleases, and reaches the mountaintop at sunset. There he meditates overnight. At dawn, he begins to walk back down, again moving as he pleases. He reaches the foot of the mountain at sunset. Prove that there is a place on the path that he occupies at the same hour of the day on the two separate journeys.

The reader might pause here to try to solve the riddle before reading further. It can be solved ingeniously by imagining the Buddhist monk walking up as his double walks down *on the same day*. In that blended space, it is clear that there is a place on the path that the two Buddhist monks occupy at the same hour of the day: The place is where he meets himself. He must of course meet himself, since someone who traverses a path in the space of a day must meet someone who traverses the path in the opposite direction in the space of the same day, however much they both walk as they please. This inference, that there must be a place that the two travelers inhabit at the same time of day, is projected *from the blend back to the input spaces* to create a point of connection between the input spaces of the two journeys, although no encounter occurs in either of them. Interestingly, people who count this blend as supplying a proof often cannot supply an alternative proof that does not make use of the blend.

It is worth pausing to observe that this is another case in which the input stories to the blend are not related as source and target. Indeed, this is a projection over stories that does not seem to involve metaphor or analogy in any central respect. There is conceptual projection from the input stories to help us create quite a different blended story—one involving two monks and an encounter. This blended space helps us to integrate the entire situation without erasing the independent input stories. It helps us organize the input stories and see relationships between them. It is also worth observing that both of the input stories count equally as topic spaces of the parable: we are interested in establishing for both of them that there is a place on the path that satisfies the requirement of the riddle. Notice also that this blend does not always fuse counterparts—the two monks in the two inputs stay distinct in the blend, although the two days are fused into one.

The blends in the boat race and the riddle of the Buddhist monk do not come from literary works, and neither can be mistaken as merely spectacular, since their purpose is to perform inferential work. They both allow the reader to reason successfully to a goal. Consider a similar case of everyday problem-solving: Suppose we hand a volleyball to someone who has played tennis but not volleyball and we say, "Serve it overhand the way you would a tennis ball." The volleyball becomes, for the moment, a tennis ball in part, but only in part. Partial blending of the volleyball space with the tennis ball space produces a suitable action.

Blending, used to reason about everyday problems, often succeeds but also often fails. If we sit down late at night to a dimmed computer screen at a desk illuminated by an architect's lamp and attempt to brighten the screen by turning the knob on the lamp instead of on the computer, we say it is a "mistake," but it is not an arbitrary or unmotivated mistake. We are very familiar with "absent-minded" mistakes like putting on our eyeglasses to hear better or punching a button on the television remote control device to turn the air conditioning off. Strange slips of action like these reveal the covert existence of momentary cognitive blends. The connections they manifest do not come from abstract analogies—they are not the transfer of an elaborate schema from one domain to another. Seeing and hearing are not "like" each other when we put on our eyeglasses to hear better; in the unsuccessful blend, seeing and hearing are fused, and they respond to the same corrective lenses. In the same way, the volleyball and the tennis ball are not merely similar to one another; in the blend, they are fused and respond to the same manipulation. Of course, it goes without saying that we know the difference: Seeing and hearing are different in the two input spaces; the volleyball served with the hand and the tennis ball served with a racket are different in the two input spaces. We know what is appropriate to each of these spaces. We often try to solve a problem by dealing with it as if it resides in the blend, but we know where it actually resides and we know how to move between the useful blend and the real problem.

These blends are not cases of misframing or reframing. If the actor is asked immediately before performing the action whether his hand and a racket are identical, or seeing and hearing are identical, or a television and an air conditioner are identical, he would of course say that they are not. He would give the same response after performing the action. The two spaces and their frames are kept quite distinct, but a blended space has momentarily been put together for the purpose of local problem-solving. When the blend produces a successful action, as in the case of the volleyball serve, the action may be permanently projected to the target, to be developed further there.

These connections are not metaphoric, either. In the metaphoric projection of seeing onto hearing, *eyeglasses* would correspond to *hearing aid*, not identically to *eyeglasses*. In the blend, however, eyeglasses come from one space but apply identically to the entity in the blended space that results from the fusing of seeing and hearing. These actions are essentially nonverbal and so clearly are independent of literary "deviation," metaphoric language, or strange idioms.

Blended spaces do cognitive work in the strongest sense. They provide inferences, emotions, and novel actions, and consequently leave their mark upon the real world. In the example of the boat race, the sailors of the catamaran were able, through the blend, to live their action as a race, and *Latitude 38* was able to cover the adventure as a race. In a series of articles in successive issues, *Latitude 38* reported on the preparation, the initial race, the initial failure, the rescue and salvage attempts, the second preparation, the second race, the details of the race and the victory, and, finally, the victory celebration. Readers of *Latitude* 38 were able to follow the "race" and to "assist," in the French sense. Everyone involved was able to plot and compare strategies that arose from considerations of the relative positions of the two ships. They could wonder whether *Great America II* was winning or losing, and they could, through projection from other spaces, actually find out: the blended space of the race comes with very precise, quantifiable truth conditions. By living as a race what is not a race, everyone involved —from the designer of the boat to the photojournalists—could feel, react, and reason differently, and perhaps more efficiently, and with more pleasure.

Wayne Booth, in *The Rhetoric of Fiction*, gives evidence of blends that lie between two specific kinds of spaces—the space of a story narrated and the space of narration. Booth does not recognize these blends as blends because his instruments of analysis include only two spaces, not a third blended space between them. Consequently, he describes the blends as "intrusions" by the space of narration into the space of what is narrated. But it is important to recognize that in general we keep the space of what is narrated and the space of narration separate, while blending them in a distinct blended space.

In the anonymous novel *Charlotte Summers*, for example, the narrator and readers are not part of the space of the story narrated; the characters of the story, their towns, and their residences are not part of the space of narration. But in the blended space, the narrator and readers can journey to the locales of the characters, to have a look at them.

> Before I introduce my Readers into the Company of Miss *Charlotte Summers*, I must make them acquainted with some of her Friends . . . for which Purpose, I must beg their Company as far as *Carmarthenshire*, in Wales. Tho' the Journey is pretty long, and, in the ordinary Way of travelling, may take up some Days, yet we Authors are always provided with an easy flying Carriage, which can waft our Readers in an Instant, much longer Journeys than this we are now setting out on.

In the space of the story narrated, the narrator does not exist and necessarily has no special powers there. In the space of narration, the narrator does exist. He has no special powers with respect to most of that space, but he does have special powers with respect to the story he is telling: He can shift the focus of time and place in the narration. In the blend, the narrator, the readers, and the characters can inhabit one world. In the blend, shifting spatial focus is identical to actually moving bodily from one place to another; shifting temporal focus is identical to moving bodily from one time to another. The power to shift spatial and temporal focus is identical to the power to move in superhuman ways from one place to another, or one time to another, and to move readers as well. We keep distinct the space of the story narrated, the space of narration, and their blend.

This flying "Carriage" is a specific blend derived from the general blend. Some of the features of the carriage come from the story narrated: It is a carriage like the carriages in the story narrated—it is a container, makes spatial journeys, and so on. But some of its features come from the space of narration, specifically, from the way the author's mind operates in that space—the "event shape" of the event performed by this blended carriage and the various "modal" relationships of what it can do and how it can do it are taken from the way the author's mind moves in the space of narration. In the blend, this carriage has features from both spaces.

Booth's *Rhetoric of Fiction* can be read (between the lines) as a taxonomy of such blends. Often these blends are easily noticed. The more interesting blends, however, are covert, and they are nearly ubiquitous in literature: Whenever a narrator moves in and out of a character's mind, shifts point of view from character to character, or provides an inside view of any sort, she is doing something impossible for the space of the story narrated, and she is doing it to a world that is not real inside the space of narration. Similarly, whenever anyone in the story, including the author, makes a statement that, given the logic of the narration, we must take to be absolutely reliable, or whenever the author confers a badge of reliability on a character, or alters "durational realism" or sequence, or tells us exactly how intensely a character experienced certain emotions, the author is thereby doing something impossible in the space of the story narrated and doing it to a world that is not real in the space of narration. The space with respect to which these actions are both possible and real is the blend.

Mental images to accompany blended spaces are easy to imagine. An advertisement for a tax consultant might talk about "tax bite" in voice-over while a visual image of an anthropomorphized Internal Revenue Service Form 1040 sinks its teeth into a terrified paycheck. Allegories and political cartoons make routine use of these impossible blendings. Gluttony is an anthropomorphized banana cream pie, Study a walking and talking dictionary.

One of the most common uses of blending is in counterfactual expressions such as "If I were you, I would have done it," said by a man to a woman who declined earlier to become pregnant: the woman did not do it, the man cannot do it, but the blend combines the man's judgment with the woman's conditions, enabling the man-woman to become pregnant in the counterfactual blend.

Personification is perhaps the most thoroughly analyzed consequence of blended spaces. If we revisit the various personifications we have considered— of the wind as a torturer, of Death as Thanatos, of the rain as a violent and spiteful destroyer, of situations we are trying to master as intentional adversaries, and so on—we will detect instantly the impossible blendings of specific information from source and target.

Let us consider a case of personification that shows these complexities of parable as well as some new complexities: Death the Grim Reaper. This personification involves robust impossible blending: The biological cause of death is simultaneously an animate, intentional skeleton who walks, carries a scythe, wears a robe with a cowl, and comes with the goal of killing you in particular. We do not confuse this interesting blend with the input space of death: no one ever actually confuses the Grim Reaper with the biological event of death. But the Grim Reaper blend is usefully connected to its input spaces and helps us think about them.

What are those input spaces? Here we make the crucial observation that nothing limits blending to only two input spaces. A blend can have as many input spaces as can be mentally juggled. Blending can also be recursive, happening in steps, so that a blend can be an input space to another blend. In the case of the Grim Reaper, there are at least four input spaces. Let us begin with two of them, which have a partial source-target relationship. They are (1) a space with an individual dying human being and (2) a space with reapers in the scenario of harvest. We can recruit a conventional metaphor to connect these two spaces, thereby putting them into a source-target relationship. That conventional metaphor is PEOPLE ARE PLANTS WITH RESPECT TO THE LIFE CYCLE; it underlies everyday expressions like "She's withering away," "He's a late bloomer," and "He's a young sprout." It guides us in connecting the person in the space of person-death with the plant in the space of reaping. EVENTS ARE ACTIONS guides us in doing more: The action-story of reaping can be projected onto the event-story of death. Dying (an event) can be understood by projection from reaping (an action).

But there is an additional input space to the Grim Reaper blend that does not stand as source or target to any other input space. This space is the very abstract story of causal tautology. We say Death causes dying, Sleep causes sleeping, Hunger causes hungering, Desire causes desiring, Lust causes lusting, Starvation causes starving, Fire causes things to be on fire, and so on. In the abstract story of causal tautology, events that belong to the same category have the same abstract cause. We saw this causal tautology earlier, in our discussion of Death-in-general as an abstract cause. But we had not yet begun to discuss blending at that point, so we skipped a crucial step there. Let us do it here.

In the abstract story of causal tautology, all the events in a given category share the same abstract cause. Of course, the abstract story of causal tautology does not stand up scientifically. There are many different individual event-stories of being ill, brought about by many different specific causes. When we blend any one of those specific stories with the abstract story of causal tautology, then, in the resulting blend, the specific event of being ill acquires an abstract cause—Illness-in-general—which is shared by every other event of being ill. This is such a standard and conventional blend that it is difficult even to recognize that any blending lies behind it. But it is necessary: When we are thinking in medical terms, we can manipulate a space in which a specific illness causes specific biological realities and a specific event of death without rooting that causality in a hypothetical Illness-in-general or a hypothetical Death-in-general; to get the abstract causes, we must use the conventional blends that draw upon the abstract story of causal tautology.

There are many individual events of human death, brought about by many different causes. Any particular event-story of death may have a particular cause—bone cancer, malaria, starvation, bleeding, stroke, suffocation, injury, and so on. When we blend any one of them with the abstract story of causal tautology, then, in the resulting blend, the specific event of death acquires an abstract cause, Death, shared by every other event of death. When we blend the event-story of Alcestis's death with the abstract story of causal tautology, then Alcestis's individual death has an abstract cause: Death-in-general.

That blend can then be an input to a second blend in which Death-in-General becomes an actor, not just an abstract cause. We have already seen a partial analysis of how this is done: EVENTS ARE ACTIONS guides us to map an action story of departure onto the event story of death as caused by Death-in-General, personifying Death-in-General as an agent who enforces that departure. Here we add the observation that the personification of Death as an agent who enforces the departure resides not in the departure story nor in the death story but only in the second blend. We can now see that the story of Alcestis's death is not just a projection of an action-story of departure onto an event-story of death. It is more complicated: it is a two-step blend. The first two inputs are the story of Alcestis's individual death and the abstract story of causal tautology. The resulting first blend is blended with the action-story of departure to produce a final blend in which Death-in-general is personified as an agent who enforces the departure. The inputs to the second blend are related as source and target.

The Grim Reaper blend also has a fourth input space, a space containing a prototypical story of a human killer killing a victim. This space stands in partial metaphoric relation to the space of the human death caused by Death-in-General. The Grim Reaper is not just a reaper and not just Death-in-general. He also has features of an intentional human killer who comes specifically to kill a specific victim.

So let us walk through the blending in the case of the Grim Reaper. Blending the individual event-story of a human being dying with the abstract story of causal tautology gives us a blended space in which the individual event of human dying is caused by Death (Death-in-general). This gives us an event-story of an individual human death with an abstract cause. We can blend *that story* with *two* different action stories, guided in each case by EVENTS ARE ACTIONS. The first of these input action stories is the prototypical story of a human killer who comes to kill a human victim. The second of these input action stories is the story of reaping grain. The resulting blend then has an entity that is simultaneously Death-in-general, a killer, and a reaper. The person who dies is simultaneously a human being dying from a specific cause (say, heart disease), a human being dying from an abstract cause (Death), the victim of a killing, and a plant that is harvested.

The Grim Reaper resides in a blend but cannot reside in any of the input spaces to that blend. The Grim Reaper is not in the input space with the individual event of human dying, since there are no plants or reapers there. Obviously, he is too specific to reside in the input space of the abstract story of causal tautology. He is also absent from the input story of prototypical killing by a killer, which does not have reapers. He is not in the input space with the story of reaping and harvest, either: the stereotype of reapers in the reaping story is incompatible with features of The Grim Reaper.

Let us consider some of these incompatibilities. Stereotypical reapers are subject to persuasion and argument. But the blending of the abstract story of causal tautology and the event story of individual human dying gives a Death that is beyond persuasion. The Grim Reaper is inhuman.

The individual authority of any actual reaper is unknown: perhaps he takes his orders from others; perhaps he is a slave. But Death has authority that is blended with the reaper to create an absolutely transcendent authority completely incompatible with that of normal reapers.

Actual reapers are numerous and essentially interchangeable. But Death is conceived of as a single abstract cause, which is projected to the blend, making Death-the-Reaper single and definite. This explains the appropriateness of the definite article: *the* Grim Reaper.

Actual reapers are mortal and are replaced by other reapers. But Death is neither. Projecting these features of Death to the blend creates a Death-the-Reaper who is immortal: the same Grim Reaper who cut our ancestors down will cut us down.

Stereotypical reapers are strong, productive, healthy, and attractive. But the killer is destructive, unhealthy, and works on *us,* so the Grim Reaper must be unattractive, or "grim."

Stereotypical reapers perform heavy labor for long intervals and wear clothing suitable to these conditions of labor. But the killer acts once only, on the person who dies, so Death-the-Reaper can wear clothing suited to repose; and this clothing can further carry connotations of the killer as grim and isolated.

Stereotypical reapers use their scythes, but the Grim Reaper is often thought of as doing his work merely by appearing. In that case, there is yet another, minor input space to the blend, in which the herald of death brings death merely by appearing. In the blend, the Grim Reaper has aspects of the reaper and the killer, but his effective action comes from the input story of the herald rather than the input story of the reaper or the killer.

Stereotypical reapers work in daylight, reaping the entire field indiscriminately, ignorant of the individual existence of plants of wheat, and they harvest rather than kill. But Death and the killer have an entirely different set of meanings, so the Grim Reaper comes for a specific person at a specific time, and he kills. He can stalk you like a killer.

Lakoff and I originally noticed a constraint on personification: We must feel about the personification the way we feel about the event, and the appearance and character of the personification must correspond to the way we feel about the event. As long as we think grimly about the event of death and its cause, we must take a grim view of Death-the-Reaper. We can now see a reason for this constraint: We project to the blend our view of the event, including its cause. In the case of the Grim Reaper, we also project to the blend an action story of killing consistent with our feelings about the event of death. The reaper in the blend is simultaneously a cause we feel grimly about and a killer we feel grimly about. The Reaper must therefore actually have these features.

If we look at the linguistic elements involved in referring to Death-the-Grim-Reaper, we see that the terms reflect the conceptual blending. The definite article "the" comes from the causal tautology, since it picks out a single general cause. The name "Death" comes from the blending of the causal tautology with the individual event of dying. The adjective "Grim" comes from both the space with the prototypical killer and the space with the individual event of human dying. The noun "Reaper" comes from the input space of harvest.

The Grim Reaper shows us again that combining in the blend is not restricted to counterparts. Reapers and skeletons are not counterparts in the input spaces: PEOPLE ARE PLANTS does not connect them, nor does EVENTS ARE ACTIONS. But Death as a cause is metonymically associated with *skeleton* as an effect. In the blend, the reaper is combined with both Death and the skeleton. Similarly, priests, monks, mourners, and members of lay brotherhoods that are associated with dying, funerals, burial, and afterlife are metonymically associated with Death. They are not counterparts of Death, but in the blend, the attire we associate with them—robe and cowl—can be the attire of the Grim Reaper. The cowl, pulled over the head of the Grim Reaper, at once evokes both connotations of death and the impression of Death as mysterious, unknown, and set apart from human society. This cognitive construction of meaning is independent of historical and scientific accuracy: maybe priests, monks, or lay brethren in fact never wore robes with cowls. What matters is only that we know the conceptual association, from any source, including cartoons. Someone who knows that association can use it to make sense of the attire of the Grim Reaper.

The possibility of combining metonymic elements—like Death and a skeleton—gives blending a great power: The blend can combine elements that contribute to the desired effect *even though those elements are not counterparts*. The combined elements "go together" in evoking the same effect even if they do not "go together" according to the counterpart connections between the input stories. Consider for example the personification of Heroism. Blending a story of heroic behavior with the abstract story of causal tautology yields a blended story in which heroic behavior is *caused* by an abstract cause, Heroism-in-general. Just as we use EVENTS ARE ACTIONS to personify Death-in-general as a reaper, so we can use it to personify Heroism-in-general as a human actor who causes heroic behavior. Nothing so far requires that this human actor be a hero. Moreover, the actor who causes the heroism corresponds to Heroism-in-general, not to any particular hero or kind of hero. However, Heroism-in-general and that causal human actor *are* indeed both associated with actual heroes. We can therefore pick such an actual hero, or a kind of hero, and use it in the blend to give Heroism-in-general a particular human form: Heroism-in-general can be Galahad or a generic veteran knight of the Round Table or a battle-seasoned samurai or Queen of the Amazons or Ajax or any other heroic person, whether specific or generic. This possibility of combining noncounterparts allows the blend to combine elements for effect even if they are not counterparts.

The Grim Reaper also shows us that when a blend involves a conventional metaphor (like PEOPLE ARE PLANTS), the recruitment of that conventional metaphor to the blend is partial, selective, and transforming. The conventional blend of the Grim Reaper does not simply recruit the conventional metaphor in which stages in the human cycle of life correspond metaphorically to stages in the plant cycle of life. Instead, the blend takes only a part of that metaphor and alters it to suit its purposes. In the conventional metaphor, the stages of a person's life correspond to the stages of plant life: Youth is a sprouting or burgeoning; full maturity is full flowering; old age is withering; and the person-death is the final decline and disintegration of the plant or of the relevant part of the plant, such as the flower. But the scenario of harvest interferes with that set of mappings.

The original analysis George Lakoff and I offered of the Grim Reaper included the observation that "the plants at the end of their life cycle are harvested." This inexact characterization came from not yet having discovered blending and its partial and flexible use of conventional metaphors. Reaping occurs not at the end of the life cycle of a plant, but at the end of its cultivation cycle, which is in the middle of its life cycle. Lakoff and I had recognized this in remarking that the "Gazing Grain" in Emily Dickinson's poem "Because I could not stop for Death" stands for maturity—it follows "Children" at school (youth) and precedes the "Setting Sun" (old age). There is a fundamental mismatch between the harvesting of the grain and the typical disintegration and death of a plant: The harvesting happens in the middle of the life cycle but the death happens at the end of the life cycle. There is also a fundamental mismatch between the harvesting of the grain and the dying of the person: Harvesting takes place at a fixed stage in the life cycle of the plant—when it has matured but has not begun to decline—yet death happens at any stage of the human life cycle.

Because of these mismatches, the conventional metaphoric connections between stages of plant life and stages of human life are ignored in the blend. In the personification of Death the Grim Reaper, it is the event of human dying we are concerned with, and so we require the Grim Reaper to be able to reap at any stage of human life. He can reap his victim in young adulthood, full flower, or old age. The conventional metaphoric connection in PEOPLE ARE PLANTS between the final stage of plant-death (in the declining plant's life cycle) and the final stage of person-death (in the declining person's life cycle) is kept out of the blend. Similarly, the fact that reaping takes place only at the middle stage in the plant's life cycle is kept out of the blend. In the blend, the stages of human life and the stages of plant life are not fused. Instead in the blend, the moment of harvest is fused with the moment of death, but that moment can occur at any point in the cycle: the Grim Reaper is a bad farmer.

Interestingly, although in principle blending could make more use of the person-plant correspondence—a painting might portray the Grim Reaper as mowing down a field of people-as-wheat (there are historical examples of this sort)—in fact the modern conventional blend does not emphasize this connection. The Grim Reaper simply arrives, and his arrival causes the dying. In this way, the Grim Reaper acts not at all like a reaper, but like any herald of death. The person who dies of course does not act like a plant.

Not just any specific information from input spaces is likely to be projected to the blended space. Prototypical information that cannot be avoided unexceptionably, given the medium of representation, is always likely to appear: In a picture of the blend, the talking donkey would probably have four legs and donkey ears, regardless of the conceptual use of this information in the parable. Much more important, however, the blended space typically includes specific details that serve as cues for projecting to the topic input space. The plough and the millstone in the tale of the ox and the donkey are specific details that do not project as specific details onto the story of Shahrazad. But they are metonymic for generic conditions of servitude and suffering, which do appear in the blend and do ultimately project onto the virgins who suffer in the story of Shahrazad. The sifted straw and the well-winnowed barley do not project as specific details onto the story of Shahrazad. But they are metonymic for generic conditions of luxury and comfort, which do appear in the blend and do ultimately project onto Shahrazad's current situation.

The varied examples we have considered make it clear that blended spaces are useful for inferential work. When we widen our scope yet further, we find blended spaces not only in literature and everyday linguistic utterances, but also in dreams and in our attempts to make sense of anything new by blending its specific details with structure from something we already know, so as to categorize it provisionally and act accordingly. The various figural projections we encountered in earlier chapters all reveal blended spaces, once we look for them. Proust's *ouverture* to *À la recherche du temps perdu*, for example, which is a projection of the spatial onto the mental, works through a fantastic blended space. In that blended space, spatial events of change, including body action, are blended with mental events of memory in strikingly impossible ways. As memories come and go, or shift into one another, the actual room that contains the sleeping narrator changes to match the memory. As a memory of one room becomes the memory of another, the wall before his eyes shifts direction and grows longer. The physical space around him takes on the aspectual nature and powers of his memory. This is an impossible blending, of the kind commonly recognized in dreams, memory, cartoons, and literature.

Blending is a dynamic activity. It connects input spaces; it projects partial structure from input spaces to the blend, creating an imaginative blended space that, however odd or even impossible, is nonetheless connected to its inputs and can illuminate those inputs. A blend can produce knowledge. It is not constructed by union or intersection of the inputs. It is not a skeletal or static mock-up of a few elements from the inputs but has a life of its own, in the sense that it contains structure that is not calculable from the inputs and that can be developed, once constructed, on its own. The blend counts as a unit that can be manipulated efficiently as a unit, providing full access to the input structures without requiring continual recourse to them.

Blending in parable has the following general principles:

- The blend exploits and develops counterpart connections between input spaces.
- Counterparts may or may not both be brought into the blend, and may or may not be fused in the blend.
- The projection from the input spaces is selective.
- Blends recruit a great range of conceptual structure and knowledge without our recognizing it.
- What has been recruited to the blend can be difficult to discover.
- A blend may have many input spaces.
- Blending is a process that can be applied repeatedly, and blends themselves can be inputs to other blends.
- Blends develop structure not provided by the inputs.
- Blends can combine elements on the basis of metonymic relation.
- The recruitment of a conventional metaphor to the blend is in general partial, selective, and transforming.
- Inferences, arguments, ideas, and emotions developed in the blend can lead us to modify the initial input spaces and change our views of the knowledge used to build those input spaces.

Now let us consider two final related questions:

- How does structure develop in the blend?
- How does structure in the blend lead us to reconsider input spaces?

Blends develop by three mechanisms: *composition*, *completion*, and *elaboration*.

In blending, we project partial structure from input stories and *compose* that structure in a blended story. We are guided in doing so by counterpart connections between the input spaces. For example, the riddle of the mountain-climbing Buddhist monk has elaborate counterpart connections between the two input spaces. Some of those counterparts, like the paths and the dates, are brought into the blend and fused. Others, like the two monks, are brought into the blend as separate entities.

In other blends, only one counterpart is brought into the blend, as in the blend for "If I were you, I would have done it," which brings into the blend the judgment of the man but not the counterpart judgment of the woman. Partial composition provides a working space for further composition.

*Completion* provides additional structure not provided by composition. Given a minimal *composition* of two boats on a course in the example from *Latitude 38*, we can *complete* the blend with a large amount of structure from our conceptual frame of a *race*. Given a minimal *composition* of two monks traversing a path during the same day starting from opposite ends, we can *complete* that structure by recognizing it as an instance of a familiar frame that contains an *encounter*. *Completion* provides the structure in the blend that gives us the solution to the riddle.

*Elaboration* develops the blend through imaginative mental simulation according to the principles and internal logic of the blend. Some of these principles will have been brought to the blend by *completion*. Continued dynamic *completion* can recruit new principles and logic during *elaboration*. But new principles and logic may also arise through *elaboration* itself. Blended spaces can become extremely elaborated, as in literary fantasies.

*Composition* and *completion* often draw together conceptual structures previously kept apart. As a consequence, the blend can reveal latent contradictions and coherences between previously separated elements. It can show us problems and lacunae in what we had previously taken for granted. It can equally show us unrecognized strengths and complementarity. In this way, blends yield insight into the conceptual structures from which they arise.

## ꞈ 6 ꞊

# MANY SPACES

*Nirad Das* (an Indian painter): You wish me to be less Indian?

*Flora Crewe* (an English poet): I did say that but I think what I meant was for you to be more Indian, or at any rate Indian, not Englished-up and all over me like a labrador and knocking things off tables with your tail. . . . Actually, I do know what I mean, I want you to be with me as you would be if I were Indian.

*Das*: An Indian Miss Crewe! Oh dear, that is a mental construction which has no counterpart in the material world.

*Flora*: So is a unicorn, but you can imagine it.

*Das*: You can imagine it but you cannot mount it.

*Flora*: Imagining it was all I was asking in my case.

*Das* (terribly discomfited): Oh, Oh, my gracious! I had no intention—I assure you . . .

*Tom Stoppard, Indian Ink*

PARABLE DISTRIBUTES MEANING across at least two stories. But now we have seen that a third story—a blended story—typically plays a role. We have also seen that a blend can have more than two inputs, and that blending can happen recursively—a blend can be blended with other inputs to create yet another blend.

In fact, parable typically distributes meaning over many spaces. The aggregate meaning resides in no one of them, but rather in the array of spaces and in their connections. We know each of the spaces, and how it relates to the others, and what each is good for. None of them replaces another. Meanings, in this way, are not mental objects bounded in conceptual places but rather complex operations of projecting, blending, and integrating over multiple spaces.

## GENERIC SPACES

We have often seen that an element in one input story can have a *counterpart* in the other. The donkey and Shahrazad are counterparts. So are *Great America II* and *Northern Light*, the two Buddhist monks, the two paths they travel, the rain and the message, and the reaper and Death. It is not possible to blend two stories without some counterpart connections between them to guide the blending.

Input stories have counterparts because they share abstract structure. Consider the boat race. There is a frame for a voyage by boat. It contains a boat, a path, a departure point, a destination, and so on. Each of the input stories for the boat-race blend has this frame structure, which provides counterpart relations between them. Different kinds of abstract structure can be shared by two stories: category structure, frame structure, role structure, image-schematic structure, and so on. Sometimes, two inputs will share abstract structure because a conventional metaphor has established that shared structure. Sometimes, two inputs will share more than one kind of abstract structure. For example, the inputs for the riddle of the Buddhist monk share frame structure (a person walking along a path) just as the inputs for the boat-race share frame structure (a boat voyage), but there is also identity structure shared in both cases: The monk in one space counts as "identical" to the monk in the other space, and San Francisco in one space counts as "identical" to San Francisco in the other space.

Now consider the expression "If I were you, I would have done it," said by a man to a woman who declined earlier to become pregnant. The two input spaces share structure: In each there is a human being, with human intentionality, possibility, and standard relations between intentionality and action. This shared structure gives counterparts: The man and the woman are counterpart human beings, even though they have different identities; their preferences are counterparts, even though those preferences are not identical; their actions are counterparts, even though their actions are not identical. In short, there is a frame structure shared by the two input spaces, and it provides counterpart relations between them.

I will say that the abstract structure shared by input spaces resides in a *generic space*. The generic space indicates the counterpart connections between the input spaces.

The central question is, is this *generic space* just a name for structure shared by the input spaces, or does it have an actual conceptual existence of its own? Can this abstract structure be manipulated and used in a way that does not entail manipulating the input space in which it resides? George Lakoff and I have given one argument for the existence of generic spaces, as follows.

When we read a proverb in a book of proverbs, and so have no reason to connect the meaning of the proverb to any specific target, we arrive at a generic reading. For example, "Look before you leap," found in a book of proverbs (or in a fortune cookie), will be interpreted generically. Similarly, "When the cat's away, the mice will play" presents a source story of mice who behave in a restricted fashion when the cat is around but who behave with fewer restrictions when the cat is gone. The generic-level information in this story can be projected to a generic space with an abstract story: One agent or group of agents constrains another agent or group of agents, and when the governing agent is inattentive, the otherwise constrained agent or agents behave more freely. We can reach this generic interpretation even if we have no specific target onto which we wish to project it. So the generic space has a conceptual existence.

Lakoff and I have called this kind of projection from a source story to a generic story GENERIC IS SPECIFIC: generic information, often image-schematic, is projected from a specific space to give structure to a generic space. Of course, this generic space "applies" to the specific space from which it came. Once the generic space is established, we may project it onto a range of specific target spaces. The generic space constructed out of "When the cat's away, the mice will play" can be projected onto stories of the office, the classroom, infidelity, congressional oversight committees, computer antivirus utilities, and so on, over an unlimited range.

Blends can be constructed if two stories can be construed as sharing abstract structure. The abstract structure they share is contained in the generic space that connects them. Consider, for example, the riddle of the Buddhist monk. Its generic space has a single journeyer taking a single journey from dawn to sunset, over a single distance along a single path. The generic space does not specify the direction of the journey (up or down), the date of the journey, or the internal form of the journey (starting and stopping, moving slower or faster). This degree of inspecificity allows the generic structure to be projected equally well onto the space of the ascent on the first day, the space of the descent on the second day, and the blended space where both journeys occur on an unspecified day. The riddle of the Buddhist monk involves two input spaces, a generic space, and a blended space.

It often takes work to find a generic space that fits two input spaces; there are often alternative generic spaces that might connect two input spaces. But in some cases, a generic space has been constructed repeatedly between two spaces. It has come to structure the two input spaces and to establish what seem to be fixed counterparts. The generic space has become fully available from each of the input spaces. In that case, the generic space becomes invisible to us. If the blend between the two spaces is conventional or minimal, the blend may also be invisible to us. In that situation, we are likely to detect only two input spaces, without a generic space or a blended space. We are also likely to detect what seems to be a direct projection between them, involving a set of fixed counterparts. This situation arises in basic metaphors like LIFE IS A JOURNEY. In basic metaphors, it looks (at first) as if the projection goes directly from one space (the source) to another (the target), without involving a generic space or a blended space. The projection seems to be one-way and entirely positive. It seems to have fixed parts: For example, the traveler projects to the person living the life; the beginning of the journey projects to birth; the end of the journey projects to death; the distance traveled projects to the amount of time lived; obstacles project to difficulties; guides project to counselors; fellow-travelers project to people with whom life is shared; and so on. These are the projections of basic metaphor analyzed insightfully by George Lakoff and Mark Johnson in *Metaphors We Live By*. The invisibility of the generic space and the blended space (except, of course, on analysis) produces a minimal phenomenon that looks like direct projection from one conceptual domain to another.

When a deeply entrenched projection is expressed in deeply entrenched vocabulary, especially vocabulary so entrenched as to seem to be the natural way to discuss the target, then we do not notice the projection consciously and have no need to notice the generic space or the blended space. For example, the phrase "intellectual progress" (from THE MIND IS A BODY MOVING IN SPACE) takes its noun from the source and its adjective from the target and can be thought of as evoking a blend, the way "fossil poetry" evokes a blend. But "intellectual progress" seems normal and "fossil poetry" seems imaginative. For "intellectual progress," the underlying generic space is absolutely established; the vocabulary of the source (JOURNEY) has been effectively shifted to this generic space during the previous history of the language and is available to all speakers now to be applied linguistically wherever the generic space is applied conceptually; the conception of the target (MIND) by projection from this generic space is very deeply entrenched; and the phrase "intellectual progress" is a conventional phrase for the target conceived in this fashion. It is accordingly difficult in this case even to notice the generic space.

By contrast, the expression "mental journey," which shares its linguistic construction (noun from source, adjective from target) and its conceptual projection with "intellectual progress," is less conventional as language, and so in this case it may be easier to see the projection and to recognize the generic space. "Ethnic cleansing," yet another example of the same linguistic construction, is not at all conventional as an expression. True, the generic projection of the scenario of cleansing is highly conventional; the resulting generic space has been applied to many specific targets and the source vocabulary has been thoroughly shifted from the source to the generic space to be applied linguistically wherever the generic space is applied conceptually to a target space. But the projection of the generic space of cleansing to the *particular* target of wholesale killing of unwanted ethnic groups is not yet conventional, and the use of its vocabulary for *this* target is not yet the natural way to refer to the target. It follows that we are more likely in the case of "ethnic cleansing" to notice the projection and the generic space, and may even recognize the blended space.

Often, the blended space is forced into view. "Walking steam-engine" refers to a human being of great mechanical vitality, industry, direction, power, and seriousness. Many things underlying this phrase are entrenched: the projection of the space of mechanical devices to a generic space; the shift of vocabulary to that generic space; the wide application of that generic space to many targets; the consequent wide application of its vocabulary to those targets; and the conventional linguistic construction used for indicating that the target input space has a human story but the source input space has a nonhuman story, as in "walking encyclopedia" and "walking time-bomb." Nonetheless, "walking steam-engine" evokes vivid specifics from the input spaces, impossibly blended. It is also an unconventional phrase. Accordingly, we *notice* the blended space.

In general, generic and blended spaces become more noticeable as the projection is less conventional, the expression is less conventional, or the projection and the expression combine noticeably what are still regarded as incompatible specifics. These circumstances are closely related: As the projection becomes conventional, so does the vocabulary it carries; and in the case of source and target input spaces, as the projection and the vocabulary become conventional, so the source category becomes extended, making the blend look less like a blend and more like an enlarged category. For example, the conceptual projections underlying "intellectual progress" extend the category of *progress* and *journey* to include mental events. Because this extension of the category is by now deeply entrenched, "intellectual" can be viewed as compatible with "progress," and "intellectual progress" can be taken as referring to an extended part of the category rather than to an aggressive blend.

Even when the projection and its expression are most deeply entrenched and least likely to be noticed, generic and blended spaces are still available. Habit has simply made us take them for granted, rendering them invisible. The generic space projected from *journey* has its own existence independent of its embedding in the target story of *the course of a life from birth to death*. It can be projected to a different target altogether. We can project it onto a particular span of life, mental activity like problem solving, or the "wandering" characteristic of daydreams. We can project it onto marriage or artwork or the building of a bookcase or evolution or computer activity or any of a vast range of other targets. We can project it just as we project the generic spaces that arise out of "When the cat's away, the mice will play" or "Look before you leap" or any other proverb that mentions only a specific source story. We can project it not just to purposeful behavior directed at a goal but indeed to any action performed by an intentional agent. "Watch your step" can be said of any action that an agent is about to perform, purposeful or not, intentional or not, consciously or not. The generic space underlying "Watch your step" consists only of an agent, an action that the agent is on the verge of performing, and a warning to pay attention.

A telling difference between a basic metaphor like LIFE IS A JOURNEY and our generic interpretation of "The girl who can't dance says the band can't play" is this: The generic space involved in LIFE IS A JOURNEY has a deeply entrenched default projection onto a particular specific target space, *the course of a life from birth to death*, while the generic space arising from "The girl who can't dance says the band can't play" is not conventionally tied to a specific target space. It is therefore easier to see the generic space in the second case, and to be aware of our application of that generic space to this or that specific target space.

When we take our data exclusively from deeply entrenched projections like LIFE IS A JOURNEY that have deeply entrenched vocabulary, the generic and blended spaces are less easily noticed, and the projection looks as if it carries positive meaning from one input space (the source) to another (the target). This has lead to the customary model of the projection of meaning as direct, one-way, and positive. This is a useful and parsimonious model, but it is adequate only in limiting cases.

Generic spaces differ linguistically from specific input spaces and blended spaces in one fundamental regard: They lack their own rich vocabulary. The vocabulary of a generic space is largely shifted to it from an input space. This vocabulary applies whenever we project the generic space onto a new space. For example, we have no generic word that means "an instrument somebody uses so constantly in his chosen work as to be regarded as defining the work." One such instrument for one such worker is an *axe*. The relation of the worker to the axe—manipulating it, trying to get it to do what he wants done—has an abstract structure, and this structure can be projected to a generic space. That generic space can then be projected to a target, such as playing a jazz instrument. In jazz, someone's instrument is called his *axe*. A saxophone is an axe, but so is a flute, a guitar, a drum set, a piano. The vocabulary of one space is shifted to the generic space, and projected from there to whatever target the generic applies to—in this case, jazz instruments. A new projection of the generic space onto a new kind of instrument (a synthesizer, for example) will not look unusual even if it is entirely novel: the vocabulary that has been shifted to the generic space is expected to apply to any target to which the generic space is projected. Such projection underlies category extension: "Axe" can now refer to the blended space that consists of all axes, including real axes.

## WAKING UP THE GENERIC SPACE

We can at will focus on the generic space and wake it up fully. Even when, as in a basic metaphor, the generic space is fully superimposed upon a conventional target, we can nonetheless easily turn that generic space into a blended space by supplementing it with specifics from the source and the target. Underlying a phrase like "She's making considerable progress as a young adult" is a conventional projection so deeply entrenched that it may be hard to see blending at work. The generic space, fully superimposed on the target, is nearly invisible. But this generic space can be turned into a blended space, as in a television commercial for an insurance company in which a person is actually on a road, encountering and going through doors labeled *school, college admissions, undergraduate education, professional school, marriage*. As she goes along, passing through each door on the road, she ages and her clothing changes to suit her present "stage of life." She acquires fellow travelers in the form of playmates, friends, husband, and children. Her parents, standing at the side of the road, hand her fistfuls of money as she trots past. She in turn hands the money to the "bursar" who stands outside the door of professional school, and so on. This is a fantastic blended space, constructed by waking up the generic space and adding to it.

Waking up the generic space is a standard tool of literature. Contrast the very skeletal generic space underlying the phrase "drug trip" with Proust's elaboration:

> When one absorbs a new drug, entirely different in composition, it is always with a delicious expectancy of the unknown. . . . To what unknown forms of sleep, of dreams, is the newcomer going to lead one? It is inside one now, it is in control of our thoughts. In what way is one going to fall asleep? And, once asleep, by what strange paths, up to what peaks, into what unfathomed gulfs will this all-powerful master lead one? What new group of sensations will one meet with on this journey? Will it lead to illness? To blissful happiness? To death?

> On n'absorbe le produit nouveau, d'une composition toute différente, qu'avec la délicieuse attente de l'inconnu. . . . Vers quel genres ignorés de sommeil, de rêves, le nouveau venu va-t-il nous conduire? Il est maintenant dans nous, il a la direction de notre pensée. De quelle façon allons-nous nous endormir? Et une fois que nous le serons, par quel

chemins étrangers, sur quelle cimes, dans quels gouffres inexplorés le maître tout-puissant nous conduira-t-il? Quel groupement nouveau de sensations allons-nous connaître dans ce voyage? Nous mènera-t-il au malaise? À la béatitude? À la mort?

Similarly, contrast the very skeletal generic space underlying an expression like "Death finally won" with Proust's elaborations:

For we talk of "Death" for convenience, but there are almost as many different deaths as there are people. We do not possess a sense that would enable us to see, moving at full speed in every direction, these deaths, the active deaths aimed by destiny at this person or that. Often there are deaths that will not be entirely relieved of their duties until two or even three years later. They come in haste to plant a tumour in the side of a Swann, then depart to attend to other tasks, returning only when, the surgeons having performed their operation, it is necessary to plant the tumour there afresh.

Car nous disons la mort pour simplifier, mais il y en a presque autant que de personnes. Nous ne possédons pas de sens qui nous permette de voir, courant à toute vitesse, dans toutes les directions, les morts, les morts actives dirigées par le destin ver tel ou tel. Souvent ce sont des morts qui ne seront entièrement libérées de leur tâche que deux, trois ans après. Elles courent vite poser un cancer au flanc d'un Swann, puis repartent pour d'autres besognes, ne revenant que quand l'opération des chirurgiens ayant eu lieu il faut poser le cancer à nouveau.

In such cases of rich blending, the generic space is awakened and elaborated in a blended space where new work is done that requires revision of the input stories.

## THE GRADIENT OF MIDDLE SPACES

A generic space stands at one end of a gradient; a richly blended space stands at the other end; the blend connects to the generic space and includes its structure. As information is blended from the input spaces into the blended space, it moves along the gradient from generic to blend. The degree of blending varies along this gradient. A "pedagogical gun" or a "walking steam-engine" may suggest a thin blend, while a lengthy allegorical poem may suggest a very rich blend.

The degree of blending is often up to the reader. Bernadine Healy resigned as head of the National Institutes of Health (NIH) shortly after the inauguration of President Bill Clinton, implicitly acknowledging that she had been asked to leave because she had been associated with the federal ban on the use of fetal tissue in scientific research paid for with federal funds. She expressed regret that the agency had been drawn into the political debate by saying, "NIH has become a bit of the Beirut of abortion and fetal tissue."

A reader who uses the popular notion of Beirut as suffering terribly and innocently because conflicting factions war over it might interpret this blend so thinly as to make it seem like no blend at all: Healy is simply saying that the NIH has suffered innocently by being caught in the "political crossfire," where again the noun comes from the source and the adjective from the target but in a phrase so conventional as to seem as normal as "intellectual progress."

But it is equally easy to imagine Healy in a bullet-scarred NIH building (the one in Bethesda, Maryland, just outside the District of Columbia) taking political rounds of ammunition, lobbed at her alternately by Republican and Democratic presidents and their political factions, from the White House and Congress, located on the Mall a few miles away. A political cartoon supporting her point of view might picture her in a helmet, ducking the incoming fire. There is a gradient of specificity between the generic space and the blended space, and we have latitude in moving along that gradient as we interpret expressions.

## CATEGORIES AND ANALOGIES

Conceptual blending is a fundamental instrument of the everyday mind, used in our basic construal of all our realities, from the social to the scientific. Let us consider some examples of social and scientific blending originally treated by Fauconnier and me.

Analogy places pressure upon conventional category structures. A successful analogy can, through entrenchment, earn a place among our category structures. The assault of an analogy on conventional categories is often expressed in the early stages by a blend-construction that draws its noun from the source and its modifier from the target. "Same-sex marriage," for example, asks us to project the scenario of marriage onto an alternative domestic scenario. People of violently opposed ideological belief will freely agree that the generic space of this projection carries information applicable to both scenarios. It might include people living in a household, dividing labor, protecting each other in various ways, and planning together.

What is at issue is not the existence of this information but rather its status. Those whose conception of conventional marriage has as a requisite component "heterosexual union" and has as its prototype "for the sake of children" will regard this abstract generic information as merely incidental or derivative in the story of traditional marriage. In their view, "same-sex marriage" will remain an analogical projection whose blended space is as fantastic and conflicted as any we have seen in Dante or Shakespeare, but which nonetheless draws legitimate abstract connections however inessential between one kind of story and an entirely different kind of story.

But others may regard this abstract information in the generic space as the central information in the story of traditional marriage. They may regard "heterosexual union for the sake of children" as merely incidental information in the traditional story. For these people, "same-sex marriage" is not an aggressive analogical construction; it simply refers to a subcategory of marriage in the way that "light wave" refers to a kind of wave.

We must be careful not to mistake the research question of how parable works in the mind for a different issue of professed ideological belief. Agreeing to treat two scenarios as belonging to the same category for purposes of protection under the law or taxation or health coverage or whatever is different from actually having a conceptual structure in which these two scenarios belong to the same conceptual category. Liberal goodwill toward diverse scenarios, on a philosophy of live and let live, is irrelevant to the phenomenon of recognizing something to be an obvious instance of a category, as when we recognize light to be obviously a wave or a heron to be obviously a bird. When we have a category that is entrenched in our conceptual structure, we do not merely agree to treat two of its central members in some of the ways we treat the other; instead, they share the same default generic structure.

Suppose the information in the generic space of "same-sex marriage"— people living in a household, dividing labor, protecting each other in various ways, and planning together—came over time to be the central information in our standard concept of *marriage*. This would mean that the generic space of "same-sex marriage" had displaced the generic space of "traditional marriage" as the essential structure of the category *marriage*. The blended space would become not a fantastic combination but rather a new and wider category. It would ultimately subsume the original input spaces.

In a situation of ideological tension over category connections, there is always the opportunity to reject the projection and invert the relative status of the two input spaces. This has happened in debates over racial, gender, social, and economic categories, and occurs in two steps. First, an attempt is made to claim that the generic space that is projected from a powerful group (white, male, aristocratic, rich, colonialist, capitalist, master) applies to less powerful groups if we project the "right" and "just" information, thereby extending the category: There becomes no "legitimate" distinction between aristocrat and commoner, for example. Such projections are often resisted by those who see themselves as belonging to the source category, but embraced by people who see themselves as belonging to the target.

However, a second possible response in the social debate occurs when those in the target reject the projection, on the claim that the two groups do not belong to a category at all. It might be claimed, for example, that violence is central to men but not to women and that any generic space that lumps them together does a disservice to women and is to be rejected; that the rich are inherently dishonest while the poor are inherently honest and that any generic space that lumps them together does a disservice to the poor and is to be rejected; that white culture is essentially a culture of ice and therefore cold while black culture is essentially a culture of the sun and therefore warm and that any generic space that is proposed as a category that applies to both of them is to be rejected; that conventional marriage involves asymmetry between the man and the woman while same-sex marriage has no such asymmetry and so any generic space proposed to lump them together is to be rejected. What is at issue here is of course not in the slightest degree any particular ideological view but rather the fact that all ideological views use parable to judge and reason. Parable is an instrument of thought and belief and consequently of argument.

The cultural tussle over the analogical pressure of "same-sex marriage" upon conventional category structures provides daily journalistic copy and stirs passions. It is an example of the role played by blended spaces in our understanding of cultural and social reality, and of our place in that reality. Blended spaces play the identical role in the world of basic science. Consider the case of "artificial life." If a mental space that includes biological life has as central information "embodied, developed through biological evolution, carbon-based," and so on, then "artificial life"—which comes from a computer lab and is not based on carbon—will always be an analogical concept, and "artificial life" will not belong to the category "life." It will be a provisional category extension, like "He's a real fish." But computer viruses, for example, share abstract structure with biological organisms. As the generic space that can be projected from biological life and imposed on computer events grows more useful, some people may be tempted to change their conception of the status of this information as carried in the source. The generic space involved in the concept "artificial life" could in principle come to constitute the central structure of the source. In that case, "artificial life" would become a subcategory of life. At present, "artificial life" is an analogical projection of evident utility that seems unlikely to displace conventional category connections. But that situation could in principle change.

Blended spaces play a routine role in the development of even the most fundamental scientific concepts. Mass and energy, once conceived as belonging to two different categories, have been reconceived. The blended space of mass that is simultaneously energy has become the new category: Mass is energy and energy is mass. Similarly, the projection of spatial structure onto the conception of time has always been profound; in our own century, the scientific role of this projection has grown considerably larger, resulting in a blend that seemed at first an impossible clash—space-time. But this blend too has come to subsume the original inputs.

## THE UBIQUITY OF BLENDED SPACES

There is a certain way of thinking about thought that has kept blended spaces from being detected. It begins with the ostensibly reasonable assumption that inference and truth go together. On this assumption, central meanings and crucial inferences that guide our action come from what we believe to be true, not from fantasy constructions like Bertran de Born in Dante's *Inferno*. To get over this blindness to blended spaces requires separating belief from the construction of meaning. It is often the case that central inferences for a "real-world" space are in fact constructed in a blended space that we do not believe to be true or real. *The truth of an input space can come from a blended space that we do not believe to be true or real.* This sounds paradoxical, but there is no reason it should, once we draw a distinction between the construction of meaning and the adoption of belief.

For example, personification—or even the minimal projection of intentionality according to EVENTS ARE ACTIONS—results in a blended space whose "truth" we hold quite distinct from the "truth" of the target space, yet inferences are clearly projected from the blended space to the all-important target space. In Hemingway's *The Old Man and the Sea*, the fisherman's hand cramps. He speaks to his hand as if it is his enemy in the struggle to bring in the fish. He taunts it. The fisherman is not demented. He does not for a moment actually believe that his hand is an intentional adversarial agent. Relative to the blended space, it is true that his hand is an intentional adversarial agent. Relative to the target space of his fishing and the work of his body in that scenario, it is not true that his hand is an intentional adversarial agent, and he has not the slightest confusion regarding the difference. He keeps the two spaces quite distinct. Nonetheless, there are certain inferences from the blended space that he does project to the target space and believe of that target space, most salient among them that he will do best to adopt the emotions and strategy of the blended space. This is an inference that bears on the target space: He, the undemented fisherman, should in the target space of what he actually believes apply himself to dealing with his hand as if it were his intentional opponent while understanding fully the weight of *as if*. He should work to an extent in the blended space, without believing it. Useful construction of meaning is not the same as adoption of belief.

This is the stance we all take when we are dealing with a recalcitrant problem or task and construct the extraordinarily useful blended space in which this problem or task is our opponent—a tax fiddle to be worked, a tire to be changed, a tent to be staked down. If in analyzing the construction of inference we restrict our focus to what we really believe to be true, we will be blind to the indispensable blended spaces in these cases. If we ask someone cursing at a tire she is trying to change whether the tire really has an intention to frustrate her, she will think we are making a joke. In the all-important target space, she understands the tire as not intentional. But her useful attitude depends upon a blended space she does not believe.

On the other hand, a blend need not be considered false or fantastic. It can come to be regarded as compatible with the source. "Working mother," "provisional government," "independent scholar," and so on might be explainable as cases where one general narrative (*mothering, government, scholarship*) is combined with another (*working, provisional activity, independent activity*) into a blended space. The hypothesis that the linguistic construction represents conceptual blending is radical. It is traditional to assume that the modifier-noun construction represents propositional expression ("red shoe") but can be adapted or stretched for exotic purposes like blending ("Irish twins"—said of two siblings born less than twelve months apart). The radical view reverses the traditional direction: The modifier-noun construction represents blending, but in special minimal circumstances, the blending can become invisible, misleading us into thinking we are dealing only with propositional structure. Consider "fire station." This is a very common noun phrase that evokes no surprise. But if we think about it, a fire station does not have fire, provide fire, or receive fire; fire is not part of it or the category that includes it. In fact, fire is in no way a feature of a fire station. But we have one general story of *fire* and another general story of people and equipment being stationed at a *station* for a purpose, and we can blend them into a story in which fire is not a feature of the station or a counterpart of the station. "Fire station" asks us to do just this.

Charts, diagrams, coins, and maps frequently provide visual representations of blended conceptual spaces. Consider the projection from magnitude of size to magnitude of importance, as in "Let's attend to the *larger* issues." A blended space is available in which the more important things appear spatially larger. A tourist map of a city may include perspectival drawings of major attractions that are inset here and there in the map—the more important the real attraction, the larger its inset picture, regardless of the relative physical size of the actual attraction. A map to literary sites of Paris might feature a drawing of Hemingway's tiny apartment that dwarfs the drawing of the huge Arc de Triomphe.

Maps are visual representations that bring together information from many different mental spaces associated with what the map represents. These spaces include street topography, names of places, latitude and longitude, appearance, water versus land, distances, directions, number of hours it takes to travel from city to city, quality of food, availability of services, hours during which events take place or buildings are open, dates of construction, weather, temperature variation, altitude, and so on. The fact that the map gives simultaneous access to these very different spaces does not automatically indicate that there is mental blending at work An outline of the landmass of the United States filled in with colored bands to indicate temperature ranges combines spatial position and color so as to give us access simultaneously to the mental space of geographical location and the mental space of weather, and it gives us a mental space *connector* from the mental space of geographical location to the mental space of weather; but it does *not* signify a mental blend in which geographical locations are simultaneously colored. The combination in the map signifies mental space connection, not mental space blending. However, such representations of mental space connections will recruit conventional blends whenever possible. For example, there is a conventional mental blend of temperature and color (hotter is redder), and it would be infelicitous to contravene that blend in the visual representation, using for example red to indicate cold and blue to indicate hot. Maps are an interesting case: They are representations that give us access to many mental spaces. Combinations of symbols on the map indicate mental space connections and correspondences. But these maps also slide, where possible, into visual representations of mental blends.

Visual representations of mental blends are often immediately intelligible. We seem to recognize their meaning passively, as if they pose no puzzle and require no work. However, once analysis detects the inferential role of the blend, it can be surprising to see how much work we actually did to interpret the drawing. *The New York Times Magazine* of August 22, 1993, carries an illustration by Brian Cronin of an article by Thomas L. Friedman, "Cold War without End." In this illustration, a bicyclist is riding a bicycle; the front half of the bicycle frame is blue with a small American flag attached; the front wheel is the globe of the world, with lines of latitude and longitude; the back half of the bicycle frame is a red hammer and sickle—the sign of Soviet political control. The back fender is the sickle blade, and the pedal is the sickle handle; the strut to the center of the rear wheel is the hammer. But there is no rear wheel! The rider is looking at the place where it should be. He is understandably dismayed.

The illustration accompanies an article that suggests that the makers of American foreign and domestic policy are troubled over how to proceed now that Soviet control has disappeared. The foundation of American policy had been conflict between the United States and the Soviet Union. That foundation is gone, and nobody seems to know what to do. The article depends on the metaphor that the making of policy is bodily movement; that the cold war was an instrument for bodily movement. This metaphor is an instance of the universal projection of stories of body movement onto stories that are not bodily or even spatial. It is clear to anyone looking at the bicycle illustration that the vehicle is flawed and that normal progress cannot be made. This inference can arise in the source space of bicycling—a bicycle without a wheel won't go. It is also clear that something that previously existed has disappeared in a dismaying fashion. This inference can arise in the target space—Soviet control over republics and satellites has simply vanished. But these two conceptual structures from the source and the target are blended into a fantastic and impossible space.

The central inference of the illustration is that Soviet control has disappeared in a way that automatically and inevitably brings a grave and manifest crisis to America, and that something must be done immediately, before the whole show comes crashing down. This inference is impossible for the source space of bicycling. Magic aside, a bicycle wheel cannot simply disappear, leaving the rider suspended in midair for a vertiginous moment that lasts long enough for him to notice the missing wheel and feel dismay. The inference is not necessary in the target—indeed, it is so counterintuitive to imagine that the disappearance of Soviet political control should be bad for American policy making that the writer must spend the entire article trotting out evidence. Yet in the blended space, the wheel that is Soviet dominion can disappear, and the disappearance of the wheel that is Soviet dominion must have inevitable, unmistakable, and incontrovertibly bad effects upon the bicycle that is the vehicle of American foreign policy. The central inference is constructed in the blended space and projected from there to the target.

Every newspaper and news magazine carries editorial columns. A cursory survey of them will reveal that a favorite routine for writing a column is to churn out a blended space, often labored. Once we see how this works, it is very easy to do, as we can show by fabricating an example. At the end of President Bill Clinton's first one hundred days in office, *The New York Times* reported that Clinton seemed unable to accomplish anything in Washington, D.C., despite his promise to hit the ground running. Not a single undersecretary had been appointed. Senator Bob Dole of Kansas, the ranking Republican on the hill, had just handed President Clinton a major defeat on a jobs bill. Clinton had lacked four votes in the Senate and had seemed ignorant of how to get them. *New York Times* columnist Russell Baker, not a fan of the often abrasive Dole, compared Clinton to President Jimmy Carter, saying essentially that a president who doesn't know how to use the powers of his office to buy four lousy votes in the Senate is simply incompetent—this would never have happened to President Lyndon Johnson.

Russell Baker frames Clinton and Dole as opponents, and that is all we need, since it gives us a generic space for *opposition* and a target space of Clinton and Dole's *political opposition*. A vivid source space might be a gunfight. In the blended space, Bob Dole becomes the Kansas gunslinger with the big iron on his hip, who, like his counterpart in the movie *Shane*, is cool, confident, utterly professional, wastes no energy, picks his fights, and knows his ground. Something like this: "Dole is the ranking gunslinger in Dodge-City-on-the-Potomac, rough at the edges but smooth on the legislative draw. When the sun of deficit negotiations got in Clinton's eyes, Dole made his move and Clinton never cleared leather. Hillary Clinton is sure to come running out with her health-care initiative to try to plug the wound, but Sheriff Clinton is bleeding his heart out on Main Street U.S.A., and Doc Greenspan at the Fed, with a barely recovering economy to protect from inflation infection, isn't about to remove the bullet so Clinton can pull himself up and go spend another ton of money. . . . "

It is not only on the editorial page that such blends are allowed. A lead sentence on page 1 of *The New York Times* for May 13, 1993, reads, "An unexpected surge in wholesale prices last month, the latest of a string of higher price reports, left many economists and investors wondering whether the inflation genie was starting to slip out of the bottle." Immediately after reading this newspaper, I called United Airlines and received the recorded while-you-wait-for-an-agent message, "Now you can tango on down to Rio, with less fancy footwork"—presumably an ad for a new nonstop flight. "Tango" and "fancy footwork" come from the source space but "on down to Rio" comes from the target space, since intercontinental travel is not possible by means of tango. I am told that the phrase also blends in elements of a Fred Astaire movie about flying on down to Rio.

## THE NATHAN BOOMERANG

In 2 Samuel 12, the prophet Nathan comes to King David. David is a judge, and Nathan approaches David in that role. Nathan presents David with the case of a certain rich man and a certain poor man.

> The rich man had very many flocks and herds; but the poor man had nothing but one little ewe lamb, which he had bought. And he brought it up, and it grew up with him and with his children; it used to eat of his morsel, and drink from his cup, and lie in his bosom, and it was like a daughter to him. Now there came a traveler to the rich man, and he was unwilling to take one of his own flock or herd to prepare for the wayfarer who had come to him, but he took the poor man's lamb, and prepared it for the man who had come to him.
>
> Then David's anger was greatly kindled against the man; and he said to Nathan, "As the Lord lives, the man who has done this deserves to

die; and he shall restore the lamb fourfold, because he did this thing, and because he had no pity."

Nathan said to David, "You are the man."

The projection must be immediately obvious to David. David had been anointed king over Israel and enjoyed many wives. Had this been too little, the Lord would have added to him as much again. But Uriah the Hittite, one of David's subjects, had only his one wife, Bathsheba. David took Bathsheba for his temporary pleasure, and she conceived a son by David, and David arranged for Uriah to be placed in the front ranks of the battle and abandoned, so as to be killed. The judgment proclaimed by David upon the rich man comes down upon his own head.

In telling his story, Nathan has pretended that it is the space of the rich man and poor man that is the target, and the space of family domesticity and affection that is the source (the ewe lamb "was like a daughter to him"). In doing so, Nathan has led David to construct a strong blended space that contains specifics of both the story of the rich man and the poor man and the story of relations between members of a family (especially "eat of his morsel, and drink of his cup, and lie in his bosom"). David thinks he knows where all this information is directed, and why: It is to clarify the iniquity of the rich man and ensure his condemnation. But then Nathan announces that the target of the projection of this blended space is not the story of the poor man and the rich man, but the story of David, Uriah, and Bathsheba.

This is veiled parable: In order to prevent the listener from resisting the projection, the storyteller veils the intended target while building up a blend with the right structure for his real purposes. In the case described by Nathan, that blend includes family affection, relations of power and its abuse, and categories of just and unjust behavior. Once this slightly blended space is fully constructed, Nathan lifts the veil from the real target and conjures David to project inferences from this blended space to it. The fit is extraordinarily compelling: The final target strongly resembles the source—both source ("it was like a daughter to him") and final target (Uriah, Bathsheba, and David) concern the destruction of a family. The establishment of counterparts has been so carefully developed by Nathan that David has no escape.

## EMBLEM

An emblem is a parable that starts from one story and projects from it a generic story that covers other stories belonging to the same conceptual domain. A story about a boy's adventures at summer camp can be interpreted as an emblem of childhood adventure. I have interpreted the story of Shahrazad and her father the vizier as an emblem: we project from it a common and abstract story of confrontation between child and parent. That generic story applies to many other stories belonging to the same domain as the original story.

When the generic space applies to a story in a different conceptual domain, we have metaphor or analogy instead of emblem. This reveals something interesting: Whether a given parable is emblematic or metaphoric depends upon what constitutes a division between conceptual domains, which is to say, upon what conceptual connections are already in place when the parable becomes active.

For example, *The Thousand and One Nights* begins with a story that can be read as either emblem or metaphor. King Shahzaman is called from his kingdom by his elder brother King Shahriyar to pay a visit. Shahzaman departs, leaving his kingdom in the hands of his vizier. But out of deep love for his wife, he finds a pretext for returning, so he may see her once more. He discovers her making love to a slave and kills them both instantly before departing on his journey. He is desolate when he arrives, declines to reveal the cause to his brother Shahriyar, and remains behind in the palace when King Shahriyar goes out to hunt. Accidentally, Shahzaman witnesses a marvelous sight: His brother Shahriyar's queen enters the courtyard with twenty slave-girls, ten of whom turn out to be slave boys who make love to the other ten slave girls, while the queen calls to herself a special slave to do the act. Shahzaman realizes he is not the only one to suffer. His mood improves. That night, Shahriyar, recognizing the change in his brother, manages to extract from him the reason for his initial despondency but not for his recovery. But at last, Shahzaman tells his brother everything. Alarmed, filled with doubt, Shahriyar spies on his wife, discovers the truth, and "half demented at the sight," says to his brother, "Let us renounce our royal state and roam the world until we find out if any other king has ever met with such disgrace."

They roam. One day, while the brothers rest under a tree, a black pillar rises from the surging sea until it reaches the sky. The terrified brothers climb the tree and watch as a giant jinnee carries a chest on his head. He places it on the shore below the tree, opens the chest to remove a box, and then opens that box to take out a "beautiful young girl, radiant as the sun."

The jinnee falls asleep in the girl's lap. She sees Shahriyar and Shahzaman and signals to them to come down and make love to her, on threat of her waking the jinnee to rip them apart should they decline. Afterward, she takes their seal rings, for a total of one hundred rings so acquired.

> "This jinnee," she added, "carried me away on my bridal night and imprisoned me in a box which he placed inside a chest. He fastened the chest with seven locks and deposited it at the bottom of the roaring sea. But he little knew how cunning we women are."

The two Kings marvelled at her story, and said to each other: "If such a thing could happen to a mighty jinnee, then our own misfortune is light indeed." And they returned at once to the city.

As soon as they entered the palace, King Shahriyar put his wife to death.

Misery loves company. The two kings read this story emblematically: Women are always cunning and deceitful. From the specific story with a specific woman and a specific male who tries to keep her, they project an abstract generic story: The female dupes the male through her cunning. This generic story is then available for projection to any other particular space, such as the specific stories of both Shahzaman and Shahriyar. The kings have a psychological interest in reading the story this way, as an emblem that provides a generic story of what women do to men.

There is of course a different projection available to us that it is psychologically impossible just now for the kings. The jinnee, serving himself, exerts extraordinary control over the young woman, "taking" her physically from one location to another on her wedding night, limiting her freedoms in specifically spatial ways. His behavior causes her to hate him, which leads her to seek revenge: She sets out to do exactly what he has so single-mindedly tried to prevent her from doing. Given this causal sequence, we can regard the jinnee as the cause of his own predicament and blame him for it. This story can be projected metaphorically onto the story of marriage generally, or at least, certainly, of marriage to kings. "Stealing" the woman like an object on her wedding night, regardless of her desires, can be projected metaphorically onto what kings do with their brides. The jinnee's locking her up and keeping her under the sea can be projected onto the kings' placing limitations (spatial and nonspatial) on their wives—Shahriyar's wife had to stay in the court while he went out to hunt. This projection is not available to Shahzaman and Shahriyar at this point: it would imply that they and not their wives are to blame for their being up a tree.

## LINGUISTIC CONSTRUCTIONS

Grammatical constructions often represent basic abstract stories. For example, consider the basic abstract story of *result*: An intentional agent performs an act on an object, with a particular result for the object. This basic abstract story is represented by the grammatical *resultative* construction, used in "Kathy pressed the wallpaper flat" and "Mike painted the kitchen yellow." Consider also the "caused motion" construction studied by Goldberg. It has the syntax

NounPhrase—Verb—NounPhrase—Preposition—NounPhrase,

as in "He hit the ball into the bleachers" or "They shoved the poor guy out of the room." The grammatical construction represents a basic abstract spatial action-story in which an agent performs a physical action that causes a physical object to move in a spatial direction. Fauconnier and I have analyzed the way in which this grammatical construction serves as a prompt to blend two things: the events referred to by the vocabulary filling the construction and the caused-motion story represented by the construction itself. In the resulting blend, the unintegrated events to which the vocabulary refers acquire the integrated event structure of the caused-motion story. For example, if we say, "He *floated* the toy boat across the pond," then even though *float* encodes only the manner of the boat's motion, and not the causal action or the causality between that action and the motion of the boat, we still know that we are being asked to conceive of a scene in which the floating of the boat is a story of caused motion. As Goldberg observes, "He *sneezed* the napkin off the table" has a verb that is a "parade example" of intransitivity, but its use in this construction prompts us to think of a scene in which sneezing physically causes the motion of an object in a direction. It does not mean, for example, that he sneezed and someone picked a napkin up off the table to hand him, because that is not a caused-motion story. We blend the physical caused-motion story with the story of sneezing.

We project from the basic abstract action story of caused physical motion an even more abstract generic story of causation that is not necessarily physical and that can be projected to target stories that may not be physical. For example, we can say, "They *laughed* the poor guy out of the room," even though *laughing* is not a physical force. We can say, "She *drove* him out of his *mind*," even if she exerted no physical force on him and even though the result is not physical motion in a spatial direction. The basic abstract story of physical caused motion involves physical spatiality; the generic story of caused motion does not, and can apply to targets that are not physical or spatial.

Grammar contains many devices for indicating what mental spaces are to be built and how they are to be connected. These devices include tenses, moods, some verbs, and conjunctions. Grammar is a set of instruments used to guide the building and blending of spaces and the projecting of generic spaces. In other words, grammar is the servant of parable. In the final chapter of this book, we will consider why it is such an apt servant.

As an example of how grammar gives us guidance in space building, space blending, and projection of generic spaces, consider the *xyz* construction, whose syntax is deceptively simple:

NounPhrase(x) be NounPhrase(y) of NounPhrase(z)

as in *Vanity is the quicksand of reason.* This simple syntax has a complex semantic and pragmatic interpretation: Construct a set of spaces and projections with the result that $x$ in a target is the counterpart of $y$ in a source, and $z$ in that target is the counterpart of an unmentioned fourth element $w$ in that source. In "Vanity is the quicksand of reason," $w$ is the traveler who travels toward a goal. As quicksand stops the traveler, vanity stops reason. The grammatical information is minimal and highly abstract—find a mapping and a missing element. The rest is left to the cognitive competence of the user, who must construct an implicit generic space and an implicit blend, in which a single element is simultaneously *reason* and a *traveler*.

An abbreviated form of the xyz construction can be seen in phrases like "Language is fossil poetry." Emerson meant by this expression that language, which seems so literal, consists of historical traces of inventive and original "poetry." Here, $x$ is *language*, $z$ is *poetry*, and $y$ is given by the modifier *fossil*. A missing $w$ (*living organism*) must be found to complete the correspondences. We construct a blended notion of something that is simultaneously language, poetry, and fossil: in the blended space, poetry *is* a living organism that can leave a fossil trace (language).

Noun phrases of this yz form ("fossil poetry") arise often. We call a suburban teenager a "mall rat." We refer to a "tax bite," a "computer jock," a "price war," a "surfing safari," or "channel surfing (or internet surfing)." The construction can be used to signal new blends, as when the Clinton administration's comprehensive effort to make executive appointments along racial and gender guidelines was called by a Republican congressional staffer a "diversity jihad." A related construction uses the standard adjective-noun syntax to indicate counterparts: "In this way he acquired a vast hoard of all sorts of learning, and had it pigeonholed in his head where he could put his *intellectual hand* on it whenever it was wanted," or, "In making these investments, you are digging your *financial grave*." Someone who has left the Touraine and its cuisine to return to the American Midwest might be said to suffer upon reentry "the gastronomic bends." A Parisian who dates one woman only on the Right Bank and another only on the Left refers to this as "French fidelity." Universities that try to raise money for research by making arrangements for technology transfer are said to be holding "technological bake sales."

## GRADIENTS

There is an aspect of parable that so far we have acknowledged only implicitly. It concerns gradients of spaces and projections. The basic metaphor DEATH IS DEPARTURE, for example, operates at one level of specificity, but above it lies EVENTS ARE ACTIONS, which projects information even more abstract, and above EVENTS ARE ACTIONS lies the most general level of projection, the general capability of projecting one story parabolically onto another.

Below DEATH IS DEPARTURE on the gradient of specificity lies the projection of the story of *an agent carrying somebody off forever* onto the story of *death*. Below that lies the projection of the story of *Thanatos intending to snatch the body at the grave and carry it off to Hades, but being wrestled out of it by Hercules* onto the story of *the near death of Alcestis,* and the projection of *someone trying to pull Alcestis by the hand toward Charon the ferryman who is waiting to carry her across the river Styx* onto *the near death of Alcestis.* A projection at any level in such a graded hierarchy can provide structure to any other projection in the same hierarchy.

## THE CONCEPT OF A CONCEPT

Parable involves dynamic construction of input spaces, generic spaces, and blended spaces, multiply linked, with projections operating over them. Inferences and meaning are not bounded in a single conceptual locus. Meaning is a complex operation of projecting, blending, and integrating over multiple spaces. Meaning never settles down into a single residence. Meaning is parabolic and literary.

This view of meaning may seem counterintuitive. If we think of concepts as little packets of meaning whose boundaries circumscribe our knowledge of them, then any sort of meaning we recognize as distributed over many spaces may seem secondary, marginal, special, or parasitic. On that view, a blended space will seem to be an exotic mental event, an exceptional quirk. But the variety of the examples we have seen shows that the dynamism, distribution, projection, and integration we see in blending are actually central and pervasive elements of everyday thought.

Consider any basic everyday concept, like *house*. It seems static and permanent, stable and unitary, cohesive and self-contained. This is an illusion, derived from an influential but mistaken folk notion of *concept*. We have no concept *house*, but we do have a word "house," and being able to use that word—like the words "fish," "marriage," "life"—requires us to construct, activate, link, and project the appropriate configurations of spaces, frames, and cognitive models. We may not perceive this multiple activation for a word like "house" because we activate again and again the same configurations of spaces and links for "house," so that one of those configurations can come to seem to be our "basic concept *house*." But in fact a great range of spaces is activated for "house": shelter from the elements, bounded interiors, security from intruders, financial investment, artifacts, aesthetic design, instrumentality for inhabitants, social residence, social place of meeting, partitioning of activities into different physical spaces, rental property, and on and on indefinitely. Any single use of the word "house" for any particular purpose will involve construction of meaning as an operation of selective integration over these various distributed stories.

Let us look at a case where it is clear that different spaces are activated for the same word in different local situations. Consider the simple $xyz$ equation, "Italian is the daughter of Latin." The source input space contains overtly only a very little structure: It has a parent and a daughter. The target input space also contains overtly only a very little structure: It has Italian and Latin. Ultimately, *parent* in this source will correspond to *Latin* in this target, and *daughter* in this source will correspond to *Italian* in this target. The result is a double personification: In the blend, Latin and Italian are human beings. But this hardly accounts for the meaning we construct on hearing this phrase. One normal interpretation might be paraphrased: "Latin existed first, and Italian came into existence second by deriving causally from Latin." It may seem as if the material needed for constructing this meaning is intrinsically in the source input space of parent-child and the target input space of Latin-Italian. But it isn't. It must be recruited and brought into the source input and the target input. It can be recruited by activating other spaces and projecting them to the skeletal source and target inputs. Onto the skeletal target input, we project a space concerning languages. In it, some languages derive from others, and in particular, Italian derives diachronically from Latin. Onto the skeletal source input of parent and child, we project a particular story of progeneration. In it, a parent bears a causal and sequential relation to the child; the parent produces the child; the parent precedes the child.

If the source input and the target input are elaborated in *these* ways, by *this* recruited structure, they share a causal and sequential structure. This causal and sequential structure will then be available to constitute the generic space that underlies the interpretation "Latin precedes and results in Italian."

But now suppose that we are talking about the study of foreign languages in a particular high school, and we observe that nearly all the students of Latin come to the subject because they encountered it in courses in Italian. We might say, "Italian is the mother of Latin." Does this assertion contradict the earlier assertion that "Italian is the daughter of Latin"? Clearly not. In the case of "Italian is the mother of Latin," what has been additionally recruited to the target input is the sequential order in which languages are *learned*, not the order in which they historically *derived*. In the space of learning languages, the sequential order of Latin and Italian is the reverse of their sequential order in the space of the history of languages. Recruiting structure from the space of learning languages to the space of Italian and Latin lets us say, "Italian is the mother of Latin," while recruiting structure from the space of the history of languages to the space of Italian and Latin lets us say, "Italian is the daughter of Latin." In general, there is no fixed structure of the target input space that the source input space must match, because the target input space has different structure under different recruitments to it.

Now let us consider the source input space. Suppose we are discussing the relative aesthetic qualities of Italian and Latin, and we comment upon the precision of Latin in Vergil, Propertius, or Horace as compared to the florid and ostentatious qualities of Italian in Bocaccio or Tasso. We say, "Well, Italian is the daughter of Latin, and her ostentatious beauty is really a rebellion against her mother's austerity." Here, we recruit to the source input space of mother and daughter not just progeneration but also social relations between mothers and daughters, and in particular adolescent rebellion over appearance and behavior. Under this recruitment of structure to the source input space, Italian is still the daughter of Latin, but in an entirely different additional sense.

In all these examples, the underlying conceptual domains—kinship and languages—are the same, but the spaces selected for recruiting additional structure to the source input space differ example to example, and the spaces selected for recruiting additional structure to the target input space differ example to example. The resulting configurations—source input space, generic space, target input space, and blended space—are different in each case.

Some recruitments to source and to target will be more common than others and thus may come to mind more quickly and give rise to highly salient default interpretations. In isolation, "Italian is the mother of Latin" will raise eyebrows. Common or default recruitments are a phenomenon of thought in general: we are always ready to use default conceptual connections as we think. It is important to recognize, however, that common, default recruitments do not give us fixed basic concepts: we can always unplug the default connections; they are, in technical jargon, "defeasible." They look stable and fixed sometimes, but only because they are entrenched. Our most entrenched concepts and connections are formed by the same mechanisms of parable we have seen in the exotic and unusual cases.

## INVARIANCE REVISITED

By now, we have detected many features of parable: input spaces (which sometimes are related as source and target); abstract structure that is shared by inputs; generic spaces that contain that shared structure; counterpart connections that exist between inputs because of their shared structure; projection from inputs to a blend; development of emergent structure in the blend; projection of structure, inferences, and affect back from the blend to inputs; and variable recruitment of structure from other spaces to the inputs themselves.

This many-space model of parable makes it possible to give a concise statement of the invariance principle: Conceptual projection, which has as one of its fundamental activities the projection of image-schematic structure from a source input to a target input, shall not result in an image-schematic clash in the target.

Invariance is a global constraint to be satisfied in building and projecting target, generic, and source spaces.

One corollary of the invariance principle is this: Once the projection is completed, the most abstract generic space, the one that contains just the image-schematic structure taken to apply to both source and target, shall not contain an image-schematic clash.

There are many ways to avoid such a clash. We have choice in what we recruit to the source, what we recruit to the target, and what we project to the generic space. We can vary all of these choices in order to meet the constraint. For example, "Italian is the mother of Latin" can be interpreted as meeting the constraint so long as we recruit to the target not the space of *historical derivation of Romance languages* but rather the space of *order of learning languages in a particular school*.

There is one way to meet the constraint that may not be obvious. Suppose a (crackpot) professor of Romance languages says, "Italian is the mother of Latin," and we respond, "You can't mean what I think you mean, you can't mean that Latin as a language derives from Italian as a language," and the professor responds, "Oh, yes, I do. Originally there was a small tribe of Etruscans who developed a new language, and it was Italian. Latin really derived from that language, although nobody recognizes this since the original speakers of Italian couldn't write—they just carved wooden sarcophagus lids all the time, and this took up such a ton of energy every day that they were always too tired to get around to learning the alphabet—so they left no documents. Later on, of course, Latin turned back into Italian, but in fact Italian never stopped being spoken up in the Apennines; it was just never written down. So you see, everyone thinks Latin is the mother of Italian, but as a matter of historical fact, Italian is the mother of Latin." In this case, we are being directed to meet the constraint of the invariance principle not by changing projections to source, target, or generic space, but rather by erasing and re-forming the image-schematic structure in the conceptual domain *historical derivation of Romance languages* so that when its structure is recruited to the target, the result will not clash with the image-schematic structure we hope to project from source to generic to target. We are unlikely to do this. Instead, we will build a separate space of *what this professor believes about Latin and Italian*, and we will note that it does not agree with what we believe.

## BLENDING AND THE BRAIN

The mental ability to combine and blend concepts has always seemed exceptionally literary and imaginative. Combining a horse with a horn to produce the impossible fantasy blend of a unicorn is a popular example of the literary imagination at work. It may seem that this process of combination must be secondary and parasitic: surely stable and integrated concepts (*horse*, *horn*) and small spatial stories (*horses run*, *horns impale*) must be in place and must have arisen by elementary processes of perception and memory before second order processes like integration and blending can work on them.

Only very recently—in the last few years—has neuroscience begun to suggest that the opposite might be true. It would be a mistake to hang too much at this stage on the specific details of the various neuroscientific theories that have arisen, but a general principle is emerging, and it is this: At the most basic levels of perception, of understanding, and of memory, blending is fundamental.

When we perceive or remember or think about a particular horse or *horse* in general, the horse seems to us whole. At the seemingly simple level of vision, a horse just looks like a visual whole. It is whole in our sight. Our recognition of it seems whole, not piecemeal or fragmented.

We expect our neurobiology to work at least loosely the way our perception seems to work, and we think (wrongly) that introspection reveals at least roughly how our perception works. *We expect our phenomenology to indicate the nature of neurobiology.* But it does not. It appears that there may be no anatomical site in the brain where a perception of a horse or a concept *horse* resides, and, even more interestingly, no point where the parts of the perception or concept are anatomically brought together. The horse looks to us like obviously one thing; yet our visual perception of it is entirely fragmented across the brain. What the brain does is not at all what we might have expected. The visual perceptions of color, texture, movement, form, topological attributes, part-whole structure, and so on occur in a fragmentary fashion throughout the brain and are not assembled in any one place. This is a surprise, like the surprise of learning that although the visual field is projected upside-down onto the retina because of the simple optics of a lens, there is no place in the brain where that image is reassembled and turned right-side-up. The qualities we believe our perception to have are in many ways not at all the qualities that neuroscientists are finding in the neurobiological activity that underlies perception.

As Gerald Edelman writes, "Objects and many of their properties are perceived as having a unitary appearance; yet these unitary perceptions are the consequences of parallel activity in the brain of *many different* maps, each with different degrees of functional segregation. Many examples could be cited; a striking case is the extra-striate visual cortex, with its different areas mediating color, motion, and form, each in different ways."

How, then, do these fragments end up seeming to us like one perception or one concept—one horse? This is known in neuroscience as the "binding problem." The binding problem is part of a more general problem, integration. For example, given that form, color, and motion are all processed differently and at different places in the brain, and that no one place in the brain receives projections from all the brain sites involved in this processing, how is it that the form, color, and motion of the horse are integrated?

Visual integration, although perhaps the archetype of integration, is only one aspect of integration. The concept of the horse, even the perception of a horse, may integrate the sound the horse makes, the way it feels to sit on a horse's back, the way it feels to ride a horse, the dynamic image schema of mounting the horse, the convexity of the horse's torso, and the sound its swishing tail makes. Nor are even these elements unitary—they also each require integration. The part-whole relational structure of the horse, its overall form, and its coloring, for example, which seem to us so unitary, also require integration.

The horse that seems one thing corresponds to a widely distributed fragmentation in the brain. Mentally, the unitary horse is a fabulous blend.

Neuroscientific attempts to solve the general problem of perceptual and conceptual integration are speculative and interesting. All of them depend upon models of integration through close timing of related neuronal events, rather than gathering of information in an anatomical site. Antonio Damasio, for example, has proposed a model of "convergence" according to which the brain contains records of the combinatorial relations of fragmentary records; the recall of entities or events arises from a reactivation, very tightly bound in time, of fragmentary records contained in multiple sensory and motor regions. Mental evocations that seem to us so unitary and solid are instead always fleeting reblendings of reactivated fragments in a very tight and intricate interval of time.

Damasio sees his speculative proposal for explaining "convergence" as generally compatible with the theory of Neuronal Group Selection proposed by Gerald Edelman and his associates, who have made an attempt to solve the binding problem (and more generally the problem of integration) by invoking a conjectural neurobiological process called "reentrant signaling." Differing in detail from Damasio's "convergence" model, reentrant signaling nonetheless also depends upon the coordination and integration of distributed fragmentary operations. In any chunk of time, reentry "involves parallel sampling from a geometric range of spatially extended maps made up of neuronal groups." Vision and perceptual categorization supply Edelman's most thoroughly worked examples. During response to the visual stimulus world, reentrant signaling

acts to coordinate inputs and resolve conflicts between the responses of different functionally segregated maps. Visual reentry allows each mapped region to use discriminations made by other regions (about borders, movement, etc.) for its own operations. This process allows the various responses to aspects of the stimulus world to remain segregated and distributed among multiple brain areas and still constitute a unified representation. Reentrant integration obviates the need for a higher-level command center, or a "sketch."

Edelman generalizes this specific model of reentry for visual areas to "include functional correlations important to concept formation, consciousness, and speech."

For our purposes here, the details of these proposals are not at issue. We must be prepared to see many future attempts to solve the problem of integration. Nor, as the study of the mind and the study of the brain themselves attempt to blend and integrate, should we leap to facile connections, making assumptions, for example, that the conceptual blending we see in the tale of the ox and the donkey must somehow be explained by simple models of integration in perception and recall.

But there is a general principle that may help to connect the study of the brain with the study of the mind: Blending is a basic process; meaning does not reside in one site but is typically a dynamic and variable pattern of connection over many elements. Our conscious experience seems to tell us that meanings are whole, localized, and unitary. But this is wrong. Blending is already involved in our most unitary and literal perception and conception of basic physical objects, such as *horse* and *horn*, and in our most unitary and literal perception and conception of small spatial stories, such as *horse moves* and *horn impales*.

When we pay close attention, most mental events appear to involve blending of one sort or another. Whenever we see something *as* something—when we look at the street and see *a woman getting into a car*—we are blending our sensory experience with abstract conceptual structure. The sensory perception and the abstract conceptual structure do not look as if they are partitioned into two different components. The perception of someone getting into a car does not seem fragmentary, with one part corresponding to the visual experience and another part corresponding to the specific action and its status as an instance of a general action. These two very different things—the sensory activity and the conceptual activity—do not seem at all like separate parcels. When they do, something has gone wrong. Perception and conception seem to us one unitary whole, but they involve blending.

Anytime we perceive something that we take to be part of a larger whole (part of a figure, part of an event, part of a small story, part of a melody, and so on), we are blending perceptual experience with the recall of that whole. Whenever we categorize new information, we are blending the new information and the established category.

When we recognize what looks like a simple event of force, we must blend together very abstract image schemas of force dynamics with parts of the specific perception. Blending abstract image schemas together is a basic conceptual operation; blending abstract image schemas with specific perceptual experience is a basic conceptual operation. When we see a car go *through* an intersection, for example, we must blend very many things, including the image schema of *path*, the perception corresponding to the car's movement, the image schema of *container*, and the perception corresponding to the bounded area of the intersection.

Temporality seems to be as dependent upon blending as is spatiality. Even a simple mental event like looking at a street and remembering the red car that went down it yesterday depends upon an impossible blend: today's perceptual experience of the street and recall of yesterday's perceptual experience of the street. This impossible blending of realities that belong to different temporal spaces is a routine part of understanding. Slightly highlighted, we can notice the impossibility and the blending, as when we are asked to blend temporal spaces to produce the "race" between *Great America II* and *Northern Light*.

☙

There is one transcendent story of the mind that has appeared many times in many avatars. In its essential lines, it claims that there are certain basic, sober, and literal things the mind does; that imaginative and literary acts are parasitic, secondary, peripheral, exotic, or deviant; and that when neuroscience gets its act together, we will come to understand that the brain does things pretty much in the ways we always expected. On this logic, since imaginative and literary acts are peripheral and exotic, they can safely be ignored while, as serious scientists, we investigate the basics.

This story, which is itself just an imaginative story, has been the pretext for offering indefinitely many "first pass" scientific models of some of our supposedly basic mental operations. These models ignore what appear to be more sophisticated and exotic mental events, like blending, on the claim—usually taken for granted—that first we must explain a few basic operations, and then we can work on explaining the more imaginative operations that are parasitic upon the basic mind.

It is possible that this story is just wrong at its core. The brain does not seem to work at all in the ways we expected it to, based on our notion of stable and unitary concepts. On the contrary, our notion of concepts as stable and unitary seems to be a false guide to neurobiology. Blending may seem exotic to us, but in fact it may have a fundamental neurobiological analogue. It should not be surprising if blending turns out to be basic, not exotic, in the everyday mind.

Certainly there is considerable evidence that blending is a mainstay of early child-hood thought.

A two-year-old child who is leading a balloon around on a string may say, pointing to the balloon, "This is my imagination dog." When asked how tall it is, she says, "This high," holding her hand slightly higher than the top of the balloon. "These," she says, pointing at two spots just above the balloon, "are its ears." This is a complicated blend of attributes shared by a dog on a leash and a balloon on a string. It is dynamic, temporary, constructed for local purposes, formed on the basis of image schemas, and extraordinarily impressive. It is also just what two-year-old children do all day long. True, we relegate it to the realm of fantasy because it is an impossible blended space, but such spaces seem to be indispensable to thought generally and to be sites of the construction of mean-ings that bear on what we take to be reality.

A scientific model of thought frequently tries to begin with what is basic, on the claim that scientists must do first things first and second things second and exotic things sometime next century. This theoretical vehicle for getting an explanation of mind off the ground has crashed and burned often. It is not implausible that the concepts behind such models are wrong, that something like imaginative blending and integration are basic, and that an explanation that cannot handle "This is my imagination dog" has no hope of ever getting to even the most basic perceptions and meanings, like the perception of a *dog* or the mean-ing of "A dog has four legs," or even what is involved in an infant's pointing at a dog and saying "Doggie!"

In the hard sciences, which attract so much emulation and envy, unusual events are not dismissed as peripheral. On the contrary, unusual events often command the most attention, on the principle that they are the most likely to reveal general processes. The usual case can be accounted for as the result of general processes working in minimal particular conditions. A scientific experi-ment that tests for fundamental mechanisms is often elaborate and weird, some-thing not likely to occur on its own (particle accelerators, odd refractions of light involving specially engineered mirrors, chemical reactions in zero gravity, and so on). Physicists who noticed that the orbit of Mercury did not quite follow Newtonian theory did not ignore it as an exotic event. On the contrary, it became the central event, calling for new theories and extraordinary new experiments. One of these experiments, for example, involved waiting for a total eclipse of the sun, in order to measure the positions of stars around the outer edge of the eclipse, so as to compare these measurements with theoretically predicted positions, to see whether the light from the stars was being bent by the mass of the sun. A more unusual, exotic, and "marginal" astrophysical event can hardly be imag-ined, but such events often constitute the touchstones of the hard sciences. Physicists interested in the fundamental laws of the universe had to voyage to the tropics to get the most revealing data. Cognitive scientists might interpret this as a parable for their research. The hard sciences do not lump apparently odd events into the category of what we don't need to explain, but rather give them special attention. It is not clear that someone in the cognitive sciences who hopes her discipline will attain to the prestige of the hard sciences should behave any differently. In particular, the methods of the hard sciences give no legitimacy to the story that we can tell in advance what is basic and what is exotic and form our theories by ignoring what we think is exotic.

The processes of the literary mind are usually considered to be different from and secondary to the processes of the everyday mind. On that assumption, the everyday mind—with its stable concepts and literal reasoning—provides the beginnings for the (optional) literary mind. On the contrary, processes that we have always considered to be literary are at the foundation of the everyday mind. Literary processes like blending make the everyday mind possible.

*How do stories "mean" across lives*
*How stories keep us alive*
*How embedded stories* ~~are used to instruct,~~ *carry projections*
*identity connectors*
*role connectors*

# SINGLE LIVES

> O Lord . . . Your years neither go nor come, but our years
> pass and others come after them, so that they all may come
> in their turn. Your years are completely present to you all at
> once, because they are at a permanent standstill. . . . Your
> years are one day, yet your day does not come daily but is
> always today, because your today does not give place to any
> tomorrow nor does it take the place of any yesterday. Your
> today is eternity.
>
> *Augustine, Confessions*

A PERSON has a single life, by which I mean not that we live only once, true as that is, but that a human being—a mind in a brain in a body—leads a singular rather than a general existence. A God's-eye view is a general view—it can belong only to a being whose existence is without limit or locale. Since God's eye is everywhere, eternal, and all-seeing, it is undifferentiated. To the eye of God, there would not be alternative ways of seeing, but only seeing pure and absolute and permanent. A human being does not have a God's-eye view. A human being has always only a single view, which is always local. This is so unacceptable as to have been sufficient reason for the invention of God.

It is astonishing that we forget so easily that we have only a single, local view. What we see of an event may look entirely unlike what a person on the other side of the event may see or entirely unlike what we ourselves actually do see when we walk to the other side, but we imagine that these views from either side are nonetheless views of the *same* story, despite the manifest differences in perceptions. This is evidence of our considerable mental capacity to integrate fragmentary information, to blend it into one mental construction.

Our sensory apparatus is located in space. We necessarily recognize a small spatial story from a particular spatial location. We can direct our sensory apparatus, and we can move our body so that our sensory apparatus is in a different location. To recognize a small spatial story—a baby shaking a rattle—is always to do so with a single focus and from a single viewpoint.

There is a basic human story here—the story of a person recognizing a story. This basic human story shows us a new aspect of parable. In this general story, there is a recognizing agent who has a single focus and a single viewpoint. Let us consider some of the structure of this story. Suppose we see a baby shaking a rattle. Sequentially, we can focus on the smile, the nose, the jerky movement of the shoulder, the frozen elbow, the hand, the rattle. Our focus changes, but we feel that, regardless, we continue to look at the *same* story: The child is playing with the rattle. We are able to unify all of these perceptions, all of these different foci. The mental spaces corresponding to the different foci will all have a child, a rattle, a rattling motion, and so on, and we connect these elements in each space to their counterparts in the other spaces. We conceive of these various spaces as all attached to a single story.

Now imagine that we walk around to the other side of the baby. Our visual experience may change substantially. It is even possible that we will see none of what we saw before, strictly speaking. Yet our new view will not seem entirely new. The space of the new viewpoint will have a baby, a shoulder, a hand, a rattle, a rattling motion, and so on, and we will connect these elements to their counterparts in the spaces of other viewpoints and other foci, allowing us to think of the different small spatial stories we see as *one story*, viewed from different viewpoints and with different foci.

As sensory beings, our view is always single and local because we have a single life and not a general life. As imaginative beings, we constantly construct meaning designed to transcend that singularity. We integrate over singularities. If we are on one side of a small spatial story, viewing "it," and a friend is on the other side, viewing "it," we can construct, mentally, a space that contains what the friend sees and connect that space to the space that contains what we see, to create an integrated space that is meant to be transcendent and unitary.

It is part of our notion of the story of someone recognizing a story with a single focus and from a single viewpoint that there are other foci and other viewpoints, and that the spaces corresponding to all the different foci and different viewpoints are connected as having the *same* story as their object. We expect correspondences to run across all these spaces. The general story of a person recognizing a small spatial story is, in these details, considerably more complicated than it seemed at first: There are many foci and many viewpoints, and the agent perceiving the story just happens to have this particular focus and this particular viewpoint.

As sensory beings, we are subject to obvious constraints on actually switching focus and viewpoint because to change them actually requires bodily movement. But once we have the story in imagination, we are not subject to these constraints. We can mentally focus on this part or that part, and move around, perceiving it from this angle or that. Subjects asked to draw an imagined event (a surfer wiping out on a wave, for example) from the front, the back, the side, above, below, and so on will all produce drawings with the expected regularities.

In imagination, we can construct spaces of what we take to be someone else's focus and viewpoint. We can, for example, in imagination, take the spatial viewpoint of one of the actors in the story. Consider a story with some actors: Grandmother watches father hand mother clothes as she dresses her son; grandmother is an observer, father is an accessory agent, mother is the principal agent, and the child is the patient—in the sense that he is the object on which the action is performed, not in the sense that he is patient as it happens! In imagination, we can switch viewpoint from grandmother to father to mother to son in the story. Consider another story: Father watches mother watch the son shake a rattle. We can take the focus and viewpoint of father, mother, son, even rattle (try it). We have single lives, but in imagination, we are suddenly free of the consequent singularity.

In the literary mind, parable projects stories onto other stories. The story in which a person with a particular focus and a particular viewpoint recognizes a story is a skeletal story of *spatial* perception. *It, too, is projected.* Most notably, it is projected onto the skeletal story of perception in *time*. For example, if we are in the second day of our three-day trip, we can "focus" on yesterday from the "viewpoint" of today, or "focus" on tomorrow from the "viewpoint" of today. We can do much more: Suppose our companion says, as we are traveling, "Imagine it's the end of the trip; how do you feel?" and we respond, "I feel sleepy. I had plenty of energy at the beginning of the trip, but now I am exhausted." Of course, the person saying this does not at the moment of speaking want to go to sleep. Instead, he is taking as his "viewpoint" in time the end of the trip and as his "focus" in time first the end of the trip ("I feel sleepy"), then the beginning of the trip ("I had plenty of energy"), and then the end of the trip again ("now I am exhausted"). He could, however, have said, "I *will feel* sleepy." In that case, his "viewpoint" in time is the moment of speaking (during the second day of the trip) and his "focus" in time is the end of the trip.

Projecting the story of perception in space (with *spatial* focus and *spatial* viewpoint) onto the story of perception in time gives us *temporal* focus and *temporal* viewpoint. Someone recognizing a story in time has, by means of this projection, a particular *temporal* focus and a particular *temporal* viewpoint.

We saw above that it is part of our notion of the story of someone recognizing a story with a single spatial focus and from a single spatial viewpoint that there are other foci and viewpoints, and that we connect the spaces that correspond to the different foci and viewpoints as all having the *same* story as their object. The same is true of perceiving a story with a single *temporal* focus and from a single *temporal* viewpoint. There are other temporal foci and temporal viewpoints; we connect the spaces that correspond to the different foci and viewpoints as all having the *same* story as their object. For example, the person "viewing" the story of his three-day trip, who shifts his temporal focus from yesterday to tomorrow, has shifted mental spaces, but he is still "viewing" the same story from those different spaces.

All stories take place in time. Counterfactual stories, stories about heaven before time was invented, imagined stories, stories about repetitive habitual events—even these stories involve temporal sequence. Although we can only *perceive* a story from a unique moment in time, namely the present, once that story is in imagination, we can understand different temporal moments of the story as if they belong to different temporal "spaces." Spaces are defined relative to spatial focus and spatial viewpoint; by projection, spaces are defined relative to temporal focus and temporal viewpoint. As we can focus on this or that spatial component of the story, so, by projection, we can "focus" on this or that temporal component of the story. Spatially, we may focus on the rattle, the eyes, the hand. Temporally, we may "focus" on the moment the baby picked the rattle up, the temporal period of rattling, or the moment the baby dropped the rattle. As we can view a story from this or that spatial viewpoint, so, by projection, we can "view" a story from this or that temporal "viewpoint." We may imagine the small spatial story of the baby's shaking the rattle from the viewpoint of the future of the story ("The baby shook the rattle"), from the viewpoint of the present of the story ("The baby is shaking the rattle"), or from the viewpoint of the past of the story ("The baby will shake the rattle").

By projecting the basic abstract story of spatial perceiving onto the basic abstract story of temporal perceiving, we understand ourselves as able to focus on one or another temporal space from one or another temporal "location" or "viewpoint." We can "focus" on the temporal space of "yesterday" from the viewpoint of "today": "I did it yesterday." We can "focus" on the temporal space of 1066 from the temporal "viewpoint" of 1066: "It's raining as William lands on English shores." We can "focus" on the temporal space of the day after tomorrow from the temporal space of today, and in the space of the day after tomorrow, there can be someone who is focusing on his yesterday (our tomorrow) from the viewpoint of our day after tomorrow, as in "He will come home tomorrow night and *we will ask him the following morning whether he has made the phone call, but he will say he did it as soon as he came home.*" The complexities of this everyday competence in narrative imagining have been surveyed by rhetoricians and literary critics for many centuries—the body of research in literary theory on focus and viewpoint is large. Focus and viewpoint have emerged relatively recently as fundamental topics in linguistics.

Let us take one small example of the phenomena of temporal focus and viewpoint. Proust begins *À la recherche du temps perdu*, "For a long time I used to go to bed early" ("Longtemps, je me suis couché de bonne heure"). This sets up a space of narration. The temporal viewpoint at the opening of the book is from this space of narration. This opening sentence also sets up a space of habitually going to bed early; this space is the temporal focus. The temporal viewpoint, in the space of narration, lies in the future of the temporal focus—the space of habitually going to bed early. From the temporal viewpoint of the space of narration, the narrator begins to describe various phenomena of memory and dreaming that belong to the space of temporal focus, like the following:

Then the memory of a new position would recur, and the wall would slide away in another direction—I was in my room at Mme de Saint-Loup's, in the country: Good Heavens, it is at least ten o'clock, they must have finished dinner! I must have overslept myself in the little nap that I always take when I come in from my walk with Mme de Saint-Loup, before dressing for the evening. For many years have now passed since Combray when, upon our tardiest homecomings, I saw the glowing reflections of the sunset on the panes of my bedroom window.

Puis renaissait le souvenir d'une nouvelle attitude: le mur filait dans une autre direction: j'étais dans ma chambre chez Mme de Saint-Loup, à la campagne; mon Dieu! il est au moins dix heures, on doit avoir fini de dîner! J'aurai trop prolongé la sieste que je fais tous les soirs en rentrant de ma promenade avec Mme de Saint-Loup, avant d'endosser mon habit. Car bien des années ont passé depuis Combray, où, dans nos retours les plus tardifs, c'étaient les reflets rouges du couchant que je voyais sur le vitrage de ma fenêtre.

In the beginning of this passage, the temporal viewpoint is the space of narration. The temporal focus is the general habitual space of nightly perception and dreaming. The temporal focus lies in the past of the temporal viewpoint. At the phrase "I was in my room," the temporal viewpoint remains in the space of narration, but the temporal focus shifts to the more local temporal space of the

*Narrative structure of the mind*

dreamer experiencing the particular dream of being in his room at Mme de Saint-Loup's. This more local temporal space is a specific space that is an instance of the general habitual space of nightly perception and dreaming. At "Good Heavens!" there is a double shift. Temporal viewpoint and temporal focus both shift to the space of the dream itself. At the phrase "they must have finished dinner," temporal viewpoint is inside the dream as the dreamer (who, in this space, does not know he is dreaming) uses narrative imagination to make sense of his immediately relevant past. It is important to see that it would have been entirely possible for the mental viewpoint to be the dreamer's while the temporal viewpoint lay with his counterpart in a different and later temporal space, as in "I concluded that they had finished dinner and that I had overslept." At "they must have finished dinner; I must have overslept myself," the temporal viewpoint is the moment of reaching these conclusions, but the temporal focus is the space of the events that are the subject of those conclusions (the finishing of dinner, the oversleeping of the appropriate moment to awaken), which the dreamer takes to lie temporally in his immediately relevant past. He marks his knowledge explicitly as resulting from his mental reasoning by saying "They must have finished dinner" rather than "They have finished dinner," and "I must have overslept" rather than "I have overslept." At "in the little nap that I always take," the temporal viewpoint and the temporal focus both float up to the temporal habitual space we might call "life at Mme de Saint-Loup's, in the country," in its function as dreamed inclusive background of the specific dreamed event of waking up in the room at Mme de Saint-Loup's. At "For many years have now passed," the temporal viewpoint remains inside that temporal space of "life at Mme de Saint-Loup's, in the country," but the temporal focus now shifts to the temporal space we might call "life at Combray," which lies "many years" in the past of the temporal viewpoint. Needless to say, by the end of the passage, temporal viewpoint and temporal focus are both extremely far from the space of narration.

Proust's report is distributed over different temporal spaces. Temporal viewpoint and focus can shift variously over such spaces. As they shift in this manner, we maintain an account of how each of these temporal spaces connects to the particular distinguished temporal space we might label "the moment of narration by Proust." The tense of the verb is an instrument for indicating temporal viewpoint and temporal focus on a story partitioned over temporal spaces. All the spaces Proust narrates lie in the past of the space of narration, but it would be a misconception to expect that his verbs would therefore have past tenses. Tense is an instrument for indicating temporal focus and viewpoint; it is to be expected that, in narrating events that lie in his past, the narrator will of course use a great range of tenses, including present tense and future tense, to indicate focus and viewpoint. The everyday mind is very good at shifting temporal focus

*Mental reasoning part of act of narration*

and temporal viewpoint; this capacity leaves its mark on the structure of language and on the artifacts of literature.

Just as the everyday mind is extremely adept at coordinating different mental spaces distinguished by spatial viewpoint and focus, so it is extremely adept at coordinating different mental spaces distinguished by temporal viewpoint and focus. We have seen many times that different spaces can be connected by structure they share; in particular, we have seen that structure shared by two input spaces, contained in a generic space that applies to both of them, establishes counterpart connections between them. One kind of shared structure can be *identity*. We saw that the two monks in the two input spaces in the riddle of the Buddhist monk were counterparts in two ways: First, each has the role of "traveler" in the frame for *traveling along a path*; second, they are viewed as the *identical* person. Following Fauconnier, we say that identity counterparts like these in different spaces are connected by an "identity connector." An identity connector does not imply that the counterparts are the same in every respect—the monk in one space is a day older than the monk in the other, for example—but rather that the counterparts share an identity.

Identity connections tie together spaces of different viewpoint and focus, whether spatial or temporal. This tying together of mental spaces by identity connectors—making them all spaces that concern the same story—greatly reduces the amount of work that needs to be done in conceiving, imagining, or telling a story. If we think of all the mental spaces involved in the story of Shahrazad, we expect that Shahriyar in any one of them connects identically to Shahriyar in any other. When we shift viewpoint or focus to a different temporal space, we do not have to build up everything in that space explicitly. For example, in imagining the marriage of Shahrazad to Shahriyar, we do not have to build explicitly into that imagined space the vizier, the relation between the vizier and Shahrazad, the relation between King Shahriyar and the vizier, and so on. All of that flows forward through identity connectors. An event established in one space as temporally ongoing flows forward through identity connectors to the appropriate future spaces.

These identity connections are assumed rather than reported. Consequently, narrative imagining operates with a huge assumed background. It operates with an immense unstated framework of whatever goes without saying. Narration typically reports changes in causal structure, event shape, role relations, or, in general, information that is not immediately established through identity connectors. It does not "interrupt" itself to report that Shahrazad is still Shahrazad, still the vizier's daughter, still lovely and intelligent. When a bit of information is reported that we assumed to have been provided through identity connectors, we often take it as a signal that the narrator means for that information to count as something extra; for if building that information into a new space were the narrator's sole purpose, he would not have reported it.

We think of a story as unitary, and of various mental spaces that are defined relative to different spatial and temporal viewpoints as simply different "perspectives" on that story, naturally belonging to a whole. There are some very interesting consequences of this thinking. Consider again that something in one of these spaces can be described by giving the description that belongs to its counterpart in another space. For example, if you are in the dark and are asked what you are looking for, you may say, "The red ball." Of course, within the spatiotemporal space of speaking, the ball cannot appear to be red because there is no light. "Red" is not a possible descriptor of the ball in this spatiotemporal space of narration. But that ball is connected, in imagination, to its counterparts in other spaces, and in those other spaces, "red" is a possible descriptor. The "red" of "red ball" spoken in darkness comes from a different mental space. When you are giving directions to someone over the telephone, you may say, "Go past the café on the right," even though the café is not presently on your right and is not presently on the right of the person you are speaking to and is indeed not universally "on the right" but is only "on the right" from the spatial viewpoint of someone driving down the street in the direction you have indicated. You and the person receiving directions can both imagine a mental space that is constructed with a certain spatial viewpoint on the street in an imagined story—namely, the story of someone making this particular journey in this particular way—and in that mental space, the café is on the right of the journeyer. Because of identity connectors, you may later say, "We are now sitting in the café on the right."

The use of descriptions from one space for counterparts in other spaces is subtly demonstrated in the passage from Proust:

> I was in my room at Mme de Saint-Loup's, in the country: Good Heavens, it is at least ten o'clock, they must have finished dinner! I must have overslept myself in the little nap that I always take when I come in from my walk with Mme de Saint-Loup, before dressing for the evening.

The temporal viewpoint of "Good Heavens, it is at least ten o'clock" is the moment of making this observation, a punctual moment. Much of the description given from this temporal viewpoint is indeed possible for the mental space of this viewpoint: "Good Heavens, it is at least ten o'clock, they must have finished dinner! I must have overslept myself. . . . " But the phrase that describes his nap does not belong to the space of this temporally punctual viewpoint. It belongs instead to the larger remembered habitual temporal space of "life at Mme de Saint-Loup's, in the country," in its function as dreamed inclusive background of the dreamed event of waking after having overslept. "The little nap that I always take when I come in from my walk with Mme de Saint-Loup, before dressing for the evening" is a description of the role *nap* as it exists in that remembered and dreamed habitual temporal space. The role *nap* lies in this habitual temporal space. The particular nap that fills that general role lies in the temporal space of having these thoughts in this dream of having awakened after oversleeping. The general role in one space and its particular filler in another are connected not by an identity connector but by a *role* connector. The descriptor Proust uses for the particular nap in a punctual temporal space can come only from its corresponding general role in the habitual temporal space.

It is natural that the literary mind should be adept at such connections across spatial and temporal spaces. A small spatial story is always recognized or executed from a single viewpoint and with a single focus. Part of our most basic cognitive capacity is to consider the spatial story as a single unit despite evident and transforming shifts of viewpoint and focus. When we see someone startle as he looks in some direction with what we assume to be some focus, we must be able to look immediately not in the same direction and not with the same focus but in the corresponding direction from our location, and with the corresponding focus from our location, so as to see what he sees, even though we do not yet know what he sees but merely hope to find out what it is. To do this, we must be able to imagine his spatial viewpoint and then calculate backward to the appropriate bearing and distance from our own spatial location. We do this instantly, as a survival capacity. The case is the same with temporal focus and viewpoint: To learn small spatial stories in a way that allows us to recognize them or execute them, we must be able to recognize the entire story from the viewpoint of any particular temporal slice or frame; we therefore require the capacity to hold various things constant, through connectors, as we switch temporal viewpoint and temporal focus from mental space to mental space.

We have seen that the basic human story of spatial viewing is projected parabolically to the story of *temporal* "viewing." Of course, these two stories combine into the basic human story of spatiotemporal viewing. *But this story too is projected.* It is projected to the schematic story of *mental* viewing. There are various kinds of mental "viewpoint" and "focus" that arise from this parabolic projection: Philosophical, political, and ideological viewpoints and foci are only some of the possibilities. Someone who inhabits a certain role in a story will have a mental "viewpoint" and "focus" appropriate to that role. In the projection of spatial stories of movement and manipulation onto stories of mental events, spatial locations and objects correspond to ideas, assertions, and thoughts. The mind "sees" or "views" ideas, assertions, and thoughts from a particular location and with a particular posture. The mind may then "move toward" an idea or "away" from a belief, "grasp" an idea or leave it "behind," and so on. Locations can also be projected onto features or states. We may think of "true" ideas as located in one place, "false" in another, "crazy but perhaps suggestive" in another, "counter-factual" in another, "hypothetical" in another, and so on. We may say that we have been "looking in the wrong places for the ideas we need" or that we have "not been positioned properly until now to see the idea clearly." We may "focus" on hypothetical reality from a particular political "viewpoint." We may "focus" on the economic story of California from the "viewpoint" of a potential investor or the alternative "viewpoint" of the governor of California.

Literary narratives are extraordinarily accomplished at indicating such mental viewpoints. The first words of *The Thousand and One Nights* read,

> It is related—but Allah alone is wise and all-knowing—that long ago there lived in the lands of India and China a Sassanid king who com-manded great armies and had numerous courtiers, followers, and ser-vants. He left two sons. . . .

The narrator takes certain mental viewpoints. First, there is the space of what the narrator relates. There is only one thing in this space that he is certain of—namely, people do tell the story of the thousand and one nights ("it is related"). This space is a parent space; what people in this space relate belongs to a child space. The child space is viewed by the narrator as a space of possibility only; the narrator will not vouch for its certainty ("but Allah alone is wise and all-knowing"). The parent space takes a temporal viewpoint on the child space: It is "long ago."

Once we decide to pay attention to these parabolic viewpoints on story spaces, we see them everywhere, in almost every phrase of a literary work. One kind of mental viewpoint concerns viewing the story space as real, unreal, or indetermi-nate. Shahrazad imagines a predictive story in which she marries King Shahriyar; she and her father view it as a hypothetical space and therefore unreal. But it becomes, in their mental viewpoint as characters in the narrator's story, real. The vizier imagines a predictive story space of the marriage; he and his daughter view it as hypothetical and unreal. He hopes it does not become real. In fact, part of it becomes (from his mental viewpoint as a character) real, the part it shares with Shahrazad's hypothetical space: Shahrazad marries Shahriyar and spends the night with him. The rest of his predictive space does not become real: Shahriyar does not order her execution. Other kinds of spaces, such as spaces viewed as both counterfactual and past ("If Shahrazad had visited England") are viewed as constrained to be permanently unreal if they are meant to correspond to conven-tional conceptions of reality. Of course, there are many cases of imaginative lit-erature in which these constraints are removed, so that in an alternative universe or a reengineered past or a world in which a time machine has appeared from the future, Shahrazad does visit England, for example.

A story space that is conditional upon another story space can be viewed as counterfactual because of the condition ("If Shahrazad had visited England . . . "), as counterfactual because of the consequence ("If Shahrazad had not married Shahriyar, the kingdom would have fallen, but it didn't fall, so I know she must have married him"), or as unreal but potentially real ("If Shahrazad marries Shahriyar, we will be saved").

A mental viewpoint can be defined by a role. When we comment on the story of Shahrazad "from the viewpoint of" Shahrazad, or the vizier, or Shahriyar, or Dinarzad, we are concerned not with their spatial or temporal viewpoints, but rather with their mental viewpoints, defined relative to their roles. Imagine the *spatial and temporal* viewpoint and focus on the wedding night that belong to the vizier, or Shahrazad, or Shahriyar, or Dinarzad. Now imagine, by contrast, the very different *mental* viewpoint and focus on the wedding night that belong to the vizier, or Shahrazad, or Shahriyar, or Dinarzad as they inhabit their roles. A given character in the story may shift mental viewpoint, so that, for example, Shahrazad may try to see the story she is engaged in "from the viewpoint" of King Shahriyar.

*The Thousand and One Nights* explores as a continual and basic theme the influence of one's relation to a story upon one's mental viewpoint and focus on that story. My favorite such exploration is the tale of the barber's fifth brother, Al-Ashar, who narrates (to himself) a daydream he imagines of his future prosperity. While he is imagining the story, he is sitting on a corner with a basket of glassware to sell. He has invested his entire patrimony in this merchandise. He imagines that he sells all his glassware and with the profit buys twice as much. In his elaborate and absorbing daydream, it does not take him long to become very rich. By the middle of the daydream, he is marrying the lovely daughter of the vizier. Throughout the entire daydream, he imagines himself not as sitting at a crossroads, but as lordly. In the daydream, the vizier bows to him, and Al-Ashar conducts himself with the greatest magnificence and generosity, like a king. His new wife wants his love, but his pride keeps him aloof:

> "I will neither speak to her nor even look at her. Presently the bride's mother will come in, kissing my head and hand, and saying: 'My lord, look upon your slave-girl, who yearns for your favour; speak to her and heal her broken spirit.' I will make no answer. She will throw herself down at my feet, kissing them again and again, and saying: 'Your slave is a beautiful virgin and she has seen no man but you. On my knees I

beg you to cease humbling her, or her heart will break!' Then the bride's
mother will rise, and, filling a cup with wine, will give it to her daughter, who will offer it to me with all submission. But I, leaning idly upon
my elbow among the gold-embroidered cushions, will take no notice
of her. With a trembling voice she will say: 'I beg you, my lord, to take
this cup from the hand of your slave and servant.' But I will maintain
my dignified silence. She will raise the cup to my mouth, pressing me
to drink from it. Then I will wave it away with my hand, and spurn her
with my foot, thus—"

So saying, Al-Ashar kicked against the basket of glassware, knocking over the contents and crashing them in fragments to the ground.

Al-Ashar narrates his daydream from the viewpoint of one who wishes to
inhabit the central role of its story. But the story of Al-Ashar's internal narration is being told by Al-Ashar's brother, the barber, as one of the stories about
his brothers that he tells in the court of the caliph, to impress the caliph with the
wisdom the barber displays as an actor in each story the barber relates and also
with his ability as a wise storyteller.

But, one step up in this nesting, this story of the barber's telling stories to
the caliph is being told by someone—the barber again!—at a dinner party, so
that he may impress the dinner guests. He is telling a story of himself telling
stories. At this dinner party, the barber is attempting to discredit the lame young
man who has just told a devastating story about the barber's garrulousness, fraud,
and incompetence and has left in a huff, refusing to stay in the same room as the
barber. So the barber's role at the dinner party gives him a certain outlook on the
story he is now narrating of his earlier narration.

The entire narrative space within which the barber does all his storytelling
at the dinner party is being related by the tailor in the court of the king. The
tailor has reason to tell a very long story, the longest story he can imagine, and
he does this by finding a way to include as an embedded story the tale of what he
comes to call the "exceptionally garrulous" barber who considers himself fabu-
lously smart when in fact everyone else thinks he is a charlatan and a blatherer.
The barber, relating at the dinner party the story of his narration of several stories to the caliph, views that story from the "mental position" of one who thinks
well of the central character, himself. But the tailor, telling the story of the barber doing the telling of his previous telling, does so in such a way that anyone
with a different "mental position" must see that the barber is "exceptionally garrulous." The barber, in the tailor's narration, is made to condemn himself out of
his own mouth:

When he had heard the tale of my sixth brother (continued the barber to the guests), the Caliph Al-Muntasir Billah burst out laughing and said: "I can well see, my silent friend, that you are a man of few words, who knows neither curiosity nor indiscretion. Yet I must ask you to leave this city at once and go to live elsewhere."

Thus, for no conceivable reason, the Caliph banished me from Baghdad.

By making the barber ridiculous but funny, the tailor makes the tedium of the barber's protracted stories hilarious. This is extraordinarily amusing to the king to whom the tailor is relating the long story, and a good thing, too, because the tailor has been brought to the king from the gallows at the moment of his hanging. At the moment of the tailor's narrating, the tailor and everyone else involved believe that the tailor killed a hunchback and is to hang for it. Everyone involved in the story of this hunchback's death has been brought before the king to explain to the king how it is that the governor has condemned and then pardoned in a row first the Christian, then the king's steward, then the Jewish doctor, before condemning the tailor for the murder of the hunchback. The tailor is telling these stories of stories of stories in order to stay alive! His narration provides, in the character of the caliph, a model of a reasonable kingly judge who maintains all civility, loves humor, has a good sense of satire, and punishes by banishing, not hanging. The tailor is providing this model in the hope that the king, who is hearing the tailor's story, will conform to it and spare the tailor.

The king to whom the tailor is telling the story is extraordinarily wonderful and cultivated and just. He marvels greatly at stories and admires them. Before the tailor begins speaking, the king hears the story of all the condemnations and the pardons; he gives "orders that the story be inscribed on parchment in letters of gold. The king asked those who were present: 'Have you ever heard a story more marvellous than that of the hunchback?'" It is this question that gives the tailor his opening to tell the longest story of stories of stories of stories you ever heard, and so to distract the king and put him into a better humor.

It certainly works. At the end of the nearly interminable story, "the King of Basrah was much amused by the tailor's story, and said: 'The young man's adventure with the Barber certainly surpasses in wonder the story of the hunchback.'" The king then orders both the barber and the corpse of the hunchback brought before him. When the king sees the barber, he bursts into a fit of laughter and says, "Silent One, we wish to hear some of your stories."

But then something very interesting, and perhaps unexpected, happens. The barber does indeed speak with great reserve and brevity. He asks to be told why the hunchback is lying dead before him. He listens to the entire explanatory story without saying a word. He asks to examine the body, and when he has done so, he says cryptically that the death of the hunchback is a wonder that should be recorded for all time. The king asks for an explanation, and the barber responds with all brevity that the hunchback is alive. Then the barber expertly revives the hunchback by extracting a piece of fish and bone from his throat. Before long, the king observes that this all makes a great story and orders that it be recorded on scrolls of parchment and saved in the royal library. He bestows honor upon everybody and raises the barber to a position of companionship and authority in his court.

The tailor, of course, in telling his stories, has been trying to lead the king to project from stories he has been telling onto the king's own situation. The caliph of the tailor's narration is cultivated, civilized, temperate, merciful, and loves a good story. This could be an emblem for the king, who could conform to that model. The person telling long tales in the narration (the barber) is merely banished by the caliph; perhaps the person telling long stories to the king (the tailor) could be merely banished, too. It is not the place of the tailor to tell the king what the king ought to do, but through the projection of stories, he can put the king in mind of a way to carry out the particular story whose ending the king will now determine.

Of course, the entire story of the hunchback, with its embedded stories of the tailor and the king, and the tailor's story of the barber, and the barber's many stories of his brothers, and the fifth brother's narration of his daydream, is being told to Dinarzad by Shahrazad, with Shahriyar listening. Shahrazad's "mental position" includes the goal of leading Shahriyar to think of ending the story of Shahriyar and Shahrazad in the way she has in mind. Her ability to use viewpoint to accomplish this is unsurpassed. She cannot flatly assault Shahriyar with her advice and opinions. Doing so might simply trigger in him the worst confirmation of the horrid views he professed when he began his practice of killing wives. But she can work through elaborate indirection. All the kings and caliphs and governors and authorities in the elaborate tale of the hunchback—the very first tale she tells Shahriyar—are thoughtful, rational, and equable. They are in no hurry, they are secure, and they love stories. They all think stories are the most worthy things in the world, and they all are certain that there is nothing more worthy for a king to do than to listen to stories, preserve them, and seek out new stories. All these kings and caliphs and governors and authorities are also marvelously well-disposed toward storytellers. Bad situations that are brought before them are transformed by their royal prudence into good for everyone involved.

However indirectly, Shahrazad cuts increasingly close to the bone. It is clear in the story of the hunchback that the tailor is motivated to tell long stories in order to entertain the king, to put him into a good humor, and thus to save his own life. If King Shahriyar can merely project this onto his own present story, he will see an extraordinarily honest admission from Shahrazad of what she is doing and how she hopes he will respond. On that reading, she is actually hoping for a lot out of him; she is hoping that he holds a reservoir of humanity and civility that can be tapped. Some of her stories are even sharper and push deeper: The barber's sixth brother has his penis and lips cut off by an enraged chieftain whose wife is discovered "dallying" with the sixth brother, and in that story, the sex is clearly initiated by the wife. Now, the big causal event of *The Thousand and One Nights* was Shahriyar's discovery of his own wife's "dallying" with a slave. Shahrazad clearly means to acknowledge the reality of stories of the sort that led Shahriyar to his practice. Does this projection justify the rage and violence of Shahriyar, by making him the counterpart of the chieftain? No, because Shahrazad, who makes it clear that the chieftain's rage is understandable, also makes it clear that something better is expected of Shahriyar: the chieftain is an uncultivated and discreditable outlaw, while Shahriyar is a king.

To my mind, Shahrazad's riskiest story is the deeply embedded story of the barber's fifth brother, Al-Ashar. Al-Ashar—he with the basket of glassware to sell—is a jerk in the opinion of everyone, possibly even himself. He is profoundly insecure about his masculinity. To feed his vanity, he daydreams about the complete submission of women to him, about his aloof command and indifference to all affection, about women who are perfect and lovely and who beg, with trembling voice, to submit to him, women who can imagine nothing better than to fall at his feet. He imagines women who have never had a thought of any man but him and who are obviously not equipped ever to have any thought of any man but him. Al-Ashar imagines a life in which there is no chance of any sort of parity between himself and his wife, and he imagines that such a life could be desirable. In his mind and story, he represents such a life as kingly. Of course, he destroys everything, losing even the little he has. Yet when he does so, neither the reader nor Shahrazad despises him. We are amused. It is a funny story. Maybe there is some hope for him. We pity him a little. We recognize how juvenile his ambitions are.

This is a daring story to be telling to a king who is a jerk, profoundly insecure about his masculinity, and who, to satisfy his obsession for control over women, has instituted an ingenious and apparently successful zero-defects program, at the cost of ever having anything like affection, companionship, or parity. It is more daring still: The woman Al-Ashar spurns with his foot in his indifference is *his wife and the daughter of the vizier*, which is of course exactly Shahrazad's double role. It is just possible that the reader who is engrossed in the story could miss for a moment this connection, but surely Shahriyar could not. Al-Ashar is portrayed as an absolute idiot for his action. The only possible mitigation in Al-Ashar's case is the fact that the woman he spurns doesn't amount to much anyway, but this fact only brings forcibly into the foreground how incomparably superior Shahrazad is in every way. Shahrazad might even be presenting the woman in Al-Ashar's daydream to Shahriyar as a portrait of what Shahriyar imagined to be his ideal woman, as a way of helping him see that he really wouldn't want her after all. From every viewpoint in the nested chain of parent narrative spaces above that of Al-Ashar, beginning with the barber, Al-Ashar is regarded as an idiot *within the story he is imagining*. And even Al-Ashar, along with everyone else, regards himself as an idiot within the completed story of his selling glassware at the crossroads.

By nesting these viewpoints so that the story of Al-Ashar stands at an elaborate distance from her own situation, Shahrazad is giving King Shahriyar some time to begin to work around to her mental viewpoint. Of equal importance, she is making it possible for Shahriyar to accept, if he chooses to do so, that she is just telling stories to her sister Dinarzad, and not challenging his authority at all. She is not necessarily requiring him to believe that she does not know what she is doing. She is instead providing him with a way out of the story he has set up for himself, if he wants one, and a set of compelling motives for taking that way out. She is trying to make it possible for him to desist from his practice and to take a wife. He needs an excuse for doing so, he needs persuasion, and he needs some models. But she has to provide these in a way that can pass for mere entertainment. Her elaborate manipulation of viewpoint allows her to perform this sleight of hand. It gives her a cover from which she is permitted to suggest to him an altogether different path toward the future of his own story. She does this through parable, prompting him to project from the stories he is hearing onto the story of his own life.

The stories she tells will be many. Some will portray civilized life at a court. Some will tell of terrible genies bottled up with nothing but their own torment, who, once the cork is popped, spew out in a black rage, intending to kill for revenge, but who finally get talked out of it by ingenious people who seem to have nothing with which to oppose the genie's power but their shrewdness and their gift for stories. Many of Shahrazad's stories will acknowledge the phenomenon of deep psychic injury. Men and women will be portrayed unblinkingly as capable of honor or perfidy, driven by virtues and lusts. This is an adult narrative: Death destroys everything. Nonetheless, what Death destroys is Delight—which presupposes that life can have some delight.

Shahrazad's manipulation of viewpoints is pyrotechnic and literary in the extreme, but it is simply a sophisticated use of indispensable and fundamental capacities of the everyday mind. We take spatial viewpoints on spatial stories. We project the story of someone's viewing a story from a spatial viewpoint onto the story of someone's viewing a story from a temporal viewpoint. We project in general the story of someone's viewing a story in space and time onto the story of someone's viewing a story from a mental position. From that mental position, we may view the story as conditional, hypothetical, nonactual, and so on. We may view it from the "viewpoint" of a particular role. We may view it, in imagination, from someone else's mental "viewpoint." We could not operate in our environment, physical or social, without extremely sophisticated imaginative abilities of viewpoint and focus on stories in imagination. The narrator of *The Thousand and One Nights* is merely asking us to use a capacity we already have, just as Shahrazad is asking Shahriyar to use a capacity he already has.

We may become engrossed, in Erving Goffman's phrase, and forget that this is a story, and get angry, and claim that Shahriyar does not deserve to be rehabilitated, that it is perfectly horrible that Shahrazad should have to go through this humiliation just because some pig is on the throne, and that the story of her life merely reconfirms all the old patterns of patriarchy. Of course. But the story makes some of those claims itself. Shahriyar never comes off well in *The Thousand and One Nights*. He is your run-of-the-mill insecure male who has only just enough intelligence to be able to see, when it is laid out masterfully before him, that he has it good and would be a fool to keep his old psychology. Shahrazad, by contrast, is an absolute genius. She is convincingly portrayed as starting from a position of no institutional power at all and bringing about what no one else of any institutional authority could possibly have done. It is Shahrazad that we admire and remember.

She accomplishes all this through parable: the conjunction of story and projection. She may have other ways for helping Shahriyar change his mind, but it is parable that we hear about and parable that she invites us to apply to our own life stories.

## ROLES, CHARACTERS, AND LIVES

> To be quite accurate, I ought to give a different name to each of the "me's" who were to think about Albertine in time to come; I ought still more to give a different name to each of the Albertines who appeared before me, never the same. . . .
>
> *Marcel Proust, Remembrance of Things Past*

For any story, we can develop a great variety of mental spaces. For the extremely simple story of the first time a baby shakes the rattle, for example, we can imagine the mental spaces of the story as viewed spatially from above, behind, ahead, or either side; as viewed temporally by his mother on his sixteenth birthday; as viewed from his mother's psychological viewpoint as opposed to the baby's

constancy —
identity connectors

psychological viewpoint; and so on indefinitely. One way to develop constancy over this great variation is, as we have seen, through identity connectors. Although all these different mental spaces of the baby shaking the rattle might look quite different, we unify them as simply different viewpoint spaces all connected by identity connectors to the same single small spatial story. The baby in any viewpoint mental space is connected identically to the baby in any other.

Role connectors are another way of developing constancy over a great variety of mental spaces. When we recognize the baby who shakes the rattle as an instance of the role *animate agent*, and the shaking as the kind of motion that animate agents cause, we are using the roles to create constancy over variation: the story of the baby shaking the rattle becomes connected to every other story in which an animate agent causes the motion of an object.

Any small spatial story comes with roles: The story of the woman throwing the stone to smash the window has roles for *thrower* (a more specific role than *animate agent*) and *missile* and *target*. To recognize a story requires recognizing its roles.

*Character* can be formed by backward inference from such a role, according to the folk theory of "The Nature of Things," otherwise known as "Being Leads to Doing." In this folk theory, glass *shatters* because it is *brittle* and *fragile*. Water *pours* because it is *liquid*. Someone *forgives* because she is *forgiving*. A dog *guards* the house because it is *watchful*. A fool acts like a fool because he is *foolish*. In general, doing follows from being; being leads to doing; something behaves in a certain way because its being leads it to behave in that way.

Someone who is typically in the role of *adversary* can, by the Nature of Things, be thought of as "adversarial." He acquires a character: *adversarial*. We develop an expectation that he will be "true to his character": his character will guide his action; his *being* will lead to his *doing*. We become primed to see him inhabit similar roles in other stories. "That's just like him," we say. Our sense of someone's general character guides our expectations of which roles he will play in which stories. For example, we know what Sherlock Holmes is likely to do in any story in which he exists. The influence of character upon assignment to role is so strong that the mere appearance of a person with a certain character in a story can induce the creation of the role: As soon as Sherlock Holmes enters the scene, we expect the story to develop a role for *detective* or *puzzle solver* even if the story has not previously had one.

*Character* is a pattern of connections we expect to operate across stories about a particular individual with that character or across stories about a group of individuals with that character. People of a particular character are expected to inhabit similar roles in different stories. We can develop a categorization of kinds of character—generous, selfish, brave, submissive, and so on. There are famous explicit surveys of character, such as Theophrastus's *Characters* and La Bruyère's *Les Caractères*. Theophrastus gives us quick sketches of the boor, the liar, the grouch, the sponge, and so on, while La Bruyère presents intricate and refined analyses of highly specific aspects of character.

Once character is established as a general pattern of connections across potential story spaces, it can serve as a generator of those spaces. As Jerome Bruner has observed, "Perhaps the greatest feat in the history of narrative art was the leap from the folktale to the psychological novel that places the engine of action in the characters rather than in the plot." Kenneth Burke made a lifelong study of the ways in which any general aspect of a story space—character, action, goal, setting, and means—could serve as the basis for building up the rest of the space. Character can generate story.

Focus, viewpoint, role, and character are concepts useful in constructing constancy across variation. They all assume that mental spaces can be connected. We have single lives, but whenever we see ourselves as having a focus or a viewpoint, inhabiting a role, or possessing a character that runs across roles in stories, we see ourselves as transcending our singularities. Our focus and our viewpoint become not singular or isolated; they connect to a central story and all its other focus and viewpoint spaces. A role in one story is not isolated but connects to the same role in other stories. A complex of roles, such as "the eternal triangle," connects to the same complex in other stories. Character is a concept that guides us in assigning an actor to the same or similar roles across multiple story spaces.

Focus, viewpoint, role, and character in narrative imagining give us ways of constructing our own meaning, which is to say, ways of understanding who we are, what it means to be us, to have a particular life. The inability to locate one's own focus, viewpoint, role, and character with respect to conventional stories of leading a life is thought to be pathological and deeply distressing. It is a principal reason for recommending psychotherapy to people not obviously insane.

There is a touchstone text for the view that knowing how to inhabit stories is the essential requirement of mature life. Peter Pan is the leader of the lost boys in Neverland. The lost boys will always be boys, and always lost, as long as they don't know stories. They can't grow up because they cannot understand how to inhabit roles in stories, how to belong to categories of characters running across story spaces, how to have lives. Peter Pan persuades Wendy to go with him to Neverland exactly by telling her that the lost boys don't know any stories:

> "You see I don't know any stories. None of the lost boys know any stories."
>
> "How perfectly awful," Wendy said.
>
> "Do you know," Peter asked, "why swallows build in the eaves of houses? It is to listen to the stories. O Wendy, your mother was telling you such a lovely story."

"Which story was it?"

"About the prince who couldn't find the lady who wore the glass slipper."

"Peter," said Wendy excitedly, "that was Cinderella, and he found her, and they lived happily ever after."

Peter was so glad that he rose from the floor, where they had been sitting, and hurried to the window. "Where are you going?" she cried with misgiving.

"To tell the other boys."

"Don't go, Peter," she entreated, "I know such lots of stories."

Those were her precise words, so there can be no denying that it was she who first tempted him.

He came back, and there was a greedy look in his eyes now which ought to have alarmed her, but did not.

"Oh, the stories I could tell to the boys!" she cried, and then Peter gripped her and began to draw her toward the window.

Trying to make sense of a life as a pattern of character running across roles in stories leads to a clear problem: People often drop out of roles in stories and often decline to inhabit the roles we expect of them on the basis of what we thought we knew about their character. People appear to perform in different ways that do not seem to belong to the same character. One way to respond to this inconstancy is to work all the harder to rebuild constancy across these spaces, on the view that of course this kind of constancy must hold. This is a mainstay of psychology, psychiatry, biography, and detective novels. If an agent seems to have the character attribute of "giving" in the role of donor in one space but the opposed character attribute of "grasping" in the role of thief in another space, we might respond to the inconstancy by trying to reconstruct the roles and infer a stable character: Ah-ha! in the case of "apparent" giving, the agent really had his own interest at heart; or ah-ha! in the case of "apparent" grasping, the agent was really trying to save the owner from some danger.

Alternatively, inconstancy across spaces can be read as a sign of the real, on the view that in reality people are uncontrolled, unpredictable, singular, inscrutable. Novelists often use inconstancy to convey objectivity and realism: if constancy reveals the narrative imagination of the author at work, then, so the simple logic goes, inconstancy should demonstrate that the narrator has not "invented" this story. It never works that way. In *The Rhetoric of Fiction*, Wayne Booth shows that novelists often try to meet various requirements like "Novels Should Be Realistic" and "Authors Should Be Objective" by tossing in variation and inconstancy—random singularities that have no role in the structure of the general story, specific events unrelated to the causal structure of the story, conflicted action by a single agent to frustrate the reader's attempt to infer underlying character, and so on. The underlying assumption is that such inconstancies can come only from the realities of individual life. Booth shows that all these techniques in fact reveal the heavy hand of the manipulative author.

Stories and the connections between them are the chief cognitive instrument for biography. A mental space that concerns a person's life seems to us to be a slice of her biography. In the slice, she has a certain role and a certain character. When we try to run connections across all these mental spaces—as when we try to predict what she will do in *this* case on the basis of what we already know of a previous space; or as when we try to imagine what she must have been like as a child on the basis of the stories she inhabits as an adult—we may encounter all sorts of incompatibilities, which therefore cannot reside in a generic space that would apply to all these mental spaces. As we run connections across all the story spaces—all these slices of biography, synchronic and diachronic—the generic space may become ever more abstract, approaching the minimum information that this human being has the role *animate agent*.

But we can get much more help from blended spaces. Blended spaces can absorb incompatibilities from the spaces they blend. In a blended space, a human being can be both donor and thief, giving and grasping. As the connections build over narrative mental spaces, the generic space becomes thinner but the blended space becomes ever more robust, intricate, and conflicted.

We do not live in a single narrative mental space, but rather dynamically and variably distributed over very many. If any one space must be selected as the place we reside, it is the blend of all these spaces. For biography, these impossible blended spaces are the most "realistic" because they come closest to signaling that life, like meaning, is not bounded in any one mental space, but involves the operations of projection, blending, and integration that run over indefinitely many activated mental spaces. "Realism" can never be the representation of uniqueness, for the simple reason that it is impossible for the everyday mind to think of the unique—the everyday mind is always, unavoidably, and fundamentally geared to constructing constancy over variation. But realism can indicate that a specific life is never contained within a single story space or even a collection of such spaces whose corresponding generic space tells us everything we want to know. The real is in the blend.

## BLENDED CHARACTERS

We have seen that character can be conceived by backward inference from behavior, on the logic that people *do* what they do because they *are* a particular kind of person. Once we have a notion of an actor's character, we can try to use it to project that actor into roles in new stories. We can try to predict what she will do in *this* story. This is an *identity* projection: the actor is connected to herself identically across all these stories.

But character can also be developed through *metaphoric* projection: "Achilles is a lion" projects the lion not to itself identically but rather, metaphorically, to something quite different—a human being. This projection is meant to imbue Achilles with a character and consequent behavior.

There is an extremely productive conceptual template that serves this type of projection. It is the GREAT CHAIN METAPHOR, which depends upon the folk notion of the Great Chain. The Great Chain is a hierarchy of attributes by type. A being can have, in ascending order, attributes of mere physical existence, attributes of part-whole functional structure, attributes of simple biology, and attributes of mental capacity. This hierarchy induces a corresponding hierarchy of kinds of beings: the category to which the being belongs is determined by the highest type of attribute it possesses. For example, barbed wire has part-whole functional structure as its highest kind of attribute, so it falls into the corresponding category of complex physical objects; but a spider, which also has part-whole functional structure, has instinct as its highest attribute, and therefore falls into the higher category of simple animals.

The folk notion of the Great Chain includes the further structure that a being at a given level in the hierarchy possesses all the kinds of attribute possessed by lower orders: For example, a spider has, in addition to instinct, simple biology (such as metabolism), part-whole functional structure (like legs and body), and simple physical attributes (like color).

The GREAT CHAIN METAPHOR is a pattern for projecting conceptual structure from something at one level of the Great Chain to something at another. "Max is a spider," for example, evokes a projection between what spiders do and what Max does. Max has social behavior; the spider has instinctual behavior. Max has certain roles in certain stories; the spider has certain roles in certain stories. We connect the two agents, their roles, their characters, and their typical stories. We connect them according to the Great Chain: "Max is a spider" is not interpreted to mean that Max is black, even though the prototypical spider is black. We assume that it asks us to make a connection between the highest attributes of the two agents: The spider's instinctual behavior projects to Max's intentional and mental behavior.

Whenever the GREAT CHAIN METAPHOR is at work, we are primed to activate a blended space in which the counterparts are blended, as in a political cartoon that portrays a corrupt politician as a spider with a human face who spins webs to catch political opponents.

Consider the tale of the ox and the donkey. The vizier creates a blend of Shahrazad and the donkey in which Shahrazad's human conviction and the donkey's unreflecting instinctive stubbornness are the same thing, so as to suggest that

Shahrazad is behaving like an ass. She should think about her plan, reconsider it, listen to his wisdom. Human beings can do these things, and she should act like a human being, not like a donkey. Shahrazad's immediate reaction to his story is so absolute and lacking in reflection as to seem to confirm his blending of the donkey's instinctive "stubbornness" and Shahrazad's intentional stubbornness:

> When she heard her father's story, Shahrazad said: "Nothing will shake my faith in the mission I am destined to fulfil."

The blend works because we have previously conceived of all donkeys by blending them with human beings. We say they are "stubborn," but they aren't. Only human beings can be stubborn. The instinctual behavior of a donkey is not at all the same thing as human stubbornness: For example, all donkeys have this behavior, not just some, and it is not subject to rational persuasion. We have conceived of this particular instinctual behavior by blending it with human stubbornness, and even given it the name "stubbornness." The conceptual ground has already prepared for blending the donkey with stubborn Shahrazad.

Douglas Sun has analyzed blended character in Thurber's story "The Moth and the Star." A young moth sets his heart on a certain star; his mother and father tell him he should instead hang around lamp bridges; they shame him for not having so much as a scorched wing:

> The moth thought [the star] was just caught in the branches of an elm. He never did reach the star, but he went right on trying, night after night, and when he was a very, very old moth he began to think that he really had reached the star and he went around saying so. This gave him deep and lasting pleasure, and he lived to a great old age. His parents and his brothers and his sisters had all been burned to death when they were quite young.

As Sun remarks, there is a central inference in this tale. If your goal is not the common goal, there may be some unpredicted benefits that outweigh the insults. This inference cannot come from the source because moths do not choose, do not know about sorrow, do not insult, do not weigh benefits, do not talk, and do not fly toward stars. The inference is not at all required of the target. In the source, it is a fixed instinctual necessity that all moths must fly toward light; but it is not true in the target that all people must instinctively strive toward a single common goal.

The moth's intentionality, his selection of his particular goal, his delusion, his pleasure, and so on all come from the target, where they are part of the human character. In the blend, the instinct of the moth from the source is blended with the character of the human being from the target to establish central inferences that are then projected to the target.

Talking animals—or, in general, blends of the human and the animal—are a principal feature of folktales and children's literature. The wolves in *The Jungle Book*, for example, are a blend of human social character and the pack instincts of wolves; even their unforgettable utterance—"Look well! Look well! Oh, wolves!"—is a blend of human language and lupine yelping. Such blends populate our imagination and memory: Sheer-Khan and Rikki-Tikki-Tavi; the lion and the hedgehog from *Aesop's Fables* ("The hedgehog twitted the lion for having only one cub in her litter; 'One,' she replied, 'but a lion'"); the serpent in the garden of Eden; and an indefinite range of cartoon characters from which readers draw homely philosophy. Talking animals seem whimsical and exotic, but they are not. They come from blending in parable, a phenomenon so basic as to be indispensable to our conception of what it means to have a human character and a human life.

# LANGUAGE

Linguistics is arguably the most hotly contested property in
the academic realm. It is soaked with the blood of poets,
theologians, philosophers, philologists, psychologists,
biologists, and neurologists, along with whatever blood can
be got out of grammarians.

*Russ Rymer in The New Yorker*

Light, heat, gravity, chemical affinity, human will, have this
in common, that they redistribute force. Their unit of
process can be represented as: term from which, transference of force, term to which. If we regard this transference
as the conscious or unconscious act of an agent we can
translate the diagram into: agent, act, object.

*Ernest Fenollosa, The Chinese Written Character*
*as a Medium for Poetry*

T HE DOMINANT CONTEMPORARY THEORY of the origin of language
proposes that genetic change produced genetic instructions for building a
special module for grammar in the human brain. Before genetic specialization
for grammar, people had no grammar at all: no grammatical speech, no parsing
of grammar, no concept of grammar. To be sure, they communicated (birds and
bees communicate), but their communication was totally ungrammatical. It was
not language. This grammar module was autonomous: it borrowed no structure
or processes from any other capacities like vision, spatial navigation, understanding of force dynamics, parable, and so on. Adherents of this theory—who form
a large group of distinguished scholars that includes Noam Chomsky, Steven

Pinker, and Paul Bloom—disagree only about which evolutionary mechanisms were responsible for the genetic specialization for grammar.

Naturally, it is a corollary of this theory that the development of language in any modern human child comes entirely from the autonomous grammar module in the child's brain, which is built entirely from the special instructions in its genes. The language the child hears prompts it to shut down the parts of the language module it does not need.

I think this theory of the historical origin of language is wrong. A carefully adjusted version of it might not in principle be absolutely impossible, but at best it offers a hypothesis of desperate last resort: Since we cannot discover a straightforward way in which language might have arisen, let us postulate the mysterious origin of a special, autonomous black box that mysteriously does everything we need to explain language, including everything we don't yet know we need.

If we reject the hypothesis that genetic specialization for grammar was the origin of language, what can we propose instead? Let us consider the possibility that parable was the origin of language, that parable preceded grammar.

Occam's razor is a basic principle of theory building, named after the man who expressed it: Make no unnecessary hypotheses. We have seen that, independently of questions of grammar, we must concede that human beings have the mental capacities I call parable. Is it necessary to add to parable something new? Is it necessary to make the additional hypothesis that special autonomous instructions arose in human genetic material for building an autonomous black box in the brain that does the entire job? Not if we consider that parable already gives us what we need. Cognitive mechanisms whose existence we must grant independently of any analysis of grammar can account for the origin of grammar. The linguistic mind is a consequence and subcategory of the literary mind.

Stories have structure that human vocal sound—as sound, not language—does not have. Stories have objects and events, actors and movements, viewpoint and focus, image schemas and force dynamics, and so on. Roughly, parable takes structure from story and gives it to voice (or bodily signs in the case of sign language). Parable creates structure for voice by projecting structure from story. The structure it creates is grammar. Grammar results from the projection of story structure. Sentences come from stories by way of parable.

Parable draws on the full range of cognitive processes involved in story. Story involves spatiality, motor capacities, the sensory modalities (sight, hearing, touch, smell, taste) and submodalities, patterns that run across sensory modalities and submodalities, perceptual and conceptual categorization, image schemas, and our other basic cognitive instruments. Parable draws on all of this structure to create grammatical structure for vocal sound. Grammar, built from such structure, coheres with it.

Grammar arose in a community that already had parable. The members of that community used parable to project structure from story to create rudimentary grammatical structure for vocal sound.

Consider the following analogy. Imagine a community of people who have trained themselves in rudimentary martial arts. All members of the community have it. No genetic instruction for specialization in martial arts exists; the competence is assembled by directing to its use preexisting capacities of muscle control, balance, walking, vision, and so on, combined with arduous work to acquire it. But once it is acquired, it seems entirely natural, and, with a little practice, inevitable.

Now suppose that into this community a special infant is born with just a little genetic structure that helps it direct these preexisting capacities to this community's martial artistry. The members of the community are better martial artists than the child and devote time to training and coaching the child, but the child has a secret edge. If the community is structured so that better martial artistry confers reproductive advantage, then the community provides an environment of evolutionary adaptiveness for the genetic change: the "martial artistry" trait is adaptive. This situation could plausibly give rise to a kind of genetic arms race in which each increment of further genetic specialization brings an increment of relative reproductive advantage. But martial artistry itself arose without genetic specialization for martial artistry.

Now imagine a community of people who use parable to create rudimentary grammatical structure for vocal sound. Everyone in this community develops story and projection, has voice, receives training from his parents, and is assimilated into the work of creating grammar through parable. Suppose that into this community a special infant is born with just a little genetic structure that helps it project story onto voice. The members of the community are better at rudimentary language than the child and devote time to training and coaching the child, but the child has a secret edge. If the community is structured so that greater facility with grammar confers reproductive advantage, then the community provides an environment of evolutionary adaptiveness for the genetic change: the "grammar" trait is adaptive. This situation could plausibly give rise to a kind of genetic arms race in which each increment of further genetic specialization brings an increment of relative reproductive advantage. But grammar itself arose without genetic instruction for grammar. It arose by parable.

❦

There are basic abstract stories. A basic abstract story is projected to create a basic kind of grammatical structure. For example, the basic abstract story in which an animate agent performs a physical action that causes a physical object to move in a spatial direction is projected to create the grammatical structure we see in

"John pushes the ball onto the court," "David tosses the can into the yard," and "Mary throws the stone over the fence." The abstract narrative structure is projected to create the abstract grammatical structure. The abstract narrative structure includes an agent, an action, an object, and a direction. The abstract grammatical structure includes a noun phrase followed by a verb phrase followed by a noun phrase followed by a prepositional phrase, with the first noun phrase as Subject and Agent and the second noun phrase as Direct Object and Patient.

The first abstract structure is conceptual and narrative. The second abstract structure is grammatical. If we think of these two structures as residing in two spaces, then there is a generic space that contains just the structure they share. This generic space is more abstract than either of them; its structure is not specifically conceptual or grammatical; it includes only elements, distinction of elements, some relations between elements, and so on.

The story in which Mary throws a stone and the story in which Bill flips a coin are different in nearly every specific detail, but we take them as sharing an abstract story structure. "Mary throws a stone" and "Bill flips a coin" are, as vocal sound, different in nearly every detail, but we take them as sharing an abstract grammatical structure. The abstract story structure and the abstract grammatical structure share generic structure.

Let us consider an example of the way in which story is projected to create grammar. Consider the small spatial stories in which Mary throws a stone, John pushes a ball, and David tosses a can. These small spatial stories are all instances of the same basic abstract story.

This basic abstract story has certain kinds of structure. One kind of structure it possesses is *distinction* of certain elements—Mary, the act of throwing, the stone. Notice that if we actually see (or imagine) Mary throwing a stone, we cannot distinguish the perception of *throwing* from the perception of *Mary* and the perception of the *stone*. Nonetheless, conceptually, in narrative imagining, we distinguish these three elements.

These three elements have *category* structure. Mary, for example, is placed into the category of animate agents; throwing is placed into the category of events; the stone is placed into the category of objects.

The story also has *combinatorial* structure. The distinguished elements of the story include Mary, the stone, the causal relationship between Mary and the throwing, the causal relationship between the throwing and the movement of the stone, the causal relationship between Mary and the movement of the stone, the event shape of the throwing, and our temporal viewpoint with respect to the throwing, all of which are *combined* as simultaneous: the act of throwing involves all of them at once. This combination has *hierarchical* structure—having a viewpoint on a story depends upon the existence of the story, for example.

In sum, the abstract story has certain kinds of structure: reliable distinction of elements, distribution of elements into categories, simultaneous combination, hierarchy, and so on. Other basic stories show recursive structure: if Paul catches the stone Mary threw, then one story (Mary throws a stone) feeds into a second story (Paul catches the stone).

Vocal sound itself—as sound, not language—does not have this structure. The elements of the story have a reliable structure of distinction but the sound "Mary throws a stone" is more or less a continuous stream that, if divided up at all, could be divided up any number of ways. The elements of the story have a reliable hierarchical structure of joined but conceptually distinguished elements (e.g., the event and the temporal viewpoint on the event) that the sound—again as sound, not language—does not mirror. The elements of the abstract story have category structure that the sound does not mirror: If Mary throws, John pushes, and David tosses, then Mary, John, and David belong to a category, but the sounds "Mary," "John," and "David" belong to no such reliable category. The causal structure in the abstract story has nothing to do with the causal structure of vocal sound. The temporal structure of vocal sound is always linear sequence but the temporal structure of this story involves highly complex simultaneity; other stories involve even more complicated temporal structure. In sum, story and vocal sound are two very different sorts of things. Story structure is projected to create structure for vocal sound that vocal sound does not intrinsically have.

The distinction of elements in the abstract story is projected to make "Mary," "throws," and "a stone" precisely distinct not as sound but as grammatical elements. The category structure in the abstract story is projected to vocal sound to put "Mary" and "a stone" into the same grammatical category—noun phrase. As sound, "Mary" and "a stone" share no reliable category, but as grammar, they do. The different roles of Mary and the stone in the story are projected to give "Mary" and "stone" different categories of grammatical relation (Subject versus Direct Object) and semantic role (Agent versus Patient). The structure of temporal foci and viewpoint in the abstract story is projected to give the sentence grammatical tense.

Abstract stories are projected to create abstract grammatical structures. The story in which Mary throws a stone is an instance of an abstract story; that abstract story is projected to create an abstract grammatical structure. The abstract story has indefinitely many instances; the corresponding abstract grammatical construction has indefinitely many instances. Mary throws a stone, John pushes a ball, and David tosses a can are all instances of the abstract story; "Mary throws a stone," "John pushes a ball," and "David tosses a can" are all instances of the corresponding abstract grammatical structure.

The abstract story, in one mental space, has conceptual structure. The abstract grammatical structure, in a second mental space, has grammatical structure. The very abstract structure they share resides in a generic space. It may sound odd to say that we blend the abstract story with the abstract grammar, but nothing is more common: In grade school, we are taught that a Noun is a person, place, or thing, a Verb is an action or event, and so on. Of course, a Noun is certainly not a person, place, or thing, and a Verb is certainly not an action or an event. Nouns and Verbs are grammatical; people, places, things, actions, and events are not grammatical. But in the blend, we join them. "Mary throws a stone" seems to be both a grammatical sentence and a story. Sentences are stories. Drawing inspiration from work done by Charles Fillmore and Paul Kay and later work done by Adele Goldberg, I call a blend of story structure and grammatical structure a grammatical *construction*. In a construction, certain story structures go with certain grammatical structures. When we want to tell that story, we use that grammar. When someone uses that grammar, it prompts us to think of that story.

Let us take a broad look at some of the principles of this "parabolic" view of language. The projection of story structure to create grammatical structure for vocal sound is not one projection but indefinitely many. There are indefinitely many specific projections of story to voice; the vastly complex network of all these specific projections is "the projection of story onto voice to create grammar." As narrative structure is not one thing but rather a mental activity that coordinates very many stories at many levels, so grammatical structure is not one thing but rather a mental activity that coordinates very many grammatical structures at many levels. The origin of grammar is the establishment of a dynamic coordinated complex of different but related grammatical structures that arise from projections of story structure. Grammar is not the beginning point of language: parable is the beginning point of language. Grammar arises originally from conceptual operations. Rudimentary grammar is a repertoire of related grammatical constructions established through parable. The backbone of any language consists of grammatical constructions that arise by projection from basic abstract stories.

Story and grammar have similar structure because grammar comes from story through parable. Let us consider some of the similarities between them.

Story depends upon constructing something rather than nothing. A reportable story is distinguished from its assumed and unreportable background. It is impossible for us to look at the world and not to see reportable stories distinguished from background, even though distinguishing in this fashion is hard to justify from the point of view of physics and biology. If we look out of the window and someone asks us what is out there, we can reply "Nothing" and mean it, so long as what we are looking at seems like background: a tree and a lawn on a quiet day. But if a lightning bolt strikes the tree, it looks very different, and becomes reportable. We believe that the same laws of physics and biology hold for both scenes and that in a scientific sense a great deal is going on in both scenes. Yet the lightning strike looks like a little story and the other scene looks like background, nothing remarkable.

This distinction of story as opposed to no story projects to the distinction of speech as opposed to no speech. Silence is part of grammar and is the counterpart of no story. We grant to certain elements of our perceptual experience special distinguished status. We think of things as happening against a background. Analogously, we think of speech as happening against a background of silence. The silence reports the background; the speech reports whatever is distinguished against the background. This is not always the case, of course: modern languages have developed many highly intricate instruments that go far beyond the basic grammatical constructions for basic stories. But radically, we report that the lightning struck the tree or that one person hugged another or that the rains flooded the tunnel or that the branch waved back and forth in the heavy wind. Reporting a nonevent is less common, unless the event was expected, in which case the nonevent is itself conceived of as an event. The form of reporting nonevents— "The lightning *did not* strike the tree"—is also much less prototypical. It would be odd to make this report if the event had not been expected; the negation pays homage to the story that did not happen rather than the nonevent that did.

Narrative imagining partitions and categorizes wholes into related elements, as when the small spatial story of Mary throwing a stone is perceived and categorized as involving different elements in different categories that stand in narrative relationships. Narrative partitioning, categorizing, and relating project to create grammatical partitioning, categorizing, and relating. The result is grammatical categories and grammatical relations.

Story groups elements. For example, the image schema *path-to-goal* groups the elements in the motion of the stone toward the window into a single unit. Story grouping projects to create grammatical grouping: "Toward the window" is a grammatical group. In English, this grammatical grouping is not simply a matter of sound adjacency. "Mary threw the rock toward the—if I'm not mistaken —window" still has "toward the window" as a grammatical group. Nonadjacency in grammatical grouping is even more evident in a language like Latin.

Narrative imagining combines finite elements into infinitely many products—Mary, John, throws, catches, pushes, flips, stone, ball, and coin, as conceptual elements of narrative imagining, combine into a great number of particular stories: Mary throws the stone, John throws the stone, Mary throws the ball, John catches the ball, John flips the coin, Mary pushes the coin, and so on. This structural property of story is projected to create a structural property of grammar: Finite grammatical elements combine into infinitely many products. "Mary," "John," "stone," and "ball," as grammatical elements, combine into a great many grammatical products: "Mary throws the stone," "John throws the stone," "Mary throws the ball," and so on.

Narrative imagining is exceptionally adept at nesting—putting one story inside another. Story nesting is projected to create grammatical nesting: "The house that Jack built fell down." Literary stories like the *Odyssey* or *The Thousand and One Nights* have stories nested to several layers, but it is hard to track all these layers at once, a fact Shahrazad exploits repeatedly to great rhetorical effect. As has often been observed, the same is true of grammatical nesting: "The house that Jack whom my aunt who came from Germany named built fell down" is hard to track.

Different basic stories are organized in a network; they are not independent of each other. They share structure. For example, the story categories Agent and Action show up in very many different basic stories. Just so, the different grammatical constructions that come from different basic abstract stories are organized in a network. They are not independent of each other. For example, the basic grammatical categories Noun and Verb show up in very many different basic grammatical constructions. Basic kinds of elements in stories have status of their own: Agent is a unit in the conceptual network of story. Just so, basic kinds of elements in grammatical structures have status of their own: Noun and Verb are themselves constructions in the network of grammar. Narrative imagining works with a network of related story structures; grammar works with a network of related grammatical constructions. Although modern language has developed many tricks, the original principle of networking persists: modern grammar is a dynamic and adaptive network of constructions, new ones evolving over time as basic ones continue to do their job.

The projection of basic stories accounts for the existence of corresponding basic grammatical constructions. *That is a small beginning*. Now we add a crucial development. We saw repeatedly in the early chapters of this book that the structure of a basic story can be projected onto other conceptual targets. For example, the structure of an agent beating an object can be projected onto the story of what the wind does to the sailor; the structure of taking an object away can be projected onto the story of Death. The target of such a projection has, by parable, structure that matches the source. Suppose a basic story projects to both a target story and a grammatical construction. Then the structure of the grammatical construction matches the structure of the target story. In that case, the grammatical construction can be used to express not only the basic story but also the target story. In sum, grammatical constructions that represent a basic story represent any conceptual target structured by projection from that story. We say both

"Mary threw the *stone* out the window" and "Mary threw the *job* out the window." The first is a small spatial story. The second is not at all spatial. The nonspatial story has structure projected from the spatial story. The grammatical construction has structure projected from the spatial story. Therefore, the grammatical construction represents both the spatial story and the nonspatial story. This phenomenon—the same grammatical construction for expressing stories of profoundly different features—is such an indispensable part of our thought and language as to seem unproblematic. But something this profound requires an explanation, and the explanation is parable.

A great range of things that are not prototypical objects, events, agents, or actions in a story can be conceived by projection as if they were. For example, times are not moving objects, but by parable we can think of them so, and this target can then be expressed by the grammatical construction that corresponds to the source: We say "The deadline is approaching" in the same way we say "The car is approaching."

The event of thinking is a process, not an object or an agent, but it can be conceived as an object-agent through parable. Conceived in this way, the target can be expressed by the grammatical constructions that correspond to the source story: We say "His thinking is moving in the wrong direction" just as we say "His truck is moving in the wrong direction." We say "I cannot grasp the idea" just as we say "I cannot grasp the handle." We say "I am turning it over in my mind" just as we say "I am turning it over in the pot." We say "I grasped the idea" just as we say "I grasped the object." We say "He accepted the explanation" just as we say "He accepted the gift."

There are other ways in which rudimentary language can be extended. A grammatical construction like Subject Noun Phrase that arose by projection from one part of story structure like Agent can be exploited to express related parts of story structure like Instrument: "John broke the stick" has a grammatical construction that can be exploited to say, "The stone broke the stick."

Where the patient in a small spatial story seems itself active in an activity induced by an agent, we may exploit the Subject position to express not the principal agent but rather the "active" patient: "The stick broke."

And so on. For parable to be the root of language means that it supplied the beginning of language. That beginning was developed and was exploited for the great additional range of communicative purposes.

❦

Let us take, as an example of how grammar comes from parable, some features of tense in English. I pick tense as an illustration because although it has been studied explicitly, intensively, and intelligently for at least two and a half millennia, and although the technical literature on tense as a facet of many different languages is voluminous, scholars of tense agree that tense is not well understood as a grammatical phenomenon. Robert Binnick begins his encyclopedic 1991 work, *Time and the Verb*, "It is no contradiction to say that we know a very great deal about tense, but understand it little. . . . It has been difficult even to know how much we do understand it, for confusing as discussions of the tenses of various languages may be, the scholarly literature concerning tense in general is, if anything, even more confusing." It seems reasonably clear that any general explanation of tense finally accepted will look substantially different from what we have now.

We explored in chapter 7 the basic human story of a person recognizing a story. In this general story, there is a recognizing agent who has a single spatial focus and a single spatial viewpoint. We saw that projecting the story of perception in space with *spatial* focus and *spatial* viewpoint onto the story of perception in time gives us an agent with a *temporal* focus and *temporal* viewpoint. Someone recognizing a story in time has, by means of this projection, a particular *temporal* focus and a particular *temporal* viewpoint.

In spatial perception, there are alternative foci and viewpoints. In temporal perception, there are alternative temporal foci and temporal viewpoints. This structure of temporal foci and viewpoints is projected to create a rudimentary grammatical system of tense. The projection of certain relations between temporal focus and temporal viewpoint creates certain constructions of tense. In English, basically, the grammatical construction of present tense corresponds to the narrative category in which temporal focus and viewpoint are the same; the grammatical construction of past tense corresponds to the narrative category in which the focus precedes the viewpoint; the grammatical construction of future tense (or technically, of verb phrase constructions that we commonly say signify "future tense") corresponds to the narrative category in which the viewpoint precedes the focus. A relative tense such as we find in "I will have run" corresponds to a complex narrative structure in which viewpoint precedes focus, but the focus itself contains a viewpoint that is preceded by its own different focus. Technically, spaces A and C precede space B; C has the event of running; A has a speaker considering B; B has an agent identical to the speaker and the runner and who is considering space C. So A is a viewpoint on B as a focus and B is a viewpoint on C as a focus. Tense lets us express such a structure of temporal viewpoints and foci as "I will have run."

Often we are told—or have reason to suspect, or assume from background knowledge—that the temporal viewpoint is identified with the actual moment of speaking, but this is an independent circumstance. Although it is the default circumstance, it is not fixed and does not have to be used. In story, the identification is optional; it is therefore optional in tense. Linguists often regard an utterance in English that makes no use of this identification as a problem, an exception that requires special explanation. I offer a different view. In the parabolic view of tense, present tense arises as the counterpart of the narrative structure in which temporal focus and temporal viewpoint belong to the same space. Only in the default case does viewpoint also correspond to the moment of speaking. Cases that do not fit the default scenario are not problems or exceptions. Let us consider some examples.

I will begin with examples that make the nonidentification of viewpoint and moment of speaking very obvious—they sound odd out of context, but people said them.

In the first example, the setting is a veranda; an old man is sitting; his old wife comes out, and, after a pause, sits down beside him; the silence grows more nervous; at last, the old man says, "It was a warm night on the banks of the intercoastal waterway. He sat alone, until she finally appeared and sat beside him. She seemed distracted and unhappy. At last, she announced—" Here, the man telling the story gestures to his wife to announce whatever it is she has to announce; the man and woman in the story are the old man and old woman on the veranda. In this example, the past tense tells us that the focus lies behind the viewpoint. From context, we know that the focus is the moment of speaking. The viewpoint is not the moment of speaking. Instead, the moment of speaking precedes the viewpoint.

Consider another lively real example with similar structure. A wife and husband are traveling in Greece; at night, they defend against mosquitos by covering the hotel window with netting; *kounoupi* is Greek for "mosquito."

> I am going to clean up, take a shower, lay down my naked body.
> What about the kounoupi netting?
> My husband took care of that while I was in the shower.

The past tense tells us the focus precedes the viewpoint: The focus is the space in which the husband puts up the kounoupi netting; the viewpoint is sometime after the focus; but we know from context that the moment of speaking precedes the viewpoint (as well as the focus).

Now consider idiomatic examples that have similar structure. Two travelers ask the train attendant to tell them the destinations of each of five trains that are sitting at platforms; the conductor tells them; the travelers think it over, and one of them asks, "That train, where *did* it go?" In this case, the focus precedes the viewpoint but we know from context that the moment of speaking precedes both of them. Later, one of the travelers can start to hop on the wrong train and the other can say, "Wait! That train *went* to Nice!" Consider also:

Which of these things do you want to give to charity?
That one goes, that one goes, that one goes, that one stays.
When?
The moment the charity truck shows up, they go.

Here, viewpoint and focus are the same and we know from context that the moment of speaking precedes both. Consider the setting in which Jane comes home and gripes at Mary that the dishes are not done. Mary says, "Today, I *will get up* early to run a million stupid errands, *clean* the bathroom, *shop* for food, *entertain* Jane's charming mother for lunch, and *prepare* dinner. Jane *will come* home and then Jane *will gripe* about the dishes. I *will shoot* her between the eyes, and the grand jury *will decline* to indict." Here, viewpoint precedes focus but we know from context that the moment of speaking is bracketed by the focus.

There are many other recognized cases in which viewpoint does not correspond to moment of speaking. In "historic present," focus is viewpoint but we know that both precede moment of speaking: "It's the late fifteenth century: Columbus has just anchored and is being rowed to the shore. He sees palm trees and a sandy beach." "It's the dawn of humankind: a smaller than average primate picks up a leg bone and smashes the head of his antagonist."

In "futuric present," focus is viewpoint but we know that moment of speaking precedes both:

So, what do you say tomorrow when you ask for a raise?
I go in, she asks me about the financing, I tell her it's finished, she beams and compliments me, and I say . . .

There are also cases in which viewpoint precedes focus and focus precedes (often by centuries) moment of speaking: "The Theran explosion *will wipe out* the Minoans, the Achaeans *will burn* Troy, Alexander *will make* the city-state obsolete, and Rome *will erase* almost everybody. But the archaeological record of everyday implements *will survive* for us to unearth and explain."

There are many such examples. They are not exceptions, but instances of the general case in which narrative imagining includes relations of temporal focus and viewpoint that are projected to create rudimentary grammatical constructions of tense. In the default instance, viewpoint may correspond additionally to moment of speaking. The existence of the default is understandable: Although we may shift temporal viewpoint in imagination, viewpoint and moment of speaking occur simultaneously in our perceptual present. But this additional default association is not the general case, and other associations are not exceptions.

This is not the standard way of analyzing absolute tenses. Typically, explanations of tense begin from the view that tense expresses the temporal relationship between the event reported and the moment of speech: past tense for events before the moment of speech, present tense for events overlapping the moment of speech, future tense for events after the moment of speech. This is the beginning frame used by Bernard Comrie in *Tense:* "past time reference is the basic meaning of the past tense"; "As far as the present tense is concerned, in its basic meaning it invariably locates a situation at the present moment." It is equivalently the standard beginning frame for analyses in the tradition of Hans Reichenbach's influential *Elements of Symbolic Logic*.

This beginning frame is often stated rather technically, as in John Dinsmore's formulation in "The Logic and Functions of the English Past and Perfect," in which he proposes that the following rule expresses the meaning of English Past:

(Past) For any time T and sentence S, at(T, pa(S)) iff at(T, S) and T < now.

Buried in this formalism is the claim that the past of a sentence is true of a certain time if and only if the sentence is true of that time and that time precedes the moment of speaking. This does not fit "My husband took care of that while I was in the shower": yes, the present-tense version of the sentence is true of the narrative mental space of taking the shower; yes, the past-tense version is true of that mental space as viewed from the viewpoint; yes, the time of that mental space precedes the time of the viewpoint; but no, the the time of that mental space does not precede the moment of speaking. On the contrary, moment of speaking precedes focus and focus precedes viewpoint.

Everyone recognizes that there are such exceptions. The typical way to handle these exceptions is ad hoc, one at a time, through local contrivance. In *As Time Goes By*, Norbert Hornstein observes that the principal exception occurs when a text "establishes a date that then acts as the anchor for the interpretation of the tenses used," as in "It was 1812, just before the Battle of Borodino. The anticipation of the coming struggle is palpable."

But "My husband took care of that while I was in the shower" does not explicitly establish a time that acts as the viewpoint. Rather, *the tense itself* indicates that the narrative mental space containing the focal event precedes the viewpoint. The relationship of this viewpoint to the moment of speaking is not part of the grammar but is rather something that we establish pragmatically. Our default pragmatic assumption may be that the viewpoint is the moment of speaking, but, importantly, that default assumption does not have to be used, as all such examples show.

The view of tense as arising from the projection of temporal viewpoint and focus requires no extra machinery beyond parable. It also saves us from ad hoc explanations. For example, how are we to explain a phrase like "John goes to work at eight o'clock every day"? Bernard Comrie, in an effort to accommodate such examples while still requiring the present tense to situate the event in the present moment, writes, "A certain property (namely, going to work at eight o'clock every day) is assigned to John, and this property is of course true of John even if at the moment he happens not to be on his way to work. In other words, the habit does hold at the present moment, and that is why the present tense is in principle an appropriate tense to use in describing this habitual situation." Aside from the fact that it is hard to see how going to work in the morning is a habit that holds at other times than morning, or that holds when one is in fact not going to work at all—as during vacations, hospital stays, and so on—this explanation will not handle a case such as the train attendant's saying "That train goes to Paris" of a train that will leave for Paris tomorrow morning from a station from which no train has previously departed for Paris and no train ever will again; nor will this explanation work for "Curtis rents the boat" said as part of the presentation of a plan for a nonhabitual future.

Comrie has the similar difficulty for the past tense—as when the waiter asks the Russian equivalent of "Who received the goulash soup?" or says in English, "Who had the roast beef sandwich?" In these cases, the tense is past but the focal event of receiving or having lies in the future of the moment of speaking. There are harder cases still. In several languages, like Russian, Comrie notes, the past can be used for imminent future events, as in "I left" when one is about to leave. English and French have a similar use for the present, as in "I am coming" or "J'y suis." Comrie's expedient, a common one, is to regard such "nonliteral" uses of tense as constituting exceptions that lie outside the scope of his analysis: "Rather, it seems that such uses of the past should simply be treated as exceptions."

Another "exception" is an extremely common use of the present perfect. Theories of tense often regard the present perfect as marking that the time of the event precedes the moment of speaking. But it can be used for events that one expects to happen, as in "John has won the race," said when John has not yet crossed the finish line, or "Clinton's won," said of the candidate before the election. A common explanation for this "exception" claims that when the preconditions of an event's taking place have been fulfilled, then it can be marked as preceding the moment of speaking even though the event is in the future of the moment of speaking.

On the theory that tense arises as a grammatical structure by projection of viewpoint and focus, none of these cases has an exceptional mechanism, they simply do not choose to connect viewpoint with the moment of speaking. "John goes to work every morning" cues us to take a viewpoint on a story of John going to work. The time of the narrative mental space is morning, and the viewpoint taken is also morning, and we know pragmatically the relation between the moment of speaking and "morning." The train attendant takes a temporal viewpoint on a story of the train's going to Paris that is the same as his temporal focus, and we know pragmatically the relation of that viewpoint to the moment of speaking. The viewpoint on the story of the customers' receiving their food lies ahead of that space; the viewpoint on the story in which the person who says "I am coming" is coming is the same as the focus; the viewpoint on the story in which John wins the race lies ahead of that narrative mental space. In all these cases, we know the relation between the temporal viewpoint and the moment of speaking pragmatically; the default pragmatic identification of temporal viewpoint and moment of speaking is simply not used.

The reasons for taking such viewpoints are not always hard to compute. For example, in the case of "John has won the race," said when John has not yet crossed the finish line, I would say that putting the event in the past of the viewpoint may serve to indicate a confidence in the event because presumably the past is fixed. Alternative analyses according to which such cases are special exceptions requiring special rules often adduce exactly these reasons. An analysis of "John has won the race" as an exception might say that the special rule is this: The "perfect" marking of the event as anterior to the moment of speaking but relevant to the moment of speaking can be used when preconditions of the event are fulfilled at the moment of speaking. These two different explanations share most of their substance. But there is a large difference in the way they frame the analysis of tense. In a view of tense as a grammatical system that arose by projection from narrative structure, the "nonliteral" cases are not essentially exceptions to the system of grammatical constructions for tense, and, more importantly, tense can have arisen through machinery whose existence we must already concede: parable.

Even a tough case like "Cows eat grass" does not look unusual on the parabolic explanation: There is a story of typicality in which everything is doing or being what it typically does or is; the time of that story is eternal; the viewpoint on that space is neither before nor after it; and we know pragmatically the relation of that story to our mental space of our own present reality or to the speaker's mental space of the speaker's reality.

The world does not occur automatically as narrative; even less does it occur automatically as a unique narrative. But it often seems to us as if it does. It may seem as if seeing reality as having a time line with a fixed viewpoint called "the present" requires no narrative imagining. But we are free to choose any other temporal viewpoint. Tense, which arises as a grammatical system by projection from the system of temporal viewpoint and focus, is an instrument for indicating our choice.

The projection of narrative structure gives rise to rudimentary language, and once rudimentary language is set up, it is extensible beyond the projections that gave it rise. Narrative structure—and, more generally, conceptual structure—is incompa rably more complicated than grammatical structure. Once grammatical structure is established by projection of narrative structure, it can be adapted to express vast ranges of conceptual structure beyond the structure that gave it rise. One way to adapt a grammatical construction is through metonymy: replacing an element with something conceptually associated with that element. For example, once "verb phrase" is set up as a grammatical construction by projection from the category of *events* and *actions* in stories, the verb phrase can be extended to accommodate not only events but also elements related to events. We say, "Mary hit the window," but also "Mary broke the window," because the window's breaking is metonymically associated (as causal result) with the action Mary performed to break it, and "Mary stoned the window," because the stone is metonymically associated (as instrument) with that action. Different constructions permit different metonymies.

A second way in which a grammatical construction is adapted is by pressuring it to accommodate other conceptual structures beyond those that gave it rise. For example, *resembles* is not a prototypical event and *John resembles Joe* is not a prototypical story, but the preexisting grammatical structure can be adapted to serve the purpose of expressing this situation in a nonprototypical sentence. *Snow is white* is not a narrative but rather a subset of information that might be relevant in a narrative, yet the grammatical structure created by parable can be adapted to serve such a propositional expression.

The view that language arises through parable in no way involves a claim that every construction or even most constructions in a speaker's system of grammatical constructions can be explained as arising through projection of narrative structure, nor does it imply that we will not find an amazing range of uses for language once language is set up and begins to evolve, nor does it imply that all grammatical constructions are isomorphs of small stories, nor does it by any means entail the claim that the only thing language can express is narrative structure. Rather, we are seeking to explain how language could arise without additional machinery, that is, without postulating hypothetical agencies and mechanisms that, conveniently, have all the properties needed to solve the problem but for whose existence we have no independent evidence. A special mechanism to do just what we need can always be conjectured in science, but such a conjecture is always suspect, a deus ex machina, and is to be introduced only as a last resort. We are not driven to that last resort. Rudimentary language arose through parable; after arising through parable, it was extended.

The view of language as arising through parable would allow for diversity of languages and grammars. Details of narrative structure vary from culture to culture and even person to person: what is universal is not all the specific narrative structures but rather stability of basic abstract stories. All cultures have stable repertoires of basic abstract stories. Some of them vary culture to culture. An accusative language (which gives Subject and Agent one grammatical coding and Patient a distinguished grammatical coding) and an ergative language (which gives intransitive Subject and Patient one grammatical coding and transitive Subject and Agent a distinguished grammatical coding) may seem to be informed by different kinds of stories, but each will seem to have a stable repertoire of basic abstract stories.

Projection is widely variable in the actual structures it projects and the ways in which it projects them. Even when two different languages project the same basic abstract story, and thereby give rise to similar grammatical constructions, the details will often be strikingly different. In English, "John loves Mary" and "Mary loves John" have different meanings, but in Latin "Iohannes amat Mariam" and "Mariam amat Iohannes" mean the same thing. In both languages, narrative relations project to create grammatical structure, but in English the result is a grammatical structure of linear word order, while in Latin it is a grammatical structure of case endings on nouns. Similarly, English has one set of constructions for representing causal narrative chains ("I make Paul eat") but French has a different and highly intricate set of double-verb causative constructions ("Je *fait manger* Paul") that English lacks.

Grammar arises as a dynamic system of projections of story structures to create a dynamic system of grammatical constructions that then can be adapted dynamically in many ways. It is likely not only that different speakers in the same linguistic community will have somewhat different grammars but even that the same person will have somewhat different grammars at different times. What matters for language as a communicative device is not that the members of a linguistic community all have the identical dynamic system of grammar but rather that the external products of grammar are perceived as fulfilling the relevant communicative needs in local situations. When they are not so perceived, then objections, corrections, and negotiations can take place to tune the systems of the conversants. On the parabolic view, grammar is a kind of dynamic repertoire, in much the same way that perceptual and conceptual categories are repertoires. The repertoires need not be identical universally or even in a community, but they do need to be stable and effective.

The level at which the projection takes place is the level of constructions above individual lexical items. A particular word like "dog" is not the projection of the concept *dog*. Rather, grammatical constructions and systems of constructions like Noun Phrase, Verb Phrase, Subject, Object, Agent, Patient, Present Tense, Progressive Aspect, Caused-Motion, Ditransitive (for example, "He baked me a cake"), Resultative (for example, "She hammered it flat") and so on arise from projection of systems of narrative structure. It is grammatical structure, not single lexical items, that arises from the projection of story.

There is a standard objection to any view that grammar arises from conceptual structure: we find in grammar various extremely odd formal quirks that seem to have no conceptual counterpart or functional explanation; therefore, so the logic goes, there must be an independent (innate) grammatical mechanism to give us 100 percent of grammar, including the quirks. But if grammar arises through parable, then grammar is based on everything involved in narrative imagining. It is based on all the sensory modalities and submodalities, on motor capacities, and on perceptual and conceptual categorization, which result in abstract structures like image schemas and dynamic integrative connections across different distributed activities in the brain. If it seems plausible that a genetically instructed grammar module would have quirks, we must a fortiori grant that the neurobiological and cognitive activity involved in all these other poorly understood systems would also have quirks—evolution is so notorious for producing quirks that the existence of quirks is a good test for separating evolved systems from rationally designed systems. Projection could project versions of those quirks when it gives rise to language. There is ample opportunity for the creation of quirks in grammar by projection from all of the systems underlying narrative imagining, without having to hypothesize an extra mechanism just to get the quirks.

There is also the possibility that some of the quirkiness may be arbitrary but necessary for consistency or efficiency in the system. Consider the analogy to copy text: We usually write to express meaning, and when we do so, it does not matter whether we write dates in the form "March 24, 1954" or "24 March 1954." Such matters are largely arbitrary. Accordingly, we resort to manuals of style for consistent decisions on arbitrary matters. There might be a great deal in grammar that works one way as opposed to another for the sake of essentially formal consistency. There is room in linguistic analysis for both parable and arbitrary formal patterns, regardless of the question of the existence of a genetically instructed grammar module in the brain.

Vast and complicated as language is, it is small compared to conceptual structure, communicative purposes, and local construction of meaning. Conceptual activity and communicative situation place a great range of constraints on language to operate effectively and efficiently, and yet to stay relatively small and manageable. As grammar evolves, it must satisfy many and varied purposes and meet many and varied constraints. Some of the pressure on grammar comes from conceptual activity, some from communicative purpose, and some from problems of internal organization of the system of grammatical constructions. A consistent and workable solution to the problem posed by all these conflicting pressures is the grammar of a language, which will not look uniformly like a set of local and simple pairings between grammatical structure and story structure. Plenty of strange opportunistic tricks, many of them ad hoc, are to be expected, with quirks as one of their manifestations.

On the other hand, there is nothing in the view of grammar as arising from the projection of story that in principle rules out the evolution of specialization for the projection of narrative structure to the particular target of voice, and therefore nothing to say that quirks in grammar as we know it could not arise from genetic specialization. But the specialization is not in principle needed to get quirks.

Linguistics typically discusses grammar at the level of the sentence. The theory of grammar as arising from parable invites us to ask whether the structure of units of discourse higher than the sentence might share structure with sentential grammatical constructions. Grammatical constructions are units of discourse; higher units of discourse contain them. A handbook like *Style*—Joseph Williams's summary of his collaboration with Gregory Colomb—which is dedicated to helping writers make their prose easier for readers to parse, tells writers that a major improvement can be achieved simply by making the subjects of clauses correspond to "the cast of characters" in the story and making the verbs that go with those subjects correspond to "the crucial actions those characters are part of." Williams and Colomb observe that readers are more likely to find prose clear and direct when it seems to present characters and their actions, thereby telling stories. What Williams and Colomb do not observe is that such prose is clearer exactly because the grammar arises from those basic stories. Readers naturally expect the stories being told to line up with the structure of the grammatical constructions being used. They read prose more easily when it follows such an alignment. Williams and Colomb recognize that many things that are not actually characters or actions are understood as such by projection, and they frame their advice accordingly. They advise those who want to write clear prose to change passages like the first version below into passages like the second version:

> Because the intellectual foundations of evolution are the same as so many other scientific theories, the falsification of their foundations would be necessary for the replacement of evolutionary theory with creationism.

> In contrast to creationism, the theory of evolution shares its intellectual foundations with many other theories. As a result, creationism will displace evolutionary theory only when it can first prove that the foundations of all those other theories are false.

The cast of "characters" in the second version includes creationism, evolutionary theory, and other theories. The actions include sharing, displacing, and proving. The second version presents characters in the story and the actions in which they are involved. The first version does not. The second version is easier to read. In my words, the grammar carries expectations about narrative structure because it is created by projection from narrative structure; the second sentence meets the inevitable expectations of correspondence better than the first.

According to Williams and Colomb, readers will regard a paragraph as more cohesive if the topics of its sentences present consistent information—which usually means referring to the characters in the story. Such paragraphs will also be more coherent if their sentences' topics present a consistent "point of view." In my terms, the larger grammar of the paragraph derives from the conceptual structure of a story, in which characters are involved in actions. Readers therefore expect the string of topics from sentence to sentence to connect the main characters, and expect one of those characters to dominate this topic string so as to present the scenario from a consistent viewpoint.

If this is right, then the prototypical grammars of clauses, sentences, and texts all derive from the same source: parable.

Everyone agrees that acquiring language helps an infant develop mentally by making it possible for the infant to express thought and to understand the expression of other people's thought. If grammar arises through parable, acquiring language could help the infant develop mentally in an additional, altogether different way. A grammatical structure corresponds to a story structure; the two structures are blended in a grammatical construction. Under parable, there can also be projection back from the blend to input spaces. The development of grammatical constructions could therefore reinforce the learning of story structure. The learning of a language may quite literally change the neurobiology of the infant in ways that are influential over cognition. This creates the intriguing possibility that speech and writing could be ways for the brain of one person to exert biological influence upon the brain of another person: thinking may be affected abidingly by experience with language.

If we use the old metaphoric conception of the brain as an agent who "deals with" language or as a container that for a moment "holds" language while examining it for storage or discard, then it is natural to think of the biology of the brain as unchanged by its dealings with language. But if we use instead the conception of the brain as an active and plastic biological system, we are led to consider a rather different range of hypotheses: The brain is changed importantly by experience with language; language is an instrument used by separate brains to exert biological influence on each other, creating through biological action at

a distance a *virtual* brain distributed in the individual brains of all the partici-
pants in the culture; early experience with language affects cognitive operations
that go beyond language.

❧

Given the current state of linguistics, there are at least two predictable responses
to the theory that language arises through parable. One is that it is trivially wrong;
another is that it is trivially true, or at least obvious, something we have always
known. I prefer the second view and am prepared not only to grant it but to make
a gesture toward documenting it. Among literary critics and poets, it is an extremely
common view, found in passages like the following from Fenollosa, where he proposes that a flash of lightning is a model (type) provided by nature of the grammatical sentence:

> The type of sentence in nature is a flash of lightning. It passes between
> two terms, a cloud and the earth. No unit of natural process can be less
> than this. All natural processes are, in their units, as much as this. Light,
> heat, gravity, chemical affinity, human will, have this in common, that
> they redistribute force. Their unit of process can be represented as: term
> from which, transference of force, term to which. If we regard this trans-
> ference as the conscious or unconscious act of an agent we can translate
> the diagram into: agent, act, object.

In typical fashion, Fenollosa sees grammar as arising by projection from
reality rather than from story. But with only minor violence to such a passage,
we can modify it into the claim that unmediated reality is not the basis of the
projection; rather, abstract stories we use to make sense of reality are the basis of
the projection.

Aristotle makes this claim explicitly in *On Interpretation*. Fenollosa views
reality as objectively narrative, and so thinks reality is the basis of the projection
to grammar. Aristotle, by contrast, says little about narrative structure but does
understand that the projection begins not from reality but from conceptual structure. The form of language, Aristotle explains, arises by projection from conceptual structure.

In its broad outlines, this is not an uncommon view today. Neuroscientist
Gerald Edelman, in elaborating the theory of neural Darwinism and neuronal
group selection, offers a very brief proposal that grammatical structure arises from
conceptual structure. Syntax arises from the projection of semantics onto pho-
nology. Edelman rejects on neurobiological grounds any notion of a genetically
programmed language module.

In its most simplistic version, the view that grammar arises by projection from story can be paraphrased colloquially by saying that sentences are small stories. The form of a sentence "is" the form of a story. Sentences are small stories that come from big stories. A noun is a person, place, or thing; a verb is an event; an adverb modifies an event; tense indicates temporal viewpoint and focus on a story; and so on. Such an ideational view of language is intuitive to anyone who has ever spoken, even though it cannot account for all of language.

At sophisticated levels, the theory that the origin of language is the projection of story is compatible with some other work in cognitive linguistics, in the minimal sense that it shares some basic assumptions with other work in the field. One of the most basic assumptions in cognitive linguistics is that linguistic structures can have conceptual bases. Perhaps the most immediately accessible analysis based on this view is Leonard Talmy's analysis of ways in which force-dynamic conceptual structure is grammaticalized in English. A view of grammar as a dynamic system of interrelated grammatical constructions appears to be broadly compatible with the theory of grammar offered by Charles Fillmore and Paul Kay. The view that some basic grammatical constructions represent some basic human stories is compatible with work done by Adele Goldberg. Although Gilles Fauconnier and Ron Langacker do not speak exactly of the projection of story, they have in different ways analyzed with great insight and in great detail the ways in which projection from conceptual structure systematically underlies various aspects of grammar. Indeed, although Langacker and Fauconnier, like nearly everyone who works on tense, offer explanations of basic tenses that start from the temporal relation between the event reported and the moment of speaking, they nevertheless explicitly make the case for tense as the grammaticalization of viewpoint and focus. Various of Fauconnier and Langacker's graduate students and colleagues have also done work on tense as arising essentially from focus and viewpoint.

It is often easy to assimilate the detailed work of a linguist who studies specific structures of language to the view that rudimentary grammar arose by parable. What is distinctive about my proposal is not the data or the analyses but rather the beginning frame. Thus, for example, although Comrie begins with a view of basic tenses as defined relative to the moment of speaking, a very little jiggle of his beginning assumptions can reposition his detailed analyses systematically to make his study compatible, I think, with the view that language arose through parable.

This impulse behind my proposal—make no unnecessary hypotheses—puts it at odds with the Chomskyan view that grammar arose because there evolved, with no help from natural selection and no help from preexisting human capacities, a species-specific, modular "organ" that is as specialized for grammar as the lungs, heart, and liver are for their particular tasks, expressed at the neurobiological level exclusively according to genetic instruction, and sharing nothing with other human capacities. There are alternative current varieties of this view, including Derek Bickerton's "language bioprogram hypothesis" "that suggests that the infrastructure of language is specified at least as narrowly as Chomsky has claimed." Bickerton draws his evidence for the "language bioprogram" from creole languages.

Any hypothesis that grammar is historically and individually the exclusive product of a special-purpose genetically provided mental organ for grammar rests upon a negative argument: We have not managed to explain how grammar arises through general processes; therefore we must posit the existence of a special genetic code that is entirely responsible for building in the brain a universal grammar organ, which will someday be located and understood in the way the retina and the lateral geniculate nucleus and primary visual cortex have been located and (partially) understood. The hypothesis of genetic instruction is not in principle impossible, but it is methodologically the hypothesis of last resort. It trades Occam's razor for God's magic hat: Against all odds, make the most cosmic and all-embracing extra hypothesis imaginable so as to solve everything at once— Let there be language.

Perhaps the main argument that grammar must arise in the individual human being exclusively from some special-purpose device, genetically coded and neurobiologically expressed, is that grammar is too arbitrary, subtle, and quirky to arise otherwise. But if the influence on language acquisition is not only the language an infant hears but also all of narrative imagining, including all of the systems from which narrative imagining recruits, there is plausibly an overabundance of sources for subtleties and quirks without conjecturing a special device to introduce them.

It is also argued that children obey subtleties of grammatical structure they have not heard, so that these subtleties must come from a special device. But if the influence on language acquisition is not only experience of language but also all of narrative imagining, including all of the systems from which narrative imagining recruits, then there is no poverty of relevant stimulus but rather a great wealth of relevant stimulus.

It is also argued that the subtleties and quirks of grammar are too universal to have arisen except through a universal mental organ for language acquisition. But story, projection, and parable are universal, and if grammar arises through parable, which recruits from universal systems such as vision, then there is no need to resort to a special conjectural mental organ to provide universality of structure.

Chomsky has been consistently unreceptive to the proposal that the hypothetical mental organ for grammar arose by natural selection. Stephen Pinker and Paul Bloom have argued in the most unhedged fashion that it does. Language, they assert, "is a topic like echolocation in bats or stereopsis in monkeys." This extra hypothesis—that natural selection is entirely responsible for the hypothetical grammar organ—might seem to put Pinker and Bloom even further away than Chomsky from my hypothesis that language arose by projection of story. But not so. In their practical attempts to explain how natural selection could have produced a genetically coded mental organ, Pinker and Bloom implicitly embrace an account of language in which grammar begins from meaning. They write, "Language is a complex system of many parts, each tailored to mapping a characteristic kind of semantic or pragmatic function onto a characteristic kind of symbol sequence."

"Mapping" is the critical term and concept in this assertion. It is usually the critical concept in any explanation of grammar as "encoding" something else, "signaling" something else, "mapping" certain structures, and so on. Yet the role of "mapping" in such explanations usually receives no comment, which is astounding. "Mapping," which I have called "projection," is a mental competence; it does not come for free in an explanation; it is instead the principal process to be explained. To speak of "mapping" is to make a theoretical commitment to a powerful and robust mental capacity of projection. Pinker and Bloom give various thumbnail sketches of such mappings that appear to me essentially compatible with a claim that grammar arises from the projection of narrative structure:

> Noun phrases . . . are used to describe things. Similarly, a verb like *hit* is made into a verb phrase by marking it for tense and aspect and adding an object, thus enabling it to describe an event. In general, words encode abstract general categories and only by contributing to the structure of major phrasal categories can they describe particular things, events, states, locations, and properties. . . . Verb affixes signal the temporal distribution of the event that the verb refers to (aspect) and the time of the event (tense).

Pinker and Bloom's explanation depends upon the existence of a mental capacity to project one kind of structure (story) onto something entirely different (vocal sound), thereby creating for vocal sound grammatical structure. Pinker and Bloom are assuming that the mental capacity for projection precedes grammar, or at least that grammar cannot arise without projection. Pinker and Bloom obscure the fundamental importance and complexity of this mental capacity by referring to it as simple "encoding" or "signaling." This mental capacity—to encode, signal, map, project—is what principally needs explaining in an account of grammar. In explaining grammar, we are not discussing simple encoding such as "We call this dog 'Harold,'" where a particular entity is given an arbitrary label. We are instead discussing the projection of vast systems of narrative structure in such a way that complex categories of *event* correspond to grammatical categories of *verb phrase*. We are discussing the projection of systems of perceiving events with temporal focus and viewpoint to create systems of grammatical structure like tense. This is not a matter of giving a particular object an arbitrary label but of projecting structural categories to impart structural categories. Pinker and Bloom are thus assuming, as part of their explanatory machinery, the existence of a robust mental capacity to project one kind of thing onto another. In my view, they are right to do so. They are wrong, however, in assuming that this mental capacity is exclusive to language, rather than part of the mental capacity I call parable.

Pinker and Bloom imagine that the kind of conceptual information that is mapped is *propositional* structure. This is a misemphasis rather than an error. Story certainly involves propositional structure. The story structure of *Mary throws the stone quickly* carries the propositional information *The throwing is quick*. But basic grammatical constructions seem to come from basic stories, with agents and actions and objects and patients and viewpoint and focus and so on, as Pinker and Bloom seem implicitly to grant in their thumbnail sketches of the way grammar "encodes" conceptual structure. These basic grammatical constructions that arise from basic stories can secondarily be used for expressing lower-level propositional structure such as "Grass is green."

Pinker and Bloom make it clear that they view their contribution as consisting entirely of the argument that natural selection explains the origin of grammar. They disavow any originality in their analyses of grammatical structures: "Any one of them could have been lifted out of the pages of linguistic textbooks." But if we lay aside Pinker and Bloom's argument about natural selection and look instead at their actual work in sketching how conceptual structure is projected to create grammatical structure, we see a treatment that appears to me (although almost certainly not to them) not far out of accord with the view that grammar arises from the projection of story.

The strong Chomskyan view of the origin of language asks us to believe that, against inconceivable odds, genetic instruction arose for a highly complex and sophisticated grammar organ, with no help from preexisting mental capacities and no help from natural selection. It asks us to believe that an extremely complex functional trait, language, is entirely genetic yet did not arise through the only mechanism of evolutionary genetics known to produce extremely complex functional traits, natural selection.

The astonishing unlikelihood of Chomsky's model of the origin of grammar prompted Pinker and Bloom to argue that Chomsky is wrong. They embrace Chomsky's picture in all respects except for their claim that natural selection is responsible for the origin of grammar.

Chomsky's argument is weak because it asks us to accept an almost inconceivably unlikely event in the absence of any evidence for that event. Pinker and Bloom's argument is weak in a different way: It skips briefly and vaguely over its central step. For natural selection to be responsible for the origin of grammar, we must have two events: First, some (minimal) genetic structure must arise that achieves penetrance to result in a trait of (minimal) grammar; second, this trait must occur in an environment in which it confers reproductive advantage. But that environment cannot be one in which a grammatical community already exists, since the origin of grammar is what we are trying to explain. The first event—the evolution of (minimal) genetic structure for (minimal) grammar—is not particularly hard to imagine, although there is as yet no compelling evidence of it. Let us look at the second step—conferring reproductive advantage.

Parable is a deeply basic capacity of human beings—we must grant this independently of any analysis of grammar. I have already sketched a scenario in which rudimentary grammar arose in a community through parable, not through genetic specialization for grammar. In that community, grammatical speech is a highly useful cognitive and cultural art. In that community, greater facility with grammar confers relative reproductive advantage, making genetic specialization for grammar adaptive. In my scenario, the origin of rudimentary grammar happens *before* any hypothetical genetic specialization for grammar. The grammatical expressions produced by the lone first genetically grammatical person are parsed at least in part *as grammar* by members of the community who have no special genetic instruction for doing so but who use parable to do so.

Do Pinker and Bloom offer a contrasting scenario, in which a lone first person with a genetic specialization for grammar has a reproductive advantage *even though no one else in the community can recognize or parse any of the grammatical structure of her utterances?* No. Such a scenario is not inconceivable—grammatical processing might assist the lone person's memory, reasoning, or imagination, and so be adaptive indirectly. But Pinker and Bloom, whose analyses covertly suggest a view of grammar as rooted in meaning, adhere overtly to a school of thought committed to the strong view of grammar as autonomous of other cognitive processes. This stops Pinker and Bloom from offering a scenario in which reproductive advantage comes from the benefit of grammatical processing to other cognitive processes. It also stops them from offering a scenario in which members of the community without genetic instruction use parable (or any other cognitive processes) to recognize and parse grammatical structure in the utterances of the first lone genetically grammatical person.

Pinker and Bloom provide no alternative to the scenario in which the adaptiveness of genetic specialization for grammar depends upon the presence of a grammatical community. All of their speculations concerning reproductive advantage depend upon a community of speakers with rudimentary grammar. This is understandable. There is no obvious way in which a lone grammatical person would have a direct reproductive advantage in a community whose other members are completely incapable of recognizing or parsing grammar by any means, general or special. The utterances directed at her would not be grammatical. Her own grammar would have no audience, since none of the grammatical structure she produced could be recognized by companions. Of course, her grammatical utterance could still be understood as ungrammatical communication, and she could still attribute grammar to the ungrammatical communication directed at her, and there could surely be reproductive advantage conferred by communication; but it is difficult to see that there would be any *additional* advantage conferred by the grammatical component.

In a brief moment in their argument, Pinker and Bloom do consider explicitly the right scenario their argument needs: a grammatical community of kin. They write, "Geschwind, among others, has wondered how a hypothetical 'beneficial' grammatical mutation could really have benefited its possessor, given that such an individual would not have been understood by less evolved compatriots. One possible answer is that any such mutation is likely to be shared by individuals who are genetically related. Because much communication is among kin, a linguistic mutant will be understood by some relatives and the resulting enhancements in information sharing will benefit each one of them relative to others who are not related." This is the only suggestion Pinker and Bloom offer of a community in which grammar is not widespread. It is still not a picture of reproductive advantage to the lone grammatical individual in a community whose other members are completely incapable of recognizing grammar by any means, presumably because Pinker and Bloom can see no such advantage.

But it is not true that such a mutation is likely to be shared by individuals who are genetically related. Consider the first genetically grammatical person. By definition, none of her ancestors or older siblings is genetically grammatical. If the genetic material expressed in her minimal grammatical competence arose by mutation from her parents' genetic material, as in a copying error in making a sperm or egg, it is extraordinarily unlikely that her younger siblings would have that mutation. If it arose because error-free sexual recombination of her parents' genetic material finally put together the right package, then later siblings would receive quite different genetic packages (especially if they do not have the same two parents). There is also the important difficulty that even if a later sibling had the right package, the first genetically grammatical infant would nonetheless still live in grammatical isolation (under Pinker and Bloom's suggestion) during the period in infancy in which she develops grammar.

If evolution could think ahead, it would certainly see that producing a genetically grammatical community, even a small one, would be enormously useful to members of that community. Pinker and Bloom are certainly right about that. But evolution cannot think ahead. It cannot think even one step ahead. As George C. Williams puts it in *Natural Selection*, "Every step of the way, as Darwin made clear, had to be immediately useful to each individual possessor. No future usefulness is ever relevant." A good natural selection story for the origin of rudimentary grammar must show that the *first* lone genetically grammatical human being had a reproductive advantage. If she was born into a community whose members had, by virtue of parable, a minimal capacity for grammar, then the reproductive advantage to her is obvious; but in that case, the origin of rudimentary grammar comes from parable, not from genetic specialization. Pinker and Bloom must disallow on principle the existence of such a community. They are therefore obliged to show benefit to the first genetically grammatical person, born into a community whose other members have zero capacity for grammar, who lack the ability even to recognize the existence of grammar, much less to parse it. This is the hard and all-important step in the argument. It is a step they skip over.

The least implausible picture Pinker and Bloom might have offered would be one in which the lone grammatical individual somehow develops grammar by using its grammar module in the absence of any grammatical utterances from other members of the community, grows up, passes the trait to one or more of her children, and converses with them in such a way that the minimal additional grammatical component that they add to communication confers, in some fashion, reproductive advantage to them, *beyond* the advantage conferred by the nongrammatical form of that communication, and skirting any costs in fitness associated with that genetic change, especially costs to the first lone grammatical person early in life, before she had a chance to reproduce and converse with offspring. This is a hazy picture, with central components missing, but nonetheless one in which genetic specialization for grammar could in principle have been adaptive even though rudimentary grammar was otherwise absent.

But there is no need to resort to such a picture. Very little grammatical competence would be needed to create an environment in which genetic specialization for grammar could be adaptive, and parable can supply a substantial grammar. The view that rudimentary grammar arises from parable provides an appropriate environment of evolutionary adaptiveness of the sort that any good natural selection story must have.

The hypothesis that human beings now living have some genetic specialization for grammar is an open question, to be decided on empirical grounds, principally in the study of genetics and neurobiology. The view of parable as the origin of grammar is not incompatible with this hypothesis. On the contrary, the parabolic account is the only one I see that straightforwardly provides the environment of adaptiveness that must be part of an adaptive account. In the parabolic environment, the lone genetically grammatical person would be surrounded by a grammatical community and would have an advantage over other members. Over time, genetic specialization in the species might take up some of the responsibility previously shouldered by parabolic mechanisms in the individual mind.

The view that parable explains the origin of language makes it possible to conceive of parabolic thinking and genetic specialization for grammar (if there is any) as historically connected in the evolution of the species and commensurate and reinforcing in the contemporary individual mind. Whether genetic specialization for grammar exists, to what degree it might exist, how it might be expressed in the individual brain under development, and how it might cooperate with other conceptual processes are all open empirical questions. But parable alone, without genetic specialization, gives us what we need for the origin of language.

ⓒ

The story I have offered reverses the view that language is built up from the sober to the exotic; that out of syntactic phrase structures, one builds up language; that out of language, one builds up narrative; that out of narrative, literary narrative is born as a special performance; and that out of literary narrative comes parable.

It works the other way around. With story, projection, and their powerful combination in parable, we have a cognitive basis from which language can originate. The dynamic processes of parable are basic to the construction of meaning and the construction of language. Story precedes grammar. Projection precedes grammar. Parable precedes grammar. Language follows from these mental capacities as a consequence; it is their complex product. Language is the child of the literary mind.

Parable is the root of the human mind—of thinking, knowing, acting, creating, and plausibly even of speaking.

# ⊸ NOTES ↢

page 3, "There was once a wealthy farmer": N. J. Dawood, trans., *Tales from the Thousand and One Nights* (Harmondsworth, Eng.: Penguin, 1973), p. 20.

page 7, C. S. Lewis on parable: See Louis MacNeice's discussion of literary critical perspectives on parable in *The Varieties of Parable* [The Clark Lectures, 1963] (Cambridge: Cambridge University Press, 1965), p. 5. C. S. Lewis's observations appear in *The Allegory of Love* (Oxford: Oxford University Press, 1936), p. 44.

page 15, "after the fact": *After the Fact: Two Countries, Four Decades, One Anthropologist* (Cambridge: Harvard University Press, 1995), p. 2.

page 16, "How do we recognize objects, events, and stories?": How we learn to partition a stimulus field into concrete objects and to categorize those concrete objects is a central problem of the cognitive sciences that has received only highly speculative answers. Gerald Edelman, in *Neural Darwinism* and *The Remembered Present: A Biological Theory of Consciousness*, describes the central difficulty: "The world of stimuli available to a newborn animal does not exist in prior information simply to be manipulated according to a set of rules, similar to those followed by a computer executing a program. While the real stimulus world obviously obeys the laws of physics, it is not uniquely partitioned into 'objects' and 'events.' An organism must contain or create adaptive criteria to develop information allowing such a partition. Until a particular individual in a particular species categorizes it in an adaptive fashion, the world is an unlabeled place in which novelty is frequently encountered." Gerald Edelman, *The Remembered Present: A Biological Theory of Consciousness* (New York: Basic Books, 1989), p. 41.

page 17, "Hanging his head down": W. H. Auden, *Collected Poems*, ed. Edward Mendelson (New York: Random House, 1976), p. 50, lines 9–12.

page 18, "Abstract reasoning": See Mark Turner, *Reading Minds: The Study of English in the Age of Cognitive Science* (Princeton: Princeton University Press, 1991), chap. 3 and 7.

page 18, "William H. Calvin": *The Cerebral Symphony: Seashore Reflections on the Structure of Consciousness* (New York: Bantam, 1990).

page 19, "We recognize small spatial stories on the basis of partial information": The possible mechanisms of such "pattern completion" are the essential subject of a highly influential two-volume work, *Parallel Distributed Processing: Explorations in the Microstructure of Cognition*, ed. David Rumelhart et al. (Cambridge: MIT Press, 1986).

page 21, "Recognizing objects . . . as having sensations": Conceiving of the *mechanisms* of sensation also appears to depend upon parabolic projection of image schemas of movement. The most common of these parabolic projections conceives of sensation as the result of small objects moving and hitting the sensory apparatus of the actor, thus making an "impression" or "impinging" upon the sensory apparatus. In antiquity, that sensory apparatus might have been regarded as the soul. In contemporary science, it is more likely to be regarded as the retina, or taste buds, or cilia in the inner ear, or sensory neurons in the skin. The modern theory of taste is a case in which an ancient image-schematic notion of sensation has come to be regarded as literal: The sensory apparatus of taste consists of certain spatial docking stations that allow molecules of only certain shapes to dock. When a molecule of the right shape encounters a docking station that it fits, the result is the particular "taste" of that molecule.

page 21, "Aristotle surveys theories": See the opening sections of book 1 of *On the Soul*.

page 23, "His model 'rejects a single anatomical site'": Antonio R. Damasio, "Time-locked multiregional retroactivation: A systems-level proposal for the neural substrates of recall and recognition," *Cognition* 33 (1989), 25–62. Quotation from p. 26.

page 24, "How to Build a Baby": *Psychological Review* 99:4 (1992), 587–604.

pages 26–27, "EVENTS ARE ACTIONS": See George Lakoff and Mark Turner, *More than Cool Reason: A Field Guide to Poetic Metaphor* (Chicago: University of Chicago Press, 1989); Turner, *Reading Minds*; George Lakoff, "The Contemporary Theory of Metaphor," in *Metaphor and Thought*, 2d ed., ed. Andrew Ortony (Cambridge: Cambridge University Press, 1993), pp. 202–51.

page 27, "Many were the men": Homer, *Odyssey*, book 1, lines 3–9. *Homeri Opera*, vol. 3 (Oxford: Clarendon, 1917), unpaginated.

page 29, "modal structure": For a full analysis of the relation of force dynamics to modality, see Eve Sweetser, *From Etymology to Pragmatics: Metaphorical and Cultural Aspects of Semantic Structure* (Cambridge: Cambridge University Press, 1990).

page 30, "The rain set early in to-night": Robert Browning, *Poetical Works* (London: Oxford University Press, 1940), p. 358.

page 33, "I feel a hand": Euripides, *Alcestis*, lines 259–64, in *Euripides IV* (Cambridge: Harvard University Press [Loeb], 1912), pp. 426–28; translation by Philip Vellacott in Euripides, *Alcestis, Hippolytus, Iphigenia in Tauris* (Harmondsworth, Eng.. Penguin, 1974), p. 51.

page 39, "George Lakoff and Mark Johnson": *Metaphors We Live By* (Chicago: University of Chicago Press, 1980).

page 40, "Yet I do fear thy nature": This example was provided by Donald C. Freeman.

page 42, Michael Reddy: "The Conduit Metaphor," in *Metaphor and Thought*, ed. Andrew Ortony (Cambridge: Cambridge University Press, 1979), pp. 284–324.

page 44, "And now, I realized": Oliver Sacks, *A Leg to Stand On* (New York: HarperCollins, 1990), pp. 206–16.

page 44, Saint John of the Cross: "En una noche oscura," in Gerald Brenan, *St. John of the Cross: His Life and Poetry* (Cambridge: Cambridge University Press, 1973), p. 144. The original poem includes the following phrases: "por el camino de la negación," "por la secreta escala," "¡Oh noche, que guiaste," "Quedéme," and "dejando me cuidado."

page 45, "*ouverture*": Marcel Proust, *À la recherche du temps perdu*, édition publiée sous la direction de Jean-Yves Tadié, 4 vols. (Paris: Éditions Gallimard, 1988), vol. 1, pp. 3–9; *Remembrance of Things Past*, 3 vols., trans. C. K. Scott-Moncrieff and Terence Kilmartin; and Andreas Mayor (New York: Random House, 1981), vol. 1, pp. 3–8. The original includes the following passages: "j'entourais complètement ma tête de mon oreiller avant de retourner dans le monde des rêves," "ma pensée, s'efforçant pendant des heures de se disloquer, de s'étirer en hauteur . . . ," "Et avant même que ma pensée, qui hésitait au seuil des temps et des formes, eût identifié le logis en rapprochant les circonstances . . ."

page 45, "And even before my thought": My translation.

page 47, Leonard Talmy: See "Force Dynamics in Language and Cognition," *Cognitive Science* 12 (1988): 49–100, and the references quoted there.

page 47, Eve Sweetser: *From Etymology to Pragmatics* (Cambridge: Cambridge University Press, 1990).

page 53, *Death Is the Mother of Beauty*: Mark Turner, *Death Is the Mother of Beauty: Mind, Metaphor, Criticism* (Chicago: University of Chicago Press, 1987).

page 53, "constraints . . . on the projection of progeneration": Turner, *Death Is the Mother of Beauty*, pp. 143–48.

page 55, "Its mother was a mainframe": I am grateful to Eve Sweetser for this example.

page 56, "mother of all battles": The expression quickly became a template for other versions: Secretary of Defense Dick Cheney, a man not known for verbal flair, reported to the American Legion that the mother of all battles had become the mother of all retreats. ABC news anchor Peter Jennings observed that for Saddam the mother of battles had become the mother of corners. *The Washington Post* of February 28, 1991, stated that the allied attack was the mother of all maneuvers and that General Norman Schwarzkopf's remarkable report to the press was the mother of all briefings. *The New York Times* of March 1, 1991, printed on its Op-Ed page the "Mother of All Columns."

page 57, "nor did Alice think": Lewis Carroll, *Alice's Adventures in Wonderland*, in *The Annotated Alice*, with an introduction and notes by Martin Gardner (New York: Clarkson N. Potter, Inc., 1960), pp. 25–26.

page 58, "Blending has been studied in detail": See Gilles Fauconnier and Mark Turner, "Conceptual Projection and Middle Spaces," UCSD Cognitive Science Technical Report 9401 (San Diego: UCSD, April 1994); Mark Turner and Gilles Fauconnier, "Blending and Metaphor" (manuscript, 1996); Mark Turner and Gilles Fauconnier, "Conceptual Integration and Formal Expression," *Journal of Metaphor and Symbolic Activity* 10, no. 3 (1995): 183–204; Gilles Fauconnier and Mark Turner, "Blending as a Central Process of Grammar," in *Conceptual Structure, Discourse, and Language*, ed. Adele Goldberg (Stanford: Center for the Study of Language and Information, in press); Mark Turner, "Conceptual Blending and Counterfactual Argument in the Social and Behavioral Sciences," in *Counterfactual Thought Experiments in World Politics*, ed. Philip Tetlock and Aaron Belkin (Princeton, N.J.: Princeton University Press, in press); Seana Coulson, "Analogic and Metaphoric Mapping in Blended Spaces," *Center for Research in Language Newsletter* 9, no. 1 (1995): 2–12; Gilles Fauconnier, *Mappings in Thought and Language* (Cambridge: Cambridge University Press, in press); Nili Mandelblit, "Blending in Causative Structures" (manuscript, 1994); Nili Mandelblit, "The Theory of Blending as Part of the General Epistemological Developments in Cognitive Science" (manuscript, 1995); Todd Oakley, "Presence: The Conceptual Basis of Rhetorical Effect" (Diss., University of Maryland, 1996); Douglas Sun, "Thurber's *Fables for Our Time:* A Case Study in Satirical Use of the Great Chain Metaphor," *Studies in American Humor*, n.s. 3, no. 1 (1994), pp. 51–61.

page 61, "Perch'io parti'": *Inferno*, canto 28, lines 139–42.

page 62, "In general, we understand proverbs": George Lakoff and I have previously analyzed this kind of projection to a generic space in *More than Cool Reason*, pp. 162–66 ("Generic Is Specific").

page 64, "So foul a sky": William Shakespeare, *King John*, act 4, scene 2, lines 108–9.

page 67, "As we went to press": "*Great America II*," *Latitude 38* 190 (April 1993): 100.

page 68: "It is even possible, as Seana Coulson has shown": Coulson, "Analogic and Metaphoric Mapping," pp. 2–12.

page 72, "A Buddhist monk": A version of this riddle appears in Arthur Koestler, *The Act of Creation* (New York: Macmillan, 1964), pp. 183–89.

page 74, "Wayne Booth, in *The Rhetoric of Fiction*": 2d ed. (Chicago: University of Chicago Press, 1983), especially pp. 3–20 and 207–9.

page 74, "in general we keep the space of what is narrated": There are in fact special cases of highly imaginative actual intrusion, as when the narrator magically enters the narrated story to interact *as narrator* with the characters.

page 75, "Before I introduce my Readers": Booth, *The Rhetoric of Fiction*, pp. 207–8.

page 79, "Lakoff and I originally noticed a constraint on personification": Lakoff and Turner, *More than Cool Reason*, p. 79.

page 81, "the plants at the end of their life cycle are harvested": Lakoff and Turner, *More than Cool Reason*, p. 75.

page 85, "Tom Stoppard, *Indian Ink*": I am grateful to Robert Keohane for this example.

page 87, "George Lakoff and I have given one argument": Lakoff and Turner, *More than Cool Reason*, pp. 162–66 ("Generic Is Specific").

page 91, "When one absorbs": Proust, *Remembrance of Things Past*, vol. 3, p. 184. French original: Proust, *À la recherche du temps perdu*, vol. 3, p. 691.

page 92, "For we talk of 'Death' for convenience": Proust, *Remembrance of Things Past*, vol. 3, pp. 197–98. French original: Proust, *À la recherche du temps perdu*, vol. 3, pp. 703–4.

page 93, "NIH has become a bit of the Beirut": " NIH Chief Announces Plans to Resign," *Los Angeles Times*, 27 February 1993, A18.

page 95, "artificial life": See John Markoff, "Beyond Artificial Intelligence, a Search for Artificial Life," *The New York Times*, 25 February 1990, Week in Review section, 5. Gilles Fauconnier alerted me to this article.

page 95, "'artificial life' will not belong to the category 'life'": A letter to the editor in *U.S. News and World Report* complains that only insane people could see category connection as arising out of the analogy between computer simulations and the evolution of living creatures. "People who begin to believe that electronic images, portrayed on a computer screen, are the same as living creatures need help." 31 May 1993, BC-20.

page 98, "Cold War without End": *The New York Times Magazine*, 22 August 1993, 28–30, 45; illustration on 28.

page 99, "This inference can arise in the target space": Actually, this inference arises in the target as understood through a *different* conceptual projection according to which the termination of something that is not a physical object—in this case, political control—is understood metaphorically as a physical object that disappears.

page 100 "An unexpected surge in wholesale prices": Sylvia Nasar, "Prices at Wholesale Surge 0.6%, Fanning Worry about Inflation," *The New York Times,* 13 May 1993, A1.

page 105, "In this way he acquired a vast hoard": Mark Twain, *Life on the Mississippi* (New York: Penguin, 1984), p. 393.

page 105, "technological bake sales": "To keep research afloat, these institutions have had to pump in big sums of their own money. And they are raising it by holding technological bake sales." Udayan Gupta, "Hungry for Funds, Universities Embrace Technology Transfer," *The Wall Street Journal,* 1 July 1994, 1.

page 110, "at the most basic levels of perception, . . . blending is fundamental": For an introduction, see Barry E. Stein and M. Alex Meredith, *The Merging of the Senses* (Cambridge: MIT Press, 1993).

page 110, "Objects and many of their properties are perceived as having a unitary appearance": Edelman, *The Remembered Present,* p. 43.

page 110, "This is known in neuroscience as the 'binding problem'": See Antonio R. Damasio, "The Brain Binds Entities and Events by Multiregional Activation from Convergence Zones," *Neural Computation* (1989): 123–32. For a popular journalistic sketch of the binding problem and of a proposal by Rodolfo Llinás to solve it, see Sandra Blakeslee, "How the Brain Might Work," *The New York Times,* 21 March 1995, Science section, B5 and B7.

page 111, Antonio Damasio and convergence: Antonio R. Damasio, "Time-Locked Multiregional Retroactivation: A Systems-Level Proposal for the Neural Substrates of Recall and Recognition," *Cognition* 33 (1989): 25–62. See also Antonio R. Damasio and Hanna Damasio, "Cortical Systems for Retrieval of Concrete Knowledge: The Convergence Zone Framework," in *Large-Scale Neuronal Theories of the Brain,* ed. Cristof Koch and Joel L. Davis (Cambridge: MIT Press, 1994), pp. 62–74; and Antonio R. Damasio, *Descartes' Error* (New York: G. P. Putnam, 1994).

page 111, "involves parallel sampling": Edelman, *The Remembered Present,* p. 65.

page 111, "acts to coordinate inputs and resolve conflicts": Edelman, *The Remembered Present,* p. 72.

page 112, "include functional correlations important to concept formation": Edelman, *The Remembered Present,* p. 70.

page 116, "O Lord": Augustine, *Confessions,* trans. R. S. Pine-Coffin (Harmondsworth, Eng.: Penguin, 1961), book 1, section 13, p. 263.

page 120, focus and viewpoint in linguistics: See, for taxonomies of linguistic phenomena involving focus and viewpoint, and for surveys of scholarship on these issues, Ronald Langacker, *Foundations of Cognitive Grammar*, vol. 1, *Theoretical Prerequisites*, (Stanford: Stanford University Press, 1987), pp. 122–26; Eve Sweetser and Gilles Fauconnier, "Cognitive Links and Domains," chap. 1 in *Spaces, Worlds, and Grammar*, ed. Gilles Fauconnier and Eve Sweetser (Chicago: University of Chicago Press, 1996); and Fauconnier, chap. 3 in *Mappings in Thought and Language*. See also Ronald Langacker, "Reference-Point Constructions," *Cognitive Linguistics* 4, no. 1 (1993): 1–38.

page 120, "Then the memory of a new position": I provide in this translation an unidiomatic crib in English of the relevant sequence of tenses in the French original. An idiomatic translation can be found in the already-cited translation (Moncrieff, Kilmartin, and Mayor) of Proust's *Remembrance of Things Past*, vol. 1, p. 7. French original: Proust, *À la recherche du temps perdu*, vol. 1, pp. 6–7.

page 123, "counterpart in another space": The foundation work on the use of a descriptor from one space for a counterpart in another space was done by Gilles Fauconnier in *Mental Spaces: Aspects of Meaning Construction in Natural Language* (Cambridge: MIT Press, 1985).

page 132, "We may become engrossed, in Erving Goffman's phrase": "Breaking Frame," chap. 10 in *Frame Analysis: An Essay on the Organization of Experience* (Boston: Northeastern University Press, 1986), pp. 345–77.

page 132, "To be quite accurate": Marcel Proust, *Remembrance of Things Past*, 2 vols., trans. C. K. Scott-Moncrieff (New York: Random House, 1934), vol. 1, pp. 708–9. (A quite different translation can be found in the 1981 three-volume Random House edition (translated by Moncrieff, Kilmartin, and Mayor), vol. 1, p. 1010.) French original: "Pour être exact, je devrais donner un nom différent à chacun des moi qui dans la suite pensa à Albertine; je devrais plus encore donner un nom différent à chacune de ces Albertine qui apparaissaient devant moi, jamais la même . . ." *À la recherche du temps perdu*, vol. 2, p. 299.

page 133, "The Nature of Things": See Lakoff and Turner, *More than Cool Reason*, pp. 169–70, and Turner, *Reading Minds*, pp. 168 and 183–89.

page 133, "Theophrastus's *Characters*": ed. and trans. Jeffrey Rusten (Cambridge: Harvard University Press [Loeb], 1993).

pages 133–34, "La Bruyère's *Les Caractères*": ed. Robert Garapon (Paris: Garnier, 1962).

page 134, Jerome Bruner: *Actual Minds, Possible Worlds* (Cambridge: Harvard University Press, 1986), p. 37.

page 134, "You see I don't know any stories": J. M. Barrie, *Peter and Wendy*, edited with an introduction by Peter Hollindale (Oxford: Oxford University Press, 1991), p. 96.

page 135, Wayne Booth: Booth, *The Rhetoric of Fiction*, chaps. 2–5, pp. 23–148.

page 138, "The moth thought [the star] was just caught": James Thurber, *Fables for Our Time and Famous Poems Illustrated* (Harper and Row, 1939), p. 17; Sun, "Thurber's *Fables for Our Time*," pp. 51–61.

page 140, "Linguistics is arguably the most hotly contested property": "Annals of Science: A Silent Childhood-I," *New Yorker*, 13 April 1992, 48.

page 140, "The type of sentence in nature": Ernest Fenollosa, *The Chinese Written Character as a Medium for Poetry*, ed. Ezra Pound (San Francisco: City Lights, 1936), p. 12.

page 145, "grammatical *construction*": For introductions to the theory of grammatical constructions, see Charles Fillmore and Paul Kay, *Construction Grammar* (Stanford, Calif.: Center for the Study of Language and Information, in press); and Adele Goldberg, *Constructions: A Construction Grammar Approach to Argument Structure* (Chicago: University of Chicago Press, 1995).

page 149, Robert Binnick: *Time and the Verb: A Guide to Tense and Aspect* (New York: Oxford University Press, 1991), p. vii.

page 152, "past time reference is the basic meaning of the past tense": Bernard Comrie, *Tense* (Cambridge: Cambridge University Press, 1985), p. 20.

page 152, "As far as the present tense is concerned": Comrie, *Tense*, p. 38.

page 152, *Elements of Symbolic Logic:* Hans Reichenbach, *Elements of Symbolic Logic* (New York: Free Press and London: Collier-Macmillan, 1947).

page 152, John Dinsmore: *Interdisciplinary Approaches to Language: Essays in Honor of S.-Y. Kuroda*, ed. Carol Georgopoulos and Roberta Ishihara (Dordrecht: Kluwer, 1991), pp. 101–17. Quotation from p. 104.

page 152, Norbert Hornstein: *As Time Goes By: Tense and Universal Grammar* (Cambridge: MIT Press, 1990), p. 11.

page 153, "A certain property (namely, going to work)": Comrie, *Tense*, p. 39.

page 153, "Rather, it seems that such uses of the past": Comrie, *Tense*, p. 20.

page 158, "the crucial actions those characters are part of": Joseph M. Williams, *Style: Toward Clarity and Grace*, with two chaps. coauthored by Gregory Colomb (Chicago: University of Chicago Press, 1990), pp. 20–21.

page 160, "Edelman rejects on neurobiological grounds": Gerald Edelman, *Bright Air, Brilliant Fire: On the Matter of the Mind* (New York: Basic Books, 1992), chap. 11.

page 161, Charles Fillmore and Paul Kay: *Construction Grammar*.

page 161, Adele Goldberg: *Constructions*.

page 161, "Indeed, although Langacker and Fauconnier": Brief but seminal comments on tense, focus, and viewpoint appear on pp. 33 and 34 of Fauconnier's *Mental Spaces*.

page 161, "Various of Fauconnier and Langacker's graduate students and colleagues": Gilles Fauconnier will give an overview of this work—by Michele Cutrer, John Dinsmore, Jeff Lansing, and Eve Sweetser—in a section titled "Time and Tense" in his forthcoming *Mappings in Thought and Language*.

page 162, "the infrastructure of language is specified at least as narrowly as Chomsky has claimed": Derek Bickerton, "The Language Bioprogram Hypothesis," *Behavioral and Brain Sciences* 7 (1984): 173–188. Quotation from p. 173.

page 163, "Language is a topic like echolocation in bats": Stephen Pinker and Paul Bloom, "Natural Language and Natural Selection," *Behavioral and Brain Sciences* 13 (1990), pp. 707–27. Quotation from p. 707.

page 163, "Language is a complex system of many parts": Pinker and Bloom, "Natural Language," p. 713.

page 163, "Noun phrases are used to describe things": Pinker and Bloom, "Natural Language," p. 713.

page 164, "Any one of them could have been lifted": Pinker and Bloom, "Natural Language," p. 714.

page 166, "Geschwind, among others": Pinker and Bloom, "Natural Language," p. 722.

page 167, "As George C. Williams puts it": *Natural Selection: Domains, Levels, and Challenges* (New York: Oxford, 1992), p. 77.

# ᴚ FURTHER READING ᴄ
# ON IMAGE SCHEMAS

## INTRODUCTION TO IMAGE SCHEMAS

Brugman, Claudia. *The Story of Over: Polysemy, Semantics, and the Structure of the Lexicon*. New York: Garland Publishing, Inc., 1988.

Gibbs, Raymond W., Jr., and Herbert L. Colston. "The Cognitive Psychological Reality of Image Schemas and Their Transformations." *Cognitive Linguistics* 6 (1995): 347–78.

Johnson, Mark. *The Body in the Mind*. Chicago: University of Chicago Press, 1987.

Lakoff, George. Case study 2 in *Women, Fire, and Dangerous Things: What Categories Reveal about the Mind*, 416–461. Chicago: University of Chicago Press, 1987.

Sweetser, Eve. *From Etymology to Pragmatics: Metaphorical and Cultural Aspects of Semantic Structure*. Cambridge: Cambridge University Press, 1990.

Talmy, Leonard. "Force Dynamics in Language and Cognition." *Cognitive Science* 12 (1988): 49–100.

Thomas, Francis-Noël, and Mark Turner. *Clear and Simple as the Truth: Writing Classic Prose*. Princeton: Princeton University Press, 1994.

Turner, Mark. "The Body of Our Thought" and "The Poetry of Connections, I." Chaps. 3 and 7 in *Reading Minds: The Study of English in the Age of Cognitive Science*. Princeton: Princeton University Press, 1991.

## IMAGE SCHEMAS IN THE BRAIN

Damasio, Antonio R. "The Brain Binds Entities and Events by Multiregional Activation from Convergence Zones." *Neural Computation* 1 (1989): 123–32.

Damasio, Antonio R. *Descartes' Error*. New York: G. P. Putnam, 1994.

Damasio, Antonio R. "Time-Locked Multiregional Retroactivation: A Systems-Level Proposal for the Neural Substrates of Recall and Recognition." *Cognition* 33 (1989): 25–62.

Damasio, Antonio R., and Hanna Damasio. "Cortical Systems for Retrieval of Concrete Knowledge: The Convergence Zone Framework." In *Large-Scale Neuronal Theories of the Brain,* edited by Cristof Koch and Joel L. Davis, 62–74. Cambridge: MIT Press, 1994.

Damasio, Antonio R., et al. "Neural Regionalization of Knowledge Access: Preliminary Evidence." *Cold Spring Harbor Symposia on Quantitative Biology* 60 (1990): 1039–47.

Edelman, Gerald. *Neural Darwinism: The Theory of Neuronal Group Selection,* passim, New York: Basic Books, 1987.

Edelman, Gerald. "Reentrant Signaling." Chap. 4 in *The Remembered Present: A Biological Theory of Consciousness.* New York: Basic Books, 1989: 64–90.

Hubel, David H. *Eye, Brain, and Vision.* New York: Scientific American Library, 1995.

Sporns, O. J., et al. "Reentrant Signaling among Simulated Neuronal Groups Leads to Coherency in Their Oscillatory Activity." *Proceedings of the National Academy of Science* 86 (1989): 7265–69.

## IMAGE SCHEMAS IN BASIC-LEVEL CATEGORIES

Edelman, Gerald. *Bright Air, Brilliant Fire: On the Matter of the Mind.* New York: Basic Books, 1992.

Graesser, A. C., et al. "Recognition Memory for Typical and Atypical Actions in Scripted Activities." *Journal of Experimental Psychology: Human Learning and Memory* 6 (1979): 503–15.

Lakoff, George. *Women, Fire, and Dangerous Things: What Categories Reveal about the Mind.* Chicago: University of Chicago Press, 1987.

Rosch, Eleanor. "Categorization of Natural Objects." *Annual Review of Psychology* 32 (1981): 89–115.

———. "Cognitive Reference Points." *Cognitive Psychology* 7 (1975): 532–47.

———. "Cognitive Representations of Semantic Categories." *Journal of Experimental Psychology: General* 104 (1975): 192–233.

———. "Coherences and Categorization: A Historical View." In *The Development of Language and Language Researchers: Essays in Honor of Roger Brown,* edited by Frank S. Kessel. Hillsdale, N.J.: Lawrence Erlbaum Associates, 1988.

———. "Human Categorization." In *Studies in Cross-Cultural Psychology,* edited by Neil Warren. New York: Academic Press, 1977.

———. "Principles of Categorization." in *Cognition and Categorization,* edited by B. B. Lloyd and Eleanor Rosch, 27–48. Hillsdale, N.J.: Lawrence Erlbaum Associates, 1978.

IMAGE SCHEMAS IN DEVELOPMENTAL PSYCHOLOGY

Edelman, Gerald. Postscript to *Bright Air, Brilliant Fire: On the Matter of the Mind.* New York: Basic Books, 1992.

Mandler, Jean M. "How to Build a Baby: II. Conceptual Primitives." *Psychological Review* 99, no. 4 (1992): 587–604.

———. "How to Build a Baby: On the Development of an Accessible Representational system." *Cognitive Development* 3 (1988): 113–36.

# ❧ INDEX ❧